TRUE STORIES OF BRITAIN'S BIGGEST STREET BATTLES

# HOOLIES

TRUE STORIES OF BRITAIN'S BIGGEST STREET BATTLES

# HOOLIES

## GARRY BUSHELL

JB

JOHN BLAKE

ke Publishing Ltd,
3 Bramber Court, 2 Bramber Road,
London W14 9PB, England

www.johnblakepublishing.co.uk

First published in paperback in 2010

ISBN: 978 1 84454 907 8

British Library Cataloguing-in-Publication Data:

A catalogue record for this book is available from the British Library.

Design by www.envydesign.co.uk

Printed in Great Britain by CPI Bookmarque, Croydon, CR0 4TD

1 3 5 7 9 10 8 6 4 2

© Text copyright Garry Bushell

Papers used by John Blake Publishing are natural, recyclable products made from
wood grown in sustainable forests. The manufacturing processes conform to the
environmental regulations of the country of origin.

# About the Author

Garry Bushell was born and raised in South East London. He started his career on the rock weekly *Sounds*, interviewing everyone from the Clash, the Jam and the Specials to Blondie, U2 and Ozzy Osbourne. The son of a fireman, he is best known for his award-winning Bushell On The Box TV column which has appeared in The *Sun*, the *People*, the *Daily Star* and now the *Daily Star Sunday*. His ITV series of the same name was Number 1 on the Night Network for two seasons, achieving audience shares of up to 68 per cent. Garry trained as a journalist on the *Socialist Worker*. He managed the Cockney Rejects; his own band The Gonads have been going for more than 30 years and his punk and Ska podcast appears sporadically on Total Rock Radio. Garry's short story, *Brutal Assault*, has just been published in the US collection *Deadlines: An Anthology of Horror and Dark Fiction*. Garry Bushell lives in Kent.

# Acknowledgements

The author would like to thank Tom McCourt, Lol Pryor, Paul Hallam, Eddie Piller, Garry Hitchcock, Paul McEvoy, Dave Cairns, Chris Weeks, Mad Marc and Garry Johnson for their help in making this book comprehensive and accurate.

# CONTENTS

# FOREWORD
## by Garry Johnson

Nineteen seventy-six was the year the British rock scene was reborn. For a brief time all the old certainties went out the window. Chaos reigned. Anything seemed possible. New bands, new ideas and new voices vied for the attention. And in this gloriously fertile maelstrom, England's great gift to the world, the youth cults were reinvigorated.

The years 1976 to 1985 witnessed a heady parade of punks, rude boys, skinheads, new mods, rockers, bikers, casuals, soullies, boneheads, New Romantics, crusties and goths. It was, as Garry Bushell wrote back then, a wonderful time to be young.

Bushell was uniquely well placed to observe this exciting period in pop history. He was a punk and a fanzine writer who landed a staff job on *Sounds* at a time when *NME* had declared punk dead. He wrote with humour and affection about bands that proved them wrong, bands like the Ruts, the Skids and the UK Subs. But he also found time for the kids in the audience. He interviewed the mods and skins and punks on the street, finding their voices just as fascinating as, and often more interesting than, the false messiahs on our stages. And, in return, the kids, these tough young peacocks, took him into their confidence. It's hard to think of any other rock writer who would have been trusted by the ICF (the West Ham Inter City Firm) or the Glory Boys as Garry was. Punks chanted his name on street demos.

Bushell was the first to enthuse about 2-Tone, catching The Specials at their first ever show and documenting the new bluebeat bonanza in the magazine *Dance Craze*. A huge lover of Ska, he defended the new bands against reggae purists and racist numbskulls alike.

Groups as diverse as Crass, U2, The Chords, The Selecter, Cockney Rejects, The Exploited, and Twisted 'fuggen' Sister had their original reviews from Garry Bushell. He was not like most music-press writers. He didn't hide behind language you'd need a degree to understand, and neither did he stick to safe venues in the West End or lavish music-biz junkets.

He was biased for sure, biased against pseuds and phoneys and in favour of the young working class.

The beat of the street floated Bushell's boat.

A former suede-head from south London, Garry interviewed the new skinheads to find out what made them tick. When the mods ran amok in Southend he was there. When the Angelic Upstarts played a shock gig inside a prison in the Northeast he was there too.

But he also covered the right-to-work marchers in *Sounds* and stuck his politics on the line, urging readers to vote Labour in 1979 and in 1983, when he interviewed a grateful Neil Kinnock for what was then Britain's bestselling rock weekly.

Garry had cut his journalistic teeth on the *Socialist Worker* with Paul Foot. He'd written for *Rebel* and for *Temporary Hoarding*. He didn't believe rock could be anything but against racism.

He had grown up on Marxism and Motown, Ska, glam rock and Black Sabbath. But he didn't preach. He listened to what people said and reproduced it faithfully. The pieces he wrote on new mod and Oi! in particular reflect that honesty and openness.

His reviews were different, of course, often savage and witty. On *Sounds*, Garry developed his lifelong love of feuds, falling out spectacularly with everyone from Crass to Boy George via the National Front, who denounced him as a 'race traitor' and published his home address.

Garry Bushell was committed to telling it like it was, no matter what.

He'll go to his grave with the label 'the Godfather of Oi!', which is fair enough. He came up with the term, compiled the albums and managed some of the bands, getting beaten up by neo-Nazis for his trouble.

But history will also record that the legacy of the Oi! bands is today's hugely popular worldwide street-punk phenomenon, which is as non-racist as it is working-class.

The *Daily Mail* proved to be as wrong about Oi! as it is about everything else.

Garry Johnson, punk poet (retired)

# Notes From a Teenage Rampage

August Bank Holiday, 1979: 11.15am. A carload of West Ham skinheads from Grays, Essex, pull up on the forecourt of the Five Bells pub at Southend-on-Sea. As they get out, stretching their legs, they are surrounded by a gang of eight older Rockabillies who have been lying in wait. It's a rat trap, baby, and they've been caught. Or so the leering Rockabillies think. They don't realise that their intended prey are the frontrunners of a 12-strong convoy of skins, Glory Boys and assorted hooligans. Parka-clad terrace legend Kevin Wells in the car behind spots what's happening and stands up through the sunroof, redirecting the other cars back round the roundabout to the pub forecourt like a determined general. Rockabilly faces drain of colour as the cars circle them and park. An awesome away-team spill-out; among them are Hoxton Tom McCourt, Barney Rubble, top mod Bob 'Bovril' Baisden, Gary Hodges and a plethora of hardcore West Side combatants including H, Bernie, Kenny, Frank and Grimbsy. It's the Sweeney of street style. If there ever was an SAS of hooligans, these guys were it.

The Rockabillies don't run, but they're not happy. The ambushers have been ambushed themselves. They shrink into a circle. Hands reach for coshes, chains and knives. They aren't nearly enough. It's all over very quickly.

Bank Holidays and beach fighting go together like pie and mash, strawberries and cream, bovver and boot. This very English tradition has been revived this particular year in the wake of the exciting mod renewal that has shaken up London and the Home Counties. Lots of youth tribes are heading for Southend – mostly mods and skins, with subsections of suedes and Glory Boys, the hard mods who follow Secret Affair, along with a sizable proportion of terrace tearaways … I'm just hoping they don't start steaming into each other – last weekend's scooter rally got called off after Northern mods clashed with their Southern rivals and then the Old Bill. Mods against mods. Everyone agrees that this is bad news. There's no need for it.

I'm here as an interested participating observer – a low-rent Hunter S. on beer and speed – to record the day's events for posterity, in *Sounds*, the music paper that has become the thinking mod's rock weekly of choice.

The car I'm in reaches the Essex coast at 10.35am. We follow the signs to Southend seafront, past the Kursaal arcade and the Minerva pub. Christ, there must be 50 bikers and Teds here already and we ain't seen a mod yet. We sink into our seats, turn up the collars of our Harringtons and keep driving. Well, what do you know? We turn the corner and see a sea of new-wave sons and daughters. The seafront is crammed with mods and skins surging down towards the Minerva and getting repelled by a thin blue line of Essex cops. The mood is good, buzzing. The chants are loud and persistent: 'We are the mods'; 'Skin'eads'; 'We are the mods'; 'Skin'eads'; 'We are, we are, we are the Mods!'

Let's park this car, find that pub on the seafront where everyone is meeting, the Hope. Life is a drink, and you get drunk when you're young …

Stand outside the pub, sinking lagers – 'Forsyte Sagas' – in the humid sunshine. About 200 mods are gathered on the seafront opposite. Sporadically they charge down the road towards 'the Grease' and get turned back. They look good. No one thinks it odd that so many late-seventies teenagers are deliberately setting out to relive the kind of seaside mayhem that so excited tabloid headline writers in the sixties. 'That was then, this is now,' says Eddie, a 17-year-old electrician from Hackney. 'Now it's our turn.'

A train load of skins with a smattering of punks turn up from Southend station. The two crowds size each other up and cheer in mutual celebration. They cheer 'cos they're smart and they're clean and this is the time to be seen. Time for action …

And a good old cockney knees-up, in the groin.

By mid-afternoon there are close on 3,000 here, although the police and the press say 1,500. The activity consists mostly of mixed mod and skin regiments making random charges in the direction of the opposition in the Minerva, spreading over roads like spilt soup on a kitchen floor, and holding back the traffic in mass displays of strength. And I'm in there with them, swept along by the mob and the excitement … When you're in the crowd, you don't see any problems; you don't fear anyone or anything. It's all jubilation – just crazy smiles and the feeling of being unshackled; of *power*. It's like the first time you invade a football pitch. There's nothing anyone can do to stop you. For the first time they – the cops, the authorities – are afraid of *you*.

Inevitably, Weller's lyrics are running through our brains: we're feeling so brave – and fired up by the deceptive invincibility of youth – we're certain we can't be stopped.

The funny thing is it's not that violent. It looks worse than it is. And naturally it will be portrayed in the newspapers as being far worse than it was. But I've been caught up in violence before, at demonstrations, and this is small beer compared with Grunwicks or Lewisham or Red Lion Square. All that really happens is that a couple of hundred kids at a time charge down the road, a few coppers say, 'You can't go no further' and the kids turn back. Revolution it ain't. But no one seems to care.

Being there, that's what counts. The laugh, the crack – tribal rival rebel revelry. A young Tilbury skinhead who paddled out a hundred yards into the sea to kip in a boat was the hero of the early afternoon.

The feel-good mood does not last. As beer flows, fights erupt like teenage spots. The skins are the most daring and also the prime targets for random arrests. One time a rocker drives his car past a gang but it gets caught up in the traffic. Skins swarm around it like angry hornets. They yell abuse and kick at the panelling with their steel-capped Doc Martens (or DMs) while the driver shoots V-signs at them, his fingers festooned with cheap, lairy rings. The cops materialise and the gang leg it. Undeterred, a uniformed officer grabs a young skinhead who had been watching from a wall and shouts, 'You're nicked!'

'I ain't done nuffin,' the kid protests, accurately. The cop knees him in the bollocks and drags him off.

Gangs rarely attempt to rescue mates who are nicked, although the arrested themselves put on a show. One skin, handcuffed in the back of a van, puts his feet on his burly captor's chest and sends him flying through the door. Another cuffed crophead makes a run for it to mass cheers before he falls arse over tit and is retrieved by the ever-angrier Essex constabulary.

Bet they both got a good going over down the station.

Stories of individual bravado buzz around the pilchard-packed pub, becoming instant mythology, embellished and magnified through noisy repetition.

The police eventually identify the Hope as Hooligan Mission Control. The hardcore are here, and so are the pill pushers and the kids flogging snide T-shirts. Just after 2pm the cops decide to shut the place down. This is the only time serious violence seems a possibility. A lot of the older West Ham chaps are in here and, as the cops mob up outside, glasses smash and the pub explodes in raucous defiance: 'Kill the Bill!'; 'I'm forever blowing bubbles!'; 'Harry Roberts is our friend, he kills coppers!'; 'I like punk and I like Sham, I got nicked over West 'Am'; 'Maybe it's because I'm a Londoner ...'

Why don't you all f-f-f-fade away ... don't try to dig what we all s-s-s-say.

I'm in the midst of it, swept along with the defiance, intoxicated by the danger, a feeling of invincibility fuelled by speed and lager.

'Come on, then, cunt-stable. Come and have a go ...'

The cops defuse the situation expertly by clearing the pub with dogs. No one fancies taking on snarling Alsatians, so people move out slowly, moodily spilling on to the pavement. It's counterproductive. Angry now, the mob storm towards the Minerva as if they mean business.

We pass the Wimpy bar with its smashed window – a skin girl is said to have thrown a Ted girl through it a few hours earlier. About a hundred yards ahead of us, the Grease have swelled to about 200 strong. A Glory Boy platoon suddenly breaks away from our flank and surges up the hill to the left. It makes the charge in *Quadrophenia* seem as threatening as Annie Walker shambling across the *Coronation Street* cobbles. The tactic is obvious – hit the Minerva from the rear. A classic pincer movement. But the cops are too smart. They see what's happening and head off the breakaway mob at the pass. Once again, the ragged army of mods, skins and football Herberts (terrace hooligans) are turned back before they reach their target. There will be no mass beach fighting today.

The two sides stare uneasily at each other, with the cops in between. I doubt it even occurs to any of them to wonder why exactly they are 'at war'. It's just accepted as natural. The rockers – the Grease – are the eternal enemy whose presence has united all the different gangs. But what are they really? Just other working-class English folk with wildly contrasting ideas of what constitutes a cool look and a good night out.

Maybe that's just the way it is. Everyone's gotta hate someone. That's how people are.

Inevitably, my mind goes back to my own youth, 11 years earlier. It was June 1968, I had just turned 13. I was at the Dreamland amusement park in Margate, Kent, with an older cousin and my friend Kevin from Charlton. There were gangs of leftover mods and rockers dotted about, along with a few mobs of younger skinheads. The mod girls looked gorgeous with their bobbed hair and slacks or skirts that came just over their knees; but love was most definitely not in the air this day. The out-of-town mods eyed the local rockers with contempt. Their displeasure was returned with a side order of venom. The tension fascinated me. The mods were more numerous, the rockers fewer but older, and probably harder. The first fight kicked off. I wasn't scared, it was exhilarating, but my cousin bundled me and Kev into an arcade. Opposite, a fella with Ted sideburns leapt over his hotdog counter to join the fray. An older kid saw his chance and seized it. He vaulted the counter, opened the till and helped himself to the takings, taking to his heels just seconds before the police arrived. Years later, the comedian Malcolm Hardee confessed to me that this opportunist tealeaf had been him.

To the papers, politicians and the TV news, hooliganism is all just pointless – either mindless violence or empty bravado. But they see youth cults only from the outside, from a distance. They see the boot go in or the window smash but they don't see the creativity and culture – the art, the music, the style, poetry, literature, friendships and the feeling, goddamn it, the feeling of being part of something, something now, something happening, something that matters. It's like judging a rhino by its horn or Dickens by Bill Sykes.

Back in the heady here and now, I contemplate the opposing tribes. Aside from the sartorial differences, the biggest rift between them is age. The rockers are generally older. They're also scruffier and tooled up; some have quiffs but mostly they have long greasy hair, a mass of leather and denim sheltering under a Confederate flag. Some of their trousers are flared.

The mods hoist up a Union Flag with The Who emblazoned across it as a counterpoint. 'They're history, we're now,' says a spotty teen, the irony completely lost on him. Sharp young Londoners start to banter.

'Look at them spotty hairy-faced bastards – and the blokes are just as bad.'

'What about that grease bag? 'E's got enough oil on his barnet to solve the fuckin' petrol crisis.'

'Look at that fat cunt, he'd 'ave to go to school to be an idiot . . .' And on it goes. And it's the same with the rockers, who think the mods are effeminate 'girls', and the skins are 'thickos'. 'My brain hurts!' yells a fella in a drape jacket pointing a heavily ringed finger at a skin. 'Look! 'Is brain hurts! Migraine! The fuckin' gumbie. Where's yer hankie, gumbie? Mum forget to pack it? Have a look! His fuckin' strides have had a row with his shoes.'

Heated slogans and obscenities are hollered before the bored cops begin to push the mod-skin crowd back again.

The Enemy are never engaged. They're never even reached. And it seems to me that most people prefer it like that. It makes them all the more perfect: pantomime baddies to hiss and boo. It's something to define yourself by: *we* not *them*.

This separation makes the few isolated skirmishes of the day seem all the more dramatic, and they are retold frequently. The arrest of West Side terrace warrior Kevin Wells is a favourite, with Wellsy being said to have taken an ever larger number of cops out with him.

It's now gone 3.15pm and the mod and skin battalions have been pushed back towards Southend Pier. Opinions are split between the hardcore, who think the day has been a waste of time because there hasn't been much fighting, and the majority, who have just enjoyed the sheer anarchy of a good old English show of strength in the sun.

It's all downhill from here. Slowly, the police push these teenage tickets back along the seafront. Hundreds line the hill up to the town centre – an army without a cause, or a general. Everyone agrees that lack of organisation and coordination are the only things that stopped the mob routing all opposition – Grease and cops. But no one does any organising.

Frustrations boil over. Small incidents with the police detonate along the front. Seventy-five people are arrested today, but there are no serious injuries and the mood is now largely positive: the kids, united, will never be defeated.

We cheer the few flotillas of scooters and clock famous faces from the new mod scene: Grant Fleming, the three lovable baboons from the fanzine *Maximum Speed*, suede head legend Hoxton Tom and his entourage, Billy H from The Chords, Yeti, old mates from Greengate, Back To Zero – these are people who have been with the movement since the start, months and months before the *Quadrophenia* film came out. I just wish every jaded hack who sat behind a desk in London dismissing mods as a commercial hype could see this now.

I can see for miles …

There are a few sporadic charges to alleviate the boredom, but most of the crowd accept that it's over. The afternoon is winding down. Nothing more is going to happen. By 4pm, the majority are leaving, either drifting home or towards Canvey 11 miles away for tonight's gig. We reach the island in 20 minutes and start looking around for Long Road, where the show will be. See a parka-clad kid sitting with his girl by his scooter. It's a beaut, a real handsome P-reg Vespa festooned with extra headlights and wing mirrors. Both the bike and the kid look familiar, and they should do – he's Robert E Lee, who graces the front cover of the Bridgehouse *Mods Mayday* live album. He obliges us, and the van containing R'n'B Herberts the Little Roosters, with an escort to the Canvey Paddocks. We kill time eating Wimpys and playing 'Love Me Tender' on the pub jukebox for a laugh. All newcomers are greeted with exaggerated accounts of the day's action, and are suckered along long enough to get the drinks in until they twig you're taking the piss and shout, 'You cunt!' without exception. At one stage, Hoxton Tom convinces a dimwit that the police had called in army reinforcements and the skins had linked arms with some navy lads on shore leave. 'It was the people walking on the water who got me though and when the Pope turned up on a Lambretta …' 'You cunt!'

The turnout for the gig is a letdown: only five or six hundred in. We were expecting a capacity crowd but it seems most people have headed back to London. Still, the bands are on top form, with promising sets from Squire and Back to Zero building to stunning performances from Secret Affair and the Purple Hearts. A perfect conclusion to an indifferent day. As ever, the Affair's cocky lyrics mirror the mood of the crowd: 'Glad just to be alive … so much I wanna change …' But what, Ian? What do you wanna change? And what are you gonna put in its place? He never says. It's more the thought of change he's embracing, the need to make room for 'the young idea', whatever that might be. Or more likely it's just the faces on *Top of the Pops* he's referring to. Bye-bye, Cliff, see ya later, Bee Gees … Make way for us? Well, there are worse ambitions.

But Paul Weller caught the grim reality for the audience more accurately when he said how hard it is to understand why the world is your oyster but your future's a clam. Yeah. Because days like today let you think you're a king, when you're really a pawn. We don't care, though, we're still buzzing from the glory pills. So much to say, so much to do. We shake hands all round and crawl out into the darkness. We fought the law and we went home, we fought the law and we went home. A day in the life of a movement. Poxy work again tomorrow.

# INTRODUCTION
## Early Doors

The sun was taking no prisoners that stifling late August day. After a Bank Holiday of bloody street fighting, the cells were crammed full of surly young hooligans awaiting trial. One of these youths caused quite a stir when he was marched into court, because of his haircut. Unlike the traditional 'donkey fringe' of his mates, his hair was clipped as closely as possible to the scalp except for 'a small patch on the crown of the head which was pulled down over the forehead to form a fringe'.

It doesn't sound such a big deal nowadays, but that's because the newspaper report that description is taken from doesn't date from the 1980s, the seventies or even the sixties.

It and the kid with the embryonic Mohican hail from the England of 1898, 112 years ago.

The history of working-class youth cults in the UK is shrouded in Fleet Street fiction, tinsel and tat mythology. Myth One miraculously links the birth of the youth cult with the appearance of Bill Hayley and co. in the mid-1950s, as if the Teddy Boys had hand-jived out of Hayley's kiss-curled skull like Athena springing from the throbbing brain of Zeus. Stuffier conservative thinkers blamed that shocking rock'n'roll 'jungle music' for bringing about a collapse of morality among the young. Marxists, meanwhile, put the rise of youth cults down to the postwar consumer boom and the creation by capitalists of an exploitative 'youth market'. The boom put pound notes in young workers' pockets, they argue, and so the manufacturing industry responded by cooking up spurious fashions and pop stars to con it all back out of them.

There's little sense in the first view and only an element of truth in the second. In fact, as researcher Geoffrey Pearson has discovered, the first youth cults can be traced back directly to the *Daily Mail*'s beloved late Victorian England. The earliest youth gangs were then known by the blanket media catchword 'hooligans', a word derived from a notoriously rowdy family in southeast London of Irish descent whose name was a corruption of Hoolihan.

Just as today, London's 19th-century hooligan street gangs were highly territorial, with crews from Chapel Street warring against their Margaret Street rivals, Fulham hoolies rucking with the neighbouring Chelsea boys and so on. August Bank Holiday, particularly the one in 1898, was a veritable beano of bruising and boozing.

What distinguished the youths from their elder working-class contemporaries was their near universal adoption of a distinct style of dress – a gang uniform of their own creation.

A youth at the very height of hooligan sartorial elegance would have sported bell-bottom trousers with a buttoned vent in the leg, iron-capped boots 'calculated to kill easily', bright neckerchiefs, metal-studded belts and the previously mentioned 'donkey fringe' haircut with a large tuft at the front. The standard look was improvised around freely. For example, hooligans in Poplar, east London, favoured plaid caps and so were known as the Plaid Cap Brigade, whereas in Battersea, south London, velvet caps were the popular choice.

There had been distinctive dress styles before, of course. Those colourful Victorian barrow boys, the cockney costermongers (street sellers of fruit and veg), for example, were renowned for their flash style. For best, these original barrow boys would wear a type of

Crombie, a cloth coat with a contrasting plush collar, a beaver-knapped top hat to replace their standard peaked work cap, a large silk neckerchief known as a kingsman, and heavy ankle boots with elaborate stitched patterns. Their famous pearly outfits had more to do with the Music Hall than the market stall, dating as they do from a later, more nostalgic era when the costers were in decline.

What distinguished the hooligans was their age: they were specifically a youth cult. The cult wasn't confined to London, either, but seems to have been a characteristic of every major city. Kids with the same style of dress and territorial attitudes were known as scuttlers in Manchester and Peaky Blinders in Birmingham – just as we saw scallies, perry boys and chaps develop independently but with many overlapping similarities in Liverpool, Manchester and London between the 1970s and 1980s.

These early delinquents were entirely of lower-class origin. More precisely, they hailed from that group of people whom the 19th-century journalist Henry Mayhew collectively labelled 'the Dangerous Class', encompassing elements of the working class, the criminal class and those hawkers, street traders and wheeler-dealers on the fringes of it. They lived in the same courts and tenements, sharing the same closed communities. What the hooligans also shared with dangerous-class elders was a penchant for back slang (which originated with the costers, although terms such as 'reeb' for beer, 'nammo' for woman and 'escalop' for police, were widely used), and an aggressive attitude to authority. The Peelers were particularly hated. Pearson reproduces a news report on the notorious August Bank Holiday upsets of 1898, which highlights the 'fierce tradition of resistance to the police in working-class neighbourhoods'. A cop who tried to make an arrest would be jumped by crowds of locals, two to three hundred strong on some occasions, shouting 'Rescue! Rescue!' and 'Boot 'im!' A newspaper report of an incident involving the Somers Town Boys (from the Euston Road area of central London) was headlined MIDNIGHT RIOTS: POLICE ATTACKED BY A CROWD OF ROUGHS. These antipolice attitudes, often assumed to be only criminal-class ones, persisted well into the 20th century – for example, resorting to the police was deemed despicable by the skinhead code of conduct, skins, like villains, knowing them as 'the filth' rather than the more homely 'Old Bill' – and date back to their very creation by Robert Peel's Metropolitan Police Act of 1829. An antipolice broadsheet handed out in 1830, for example, gave notice to 'Peel's bloody gang', or the 'Blue Devils', as they were also known, that 'a subscription has been entered into to supply the PEOPLE with STAVES of a superior effect either for defence or punishment, which will be in readiness to be gratuitously distributed whenever an unprovoked and therefore unmanly and bloodthirsty attack be made upon Englishmen by a force unknown to British Constitution legislating for their individual interests, consequently in opposition to the Public good.'

Back in 1898, 'hooligan' was the latest 18-carat, headline-grabbing bogeyman. Politicians, newspaper editors and churchmen queued up to put the cause of the hooligans' battling ways and immorality down to 'Penny Dreadfuls' (the Victorian equivalent of horror comics, which featured such roguish folk legends as 'Spring-Heeled Jack, the Terror of London'), the good old Music Hall, of course, and, according to the 1909 Poor Law Commission 'too much pocket money'.

A quarter of a century later, Hollywood and the radio were to take their share of the blame for delinquency, with conservative commentators wistfully, albeit ironically, stating much as they do now that 'things weren't like this 20 years ago'. More recently, gory films, PC games and sometimes even the emasculated old music press have been named and shamed as the source of teenage turmoil and turbulence. And in the 1950s it was rock'n'roll, which brings us neatly back to that first big myth again – the deeply prevalent idea that Teddy Boys, the first universally recognised nationwide youth cult, were somehow the product of this dangerously alien new music. (See Chapter 1, 'In the Beginning There Was the Ted').

What is undeniably true is that the rise of the Teds wouldn't have happened without the growth of the mass media and the new affluent society. Between October 1951 and October 1963 wages in the UK are estimated to have risen by 72 per cent (prices rose by 45 per cent). After years of austerity, we had full employment, and ownership of consumer goods such as cars, washing machines, record players and TV sets became widespread. Adolescents were the real winners. In the first five years after the end of World War Two, the average teenage wage had shot up at twice the rate of adults', and this trend carried out right through the 1950s, reaching a peak in the 1960s.

Up until the fifties, teenagers didn't exist as a distinct consumer group.

The novelist Colin MacInnes said that before then, in his era, there were 'big boys and girls or young men and women – but no such thing as a teenager'. The boom changed that. Now the kids had money and, more than that, dreams, aspirations and expectations. Never again would the young working class put up with the type of lives their parents and grandparents had taken for granted. The new teenagers refused to 'know their place' and 'respect their elders'.

These kids were lippy, headstrong, dangerous and subversive. They turned insubordination into a lifestyle choice and carved out their own look, their own space and identity. The cults and styles that working-class youth went on to create and adopt were visible symbols of their sense of being distinct from what had gone before. The Teds, like the later skinheads, were an entirely proletarian phenomenon, which is why they were so feared.

But did they achieve anything of worth?

Some argue that teenage rebellion, this revolt into style, was ultimately pointless – just an adolescent phase that changed nothing. Wasn't it all just dressing up and dancing, fucking and fighting? To which you might respond that life would be pretty dull without all of the above. But youth cults were far more important than that: they have turned the old world on its head; they've sparked revolutions in culture, art and in expectations. And not just in the UK, either.

Youth styles and attitudes created on the backstreets of Britain have spread across the globe. Today there are mod scenes in Moscow, Oi! scenes in Beijing and punks and skinheads everywhere from Tokyo to Buenos Aires. Hooligans in Bangkok write 'Cockney Rejects' on walls and draw crossed hammers next to them. Rioters in Seattle wear badges of anarchist bands like Conflict and Crass. Scooter clubs in Italy fly the Union Flag and listen to The Jam.

Hooligan British youth have stamped their influence on our entire global culture.

This book tells their story.

# CHAPTER ONE

# IN THE BEGINNING, THERE WAS THE TED: FROM BILL HALEY TO NOTTING HILL

You're young, tough and working-class. You're earning money, but you're bored. Your world is so black and white and austere you could be living in a Pathé newsreel. And then one night at the pictures you hear it: 'Put your gladrags on and join me, hon, we'll have some fun when the clock strikes one …'

Everyone is up from their seats and dancing in the aisles. You too. This is the music you love, and you're hearing 'Rock Around the Clock' on proper speakers for the very first time. Excited, you reach for your razor and you cut the nearest cinema chair, stabbing it and slashing it. And your mates are dancing too, and so is that girl you've always fancied. Life could not be sweeter.

And now the police are here, trying to drag you away, drag you out of your own local fleapit. Why? You're just having a good time. And so, when the copper pushes you, you fight back …

Teddy Boys reached their peak in Britain in 1956, and became forever tarnished by their association with the Notting Hill race riots two years later. But where did they come from and why did they catch on? The first major myth of youth-cult history is that the Teddy Boys were a by-product of rock'n'roll. Not so. The Teds had been in existence for years before the arrival of hammy Bill Haley. It just took the release of the movie *Blackboard Jungle* in 1956 to drag them to the attention of a cowering nation. Its use of Haley's 'Rock Around the Clock' over the opening credits electrified young audiences. Kids danced in the aisles, seats were slashed in the excitement, and everything got blown out of all proportion. The police reacted savagely – and were met with unexpected resistance. At the Elephant and Castle Trocadero in south London, frenzied teenagers started hacking at the seats with cut-throat razors. Cops who were called to break up the crowd found themselves pelted with bottles and lighted fireworks. Two officers were injured and nine Teds were arrested.

Similar scenes occurred all over the UK. Down the road in Lewisham, the Teds yanked out the front seats at the Gaumont Theatre and proceeded to slice them up. A few miles away in Stratford, east London, police ejected an estimated 120 teenagers from the Gaumont. Out of control and high on life, the Teds continued to jive and party defiantly on the flower gardens outside.

At Manchester's Gaiety Theatre, Teddy Boys in the balcony hurled lighted cigarettes at kids in the stalls below. At Bootle, police drew truncheons to escort 'delirious' kids out of the cinema. Worried councillors quickly banned the film in Blackpool, Birmingham and Belfast; and the Teddy Boy was nationally recognised as the face of delinquency. Public Enemy Number One.

But where had they come from – and why? The Teds actually predated rock by quite a few years. They had grown out of the territorial gangs that had long been a part of young, working-class, inner-city life. Pre-Ted but postwar, the national press was awash with a new youth threat – the Cosh Boy, a species of juvenile hoodlum who livened up his boring life with random violence. The young Reggie and Ronnie Kray, for example, figured prominently in the Hackney youth battles of the early 1950s. 'It was just kids running free,' Ronnie once told me. 'It was finding your feet, carving out a name for yourself with your fists, and anything else that came to hand.'

What the gang fights offered was high-adrenalin excitement in the very drab postwar world. London especially was riddled with hideous bomb sites. National Service loomed like a coming court conviction, and rationing, and with it those never-ending queues, was a fact of life until 1954. Popular culture wasn't coming from the streets, but from the Establishment. It was tailored for young adults 'training' to become 'real' adults. Entertainment for the young working class was particularly ropey, being mostly confined to massive dance halls like the Mecca, the Locarno and the Palais: big bands and ballroom dancing. BBC radio's po-faced Light Programme was equally grim. Films were tame and clothes were a nightmare, with foul dungaree and tartan designs mass-produced to distinguish Joey Teen from his old man in his floppy demob suit.

Only the spivs with their US dress had any sense of style at all.

Of course, the Marxists were right when they said the consumer boom of the 1950s changed all this. Youth wages were growing, but capitalism didn't create the Teddy Boy cult for young workers – they stole it for themselves from right under the noses of the Establishment, contemptuously rejecting the patronising crap that was being created by clothing companies for them.

At the fag end of the 1940s, Savile Row had tried to revive Edwardian men's fashion among the upper classes. The style had first been resurrected in homosexual circles. Savile Row's espousal of it resulted in its brief, limited popularity among young Guards officers and the like, for whom the long Edwardian jackets with their velvet collars evoked a sense of nostalgia for the pre-World War One so-called golden age of Edward VII's reign. It hadn't exactly been a laugh a minute for the working classes, but it was working-class kids who really picked up on the fashion, lifting it right from under the toffs' noses to create their own identity as Teddy Boys (Teddy being an obvious contraction of Edwardian).

Skinny youths from inner-city London – the Elephant & Castle first, with Clapham and Tottenham not far behind – crossed cosh-boy aggression with a dedication to fashion, creating a phenomenon all of their own. The effect was astonishing – simultaneously foppish and vicious.

Society soon recognised this shocking development with newspaper articles in 1953 identifying Edwardian suits as the distinguishing mark of 'the craze that leads to gaol'. In south London especially, the Teds were involved in vast inter-gang territorial battles, leading to some dance halls banning Teddy suits altogether. During that same year, questions were asked in the House of Commons and a 17-year-old kid called John Beckley was stabbed to death by Teds on Clapham Common.

It wasn't a one-off. There were incidents all over the southeast of England. In Essex, Teds smashed up a train on the Barking–Southend line. In Epping Forest two brothers, both Teddy Boys, robbed another teen with a loaded air rifle. In April 1954, 55 youths were taken in for questioning after two rival mobs of Teds met for a rumble at St Mary Cray railway station in Kent after a dance. Their arsenal of weapons included house bricks and socks packed with sand and coins.

The previous month, a 16-year-old youth was convicted at Dartford Magistrates' Court in Kent of robbing a woman 'by putting her in fear'. The chairman of the bench told him, 'There are a lot of so-called pleasures of the world which demand a lot of money. You tried to get hold of money to pay for ridiculous things like Edwardian suits. They are ridiculous in the eyes of ordinary people. They are flashy, cheap and nasty and stamp the wearer as a particularly undesirable type.'

Flashy maybe, but cheap? Hardly. Young Teds would spend their entire wages on clothes. Different areas sported different-colour drape jackets (or just drapes with different-colour collars, or even just different-colour socks) to identify them as a gang distinct from other gangs. For full peacock glory, these frock coats were augmented by fancy embroidered waistcoats, moleskin collars and 'drainpipe' trousers so tight they were a second skin. Like the mods a decade later, the Teds were obsessed with looking good, looking right.

At first narrow ties were favoured but, as the American influence grew, the gambler's bootstring became more popular, held together with a variety of different medallions – American eagles, death heads and suchlike. The look became vulgarised until the Ted was more like a US gunslinger than an English Edwardian nob. The urban cowboy was here. The shoes that went with the look were also American: brothel creepers (a.k.a. beetle crushers), which had thick foam-rubber undersoles. The hair had to be right, too. The Teds pioneered their own versions of the US Marine crew cut like the spiky-top and the silver dollar, the latter being the shortest but both styles being heavily greased back. Film star Tony Curtis donated a much-imitated style, but the cut that evolved as the standard male look had a frontal quiff and a DA (duck's arse) cut at the back with the hair lovingly greased to meet in the middle. Sideburns caught on, too.

The original Teddy Girl look included hobble or pencil skirts, black, seamed nylon stockings and coolie hats. Like the men, they adopted drape jackets. Some adventurously wore slacks. Brooches and lace-up espadrilles were popular, and, later, American-style circle skirts and toreador pants caught on.

Although the Teds are the youth cult normally associated with the fifties, there were smaller, less well-publicised localised alternatives such as the Vicky Boys in Hammersmith, who looked to Victorian rather than Edwardian fashion for their uniform. They favoured a short jacket with thin lapels, a loud waistcoat, starch-collared shirts and thin ties – an obvious forerunner of the Italian look that became nationally popular later in the decade. Like Ted, the Vicky look was an exclusively working-class fashion, middle-class kids being more prone to express their dissatisfaction through CND and folk music – standard protest – or they took to jazz. Duffle coats were disgustingly prominent.

Nationally, the Teds were the only sharp dressers and the only action going.

'Straight' society didn't know what to make of it all. Why was juvenile crime on the up and up, at the same time as juvenile wages?

These kids were like a secret society, a teenage Mafia, impenetrable to the adult experts. Scotland Yard compiled a report on the Ted phenomenon for the Home Office. Pulpit preachers blamed the collapse of Christianity for these devils in drapes. Newspaper pundits belched forth acres of shock-horror column inches. For the first time kids all over the country were able to read about other kids as though they were an alien breed.

Until the mid-fifties the Teds were a very small minority, however. And then Ted met rock'n'roll head-on. It was a union forged in teenage heaven.

Rock'n'roll was liberating: the manic mixed marriage of black American R&B and white American country. In it, the Teddy Boys discovered music as wild and untamed as they appeared to the authorities to be. They took to rock as enthusiastically as they took to the new breed of American actor – men like James Dean, whose death in 1955 while he was still young and beautiful guaranteed his immortality, and Marlon Brando, whose movie *The Wild One*, about a marauding motorcycle gang, was banned in Britain for over a decade.

One piece of dialogue from the film summed up the Ted mood perfectly. A girl asks the Brando antihero, 'Hey, Johnny, what are you rebelling against?'

Brando shrugs and says, 'Whaddya got?'

Rock'n'roll was the only music energetic and exciting enough to do the Teds justice. George Melly captured the essence of the new sound when he called it 'screw-and-smash music'. Or more coarsely, fuck-and-fight.

Naturally, the Establishment and reactionaries hated it as much as they hated the Teds themselves. But, the more the papers sensationalised it and the authorities put it down, the more it grew. In America, groups like the Alabama White Citizens Council issued severe statements warning that 'the obscenity and vulgarity of the rock'n'roll music is obviously a means by which the white man and his children can be driven to the level of the nigra – it is obviously nigger music.' In Britain the naturally more polite *Any Questions* radio panel preferred to label it 'the logical extension of jungle music'.

This unsavoury racialist element pervaded the opinions of even the most respectable criticisms. Liberal MP Jeremy Thorpe likened rock'n'roll to 'Mau Mau music', a reference to Kenyan terrorists/freedom fighters (delete to suit your prejudices) in Africa, while leading classical conductor Sir Malcolm Sargent snorted that it was 'nothing more than primitive tom-tom thumping'. He went on, 'Rock'n'roll has been played in the jungle for centuries.'

All of which is pretty ironic when you consider that a few years later the Teds would be blamed for Britain's first postwar race riot at Notting Hill in west London.

It's hard for us now to appreciate just how threatening and otherworldly rock'n'roll appeared. It wasn't just old fogeys who were outraged, either. Even Old Blue Eyes saw red. 'Rock'n'roll smells phoney and false,' Sinatra raged. 'It is sung, played and written for the most part by cretinous goons ... and by means of its almost imbecilic reiteration and sly, lewd – in fact, plain dirty – lyrics, it manages to be the martial music of every sideburned delinquent on the face of the earth.'

The Teds weren't bothered: 1956 was their year, the year Teddy Boys blew up into a mass cult, and the Americanisation of their look moved up a gear.

The spark was a very ordinary Bill Haley movie called *Rock Around the Clock*, which sent the mass media into a frenzy. It was made quickly to cash in on Haley's chart success. As a film, it stank. It was cheaply made with next to no plot. But somehow the papers conspired to make the genial but balding and boring Bill Haley look like some sort of fire-breathing, baby-gobbling subversive. More riotous behaviour in cinemas followed and by September Haley had five singles in the Top Twenty.

The title track of the film has now sold in excess of 20 million copies worldwide.

Increased youth spending power saw record sales soar. Businessmen recognised the youth market as a separate consumer group and rushed to supply the new demand coming up from the streets. Rock'n'roll was the main beneficiary. First heard in Britain via Radio Luxembourg, by 1956 it became the first genuine teenage music.

With the coming of Elvis Presley, the Teds got the icon on the cake, the first real rock heartthrob. Elvis was the poor white truck driver who became the megastar of megastars, embodying the rags-to-riches rock dream along the way. In 1954, aged just 19, he recorded 'That's All Right Mama' at Sun Studios, Memphis, fulfilling producer Sam Phillips's dream of finding 'a white guy who sings like a Negro.' That recording was the moment when the embryonic new music found its perfect embodiment.

There were black performers who were more creative, such as the duck-walking wordsmith Chuck Berry, whose style influenced everyone from the Beatles to the Beach Boys, or the hysterically hyperenergised Little Richard Penniman, but at the time whiteness itself was a pre-requisite of mass acceptance.

It's important to emphasise that rock'n'roll was part of a rich two-way flow between black and white musicians at this time, however. Berry admitted his sublime first hit 'Maybelline' was inspired by 'Ida Red' by white western-swing performer Bob Wills.

Besides, Elvis was more than just another singer. He had everything that Malcolm McLaren was to correctly identify as the mainstays of rock'n'roll immortality – Sex (such was the suggestive power of his strutting hips that on TV he would be screened from the waist up), Style (Presley was cool personified) and Subversion (he oozed it – until he got drafted down the middle of the road). A Des Moines Baptist preacher denounced Elvis as 'morally insane'; several cities concurred, and banned him altogether.

With mass appeal, Teddy Boys inevitably changed. Once, Ted was about fighting and fashion, now it was more to do with music and dancing. Gradually it became publicly acceptable. By 1957 Princess Margaret could be seen tapping her royal tootsies to those despicable jungle rhythms as Jayne Mansfield bust out all over *The Girl Can't Help*

*It*. The *Daily Express* considered it front-page news. In less than two years, rock'n'roll had achieved, if not society's approval, then at least its tolerance.

That same year the *Daily Mirror* got in on the act, organising the Bill Haley Special train that brought the man himself to Waterloo to be met by 3,000 screaming fans. Hysteria plagued his European tour. More seats were slashed, aisles were jived in, and in Berlin film cameras captured scenes more reminiscent of the Sham 69 concerts of 1978 than *Rock Around the Clock*. Chairs were trashed and the stage was invaded with Germanic gusto.

But Haley was his own undoing. Rock journalist Nik Cohn wrote: 'the only trouble was Haley himself, he turned out to be a back-dated vaudeville act … and when the shouting and stamping had all died down, everyone finally had to face facts and Haley was through.' The spell he'd cast over British kids since 1955 was broken, and after that Elvis Presley, who really did reflect the untamed youth of the Teds, was the one true King.

Many of the original Teds had ditched the cult by now, moving on in the only way acceptable to any gang – by getting spliced and having kids. The new wave of Teds had a different understanding of the Teddy Boy ethic. Fighting continued in backstreets, arcades and fairgrounds, but now the music had become the main thing. Teds had lost their subversive edge in the eyes of the media, and, although the term was to stay synonymous with 'hooligan' for some time to come, the image of the Teds became almost cuddly.

They did regain an element of notoriety at the tail-end of their popularity when some Teds were involved in London's first serious racial disturbances. Between 1955 and 1957 a total of 132,000 black Commonwealth immigrants had arrived in Britain to meet the needs of the expanding economy; 80,000 of these were West Indian. In the west London suburb of Notting Hill, where black families were being housed, working-class whites responded by evicting them in a protest against 'queue jumping'.

The trouble reached a crisis point over the August Bank Holiday of 1958 with the notorious Notting Hill race riots, triggered by 300-400-strong 'Keep Britain White' mobs, many of them Teddy Boys armed with iron bars, butchers' knives, razors and weighted leather belts who went 'nigger hunting' among the West Indian residents of Notting Hill and Notting Dale. The first night left five black men unconscious on the pavements. It was a miracle nobody died. The violence continued over the weekend as black men responded in kind. West Indian Thomas Williams was stopped by the police and found to have a lump of iron down his left trouser leg, an open razor blade in his inside breast pocket and a petrol bomb in his right pocket. He told the arresting officer, 'I have to protect myself.'

108 people were charged with offences ranging from grievous bodily harm to affray and riot and possessing an offensive weapon: 72 were white, 36 'coloured'.

In the aftermath, ITN dispatched Reginald Bosanquet and black journalist Ernest Ickle to investigate. Their report, which seems remarkably even-handed by contemporary standards, found that there were 'genuine grievances on both sides'. Ickle spoke to white residents, Bosanquet to black ones. Ickle found that the whites were agitated by the small minority of black immigrants who were involved in prostitution in the area. They complained of 'girls on the game', black men 'living off women' and 'houses run as brothels'.

Rioters at the time insisted that the spark that set off the three nights of violence was a local white girl being beaten up by a black pimp. Not that this excuses, for example, the attack on Majbritt Morrison, a young Swedish girl whose only 'crime' was to have married a Jamaican. Majbritt was pelted with stones, glass and wood and struck in the back with an iron bar as she tried to get home. Very chivalrous.

The local cops blamed 'ruffians both white and coloured who took the opportunity to indulge in hooliganism'.

The contemporary police statements show that the mobs of yobs were openly defiant of the cops. PC Victor Coe said he had seen a Teddy

Boy called David Slater in Artesian Road 'sitting astride a motorcycle in company with a crowd of about fifty youths dressed in Edwardian-type clothing. I told him to move and he said, "Why the hell should I?"'

Detective Sergeant Walters reported on the third night that there was a 'large group of coloured men' walking along Ladbroke Grove. He described them as 'a mob [who] were shouting threats and abuse, and openly displaying various most offensive weapons, ranging from iron bars to choppers and open razors'. One of them, Denton Boyd (later sentenced to 12 months' imprisonment) had an axe in his hand and was shouting, 'Come and fight,' and, 'What about it now?'

In Notting Dale, a white greengrocer's wife faced down an angry crowd to save black student Seymour Manning from a beating.

The disturbances finally petered out on 5 September. Nine white youths were tried at the Old Bailey and received four-year sentences.

Racial clashes involving Teds (among others) and blacks made no sense at all when you considered how greatly rock'n'roll was indebted to working-class US black culture, but had a regrettable logic when you look at it from the point of view of what had inspired earlier clashes between rival white youths – territorial attitudes and the quest for excitement. Teds were involved in disturbances at Notting Hill and similar incidents in Nottingham – most street-fighting youth at this time would have been Teds, so this figures. But such incidents were atypical and were neither repeated nor translated into support for extreme right-wing politics. Sir Oswald Mosley, the pioneer British fascist, returned from Eire to launch his 'biggest postwar campaign' at the Notting Hill election of October 1959. For the first time in his electoral career he lost his deposit.

Notting Hill's West Indian carnival was launched at the August Bank holiday of 1959 as a direct response to these riots. Twenty years on, the Notting Hill and Ladbroke Grove areas of London were bastions of anti-racist or at least non-racist skinhead feeling.

# CHAPTER TWO

# IN THE BEGINNING:
# MODS AND ROCKERS

'WILD ONES INVADE SEASIDE – 90 ARRESTS.
POLICE CHIEF SENDS SOS FOR REINFORCEMENTS'
*Daily Mirror* front page, 30 March 1964

Everyone knows what mod was about, don't they? Mobs of immaculately dressed Herberts smashing up a seaside town, the loud anthemic rock of The Who, the colour and pizzazz of Carnaby Street when England swung like a pendulum does ...

Inevitably, it's far more complicated than that.

Original mod was very sixties, very forward-looking; very much of its time. Whereas skinhead a few years later would be uncompromisingly working-class, mod was about aspiration, improving your life, not settling for the job your dad did. Although mod hit the headlines in 1964, its roots went back years earlier to a small group of north London teenagers, many Jewish, who combined their interests to create a unique and exclusive style. Mod was to become a street fashion but lower-middle-class kids were the originators – exhibitionists one and all. At the start they were rebelling against mass tastes and everyday expectations. Theirs was a revolt into style. Ironically, young pioneers like Wayne Kirven, Steve Sparks and John Simon took influences as diverse as American jazz, French cinema and Italian cool to create something quintessentially English.

In his 1959 novel *Absolute Beginners*, Colin MacInnes calls a young jazz fan who dresses in sharp Italian clothes a modernist – this is thought to be the first time the name was used in print. The name derived from modern jazz (Miles Davis and Charlie Mingus being prime examples). French New Wave films, such as Jean-Luc Godard's 1960 movie *À bout de souffle* starring Jean-Paul Belmondo and Jean Seberg, were much admired.

But what united these individual young dandies was their shared obsession with clothes. Stylish Italian waiters riding around Soho on their scooters in their bum-freezer jackets were their inspiration; they begat what John Simon calls 'the cult of the male peacock'. The mod pioneers weren't as yet a group, but rather a sprinkling of highly individual stylists who paid huge attention to detail. They wanted to stand out, so they sought out unusual clothes, such as the green button-down shirt that Miles Davis wore on the *Milestone* album. And they had suits made – smart, round-shouldered, single-breasted whistles with two-and-a-quarter-inch lapels and slanted two-inch flap pockets. The trousers were low-fitting with slanted frog-mouth pockets.

The look was as eye-catching as it was unique. In 1962, *Town* magazine ran an article about these style-crazy teenage trendsetters, with the subhead 'YOUNG MEN WHO LIVE FOR CLOTHES AND PLEASURE'. Among them was Wayne Kirven, then 17, and 15-year-old Marc Feld, who regarded himself as a young Beau Brummel. You may know him better by the stage name he adopted later: Marc Bolan.

Inexorably, the mod style developed. The suits were constantly amended. Bell bottoms came in briefly. Fred Perry-style sportswear was adopted as a distinctively mod item – because it was ideal for dancing in sweaty clubs – and, soon after, Levi's jeans, which were expensive by contemporary standards. Italian haircuts became fashionable at the turn of the decade, followed by the Perry Como cut, the college boy and then the French crew cut. Scooters began to be identified with the look around 1959. Gangs of scooter boys could be seen by 1960, and with them parka coats. Hush Puppies and ski pants were a popular look for girls around this time.

The old world – of grey austerity, rationing, and a too rigid class system – was a drag. Mod rebelled against that drabness, and against the inevitability of being stuck at the bottom of life's dunghill. In their book *On Fashion*, Shari Benstock and Suzanne Ferriss argue that mod 'mocked the class system that had gotten their fathers nowhere'. The young mods worshipped leisure and consumerism. Nine-to-five work was just something they did to pay for their clothes and their all-night clubs. Hundreds of chemist shops would be broken into for the uppers to keep them going.

In his well-researched and recommended book *Mods*, Richard Barnes pinpoints 1962 as the year mod changed from being a scattering of individuals into a youth cult as such. After that, the look developed at an even faster pace. City-gent suits complete with brollies caught on briefly, followed by the 'waisted' English suit, and, as the cult became increasingly street-level, so casual clothes like cycle shirts and cycle shoes came in. The Lonsdale sports shop in Beak Street, London became popular, as did backcombing the hair. This time also saw the emergence of the Ace Face mod, the elite stylist who was a fashion leader, as opposed to the ticket, the younger mod who followed the trends. East End face Barrie 'the Mod' Taylor recalls, 'Mod was all about obsession. It was intense. You had to look dead right. We were neat and we were clean – the polar opposite of the rockers.'

He goes on, 'The mod shirt of choice had a button-down collar. The only ones we could get at the start were American, Brooksweave. And they cost £4 apiece, which in those days was a lot.' The button-down collar had been developed by the clothing company Brooks Brothers as a way of keeping collars from flapping about while one was on one's nag playing polo. The British designer Ben Sherman successfully marketed a cheaper home-grown version using tartans and candy stripes. Ironically, a shirt developed for posh Americans was to become one of the enduring symbols of both mod and skinhead street fashion.

Mod's musical allegiances changed too. American Forces radio had first introduced mods to the underground sounds of black American music, the blues and then rhythm and blues, out of which grew the true mod music: 1960s soul as pioneered by assembly-line car worker turned music magnate Berry Gordy and his Tamla Motown label (not to mention Stax, Volt and the other Atlantic labels, Dial, Fame and Music Enterprises).

Gordy was an incredible character. In 1959, he had only a few hundred dollars to his name, but he was a hustler and he employed a network of enthusiasts: Tamla's receptionist Janie Bradford doubled as a talent scout; singer Mable John drove Gordy around before he could afford a car; and the incredible William 'Smokey' Robinson knocked up 'answer' songs aping recent hits. The Miracles' 'Shop Around' was their first million seller in 1961, and the Marvelettes had their first Number 1 with 'Please Mr Postman' that same year. After that the success never stopped, with smash singles from the Supremes, The Temptations, Stevie Wonder and more. Tamla Motown was the Hit Factory, outselling even The Beatles. It gave R&B a stylish pop sheen, making it easily accessible to a young British audience – unlike the harder, rawer and more raucous sounds of James Brown, whose funk was undiluted and uncompromising. (If Elvis made love to the microphone, James Brown humped it to death – and back to life again.) Brown's 1962 *Live at the Apollo* was the first million-selling R&B album; he inspired everything from disco to hip-hop. His influence can't be overstated.

In England, a highly derivative R&B scene developed, spawning The Rolling Stones and The Pretty Things, but their scruffiness and lack of authenticity meant they were scorned by the hardcore mods.

The first band to score real credibility were The Who (formerly the High Numbers) from west London. They had their image contrived for them by leading ace face Pete Meaden (who defined mod succinctly as 'clean living under difficult circumstances' and who was given a meagre £50 by Who manager Bill Curbishley to kit the band out authentically). What made The Who special was their guitarist Pete Townshend, a former Young Communist whose lyrics combined mod angst and the sense of the young as a class apart. He had a knack of writing songs that mirrored the thinking of a typical Shepherd's Bush mod. Dressed in Union Flag suits, Townshend smashed his guitar on stage and wrote anthems that perfectly captured teenage frustration, songs like 'I Can't Explain', 'Anyway Anyhow Anywhere' and, best of all, the 1965 stuttering scorcher 'My Generation' with its barely concealed taboo-busting innuendo, 'Why don't you all f-fade away?'

When pin-up Who singer Roger Daltrey raged, 'I hope I die before I get old', a million teenage boys appreciated the sentiment.

Mod turned scooterist Barrie Taylor recalls, 'The Who were the loudest band any of us had ever heard and the most exciting thing I'd ever seen. My ears still bleed just thinking about it. They played in front of a mountain of amps. It was the musical equivalent of a smack in the mouth.'

Other rock bands were formed by mods or were associated with the mod look, principally The Kinks, the Yardbirds and Small Faces, who were East End mods, small and neat with a tendency to jump on any passing arty fad. But even they weren't really accepted by the mod purists. To the hardcore, there were only ever two components to genuine mod music: American soul, the blacker the better, and Jamaican ska, which was also to become the defining music of the skinheads.

The years 1963–65 were the golden ones of mod, with the scene developing at a frightening pace. This was the time of Carnaby Street, before commercialisation killed it, coffee bars, dances, amphetamines to keep you moving for whole weekends without sleep. London's Soho was Mecca for the mods. The club scene was thriving.

Barrie Taylor says, 'We had the Allnighter [at the Flamingo in Wardour Street], which played a lot of bluebeat, the Scene, which was the main mod club, and La Discothèque. The Marquee, also then in Wardour Street, was an important venue for live R&B.'

But mod meant more than music and fashion. It meant an explosion of creativity and the possibility of upward mobility for sharper working-class kids. Ronan O'Rahilly opened his Radio Caroline pirate station on Easter Sunday 1964 in memory of his granddad, who'd died during the IRA's Easter rising of 1916. Cathy McGowan made TV history presenting *Ready Steady Go* – the first (maybe the only) pop TV show to move at teen pace and avoid patronising.

Tom Wolfe spelled out the ethics of Mod with poetic precision in his essay 'The Noonday Underground':

*What is it with this kid? Here he is, 15 years old and he is better dressed than any man in the office. He has on a checked suit with a double-breasted waistcoat and a step-collar on it and the jacket coming in at the waist about like so, and then trousers that come down close here then flare out here, and a custom-made shirt that comes up like ... so at the neckband, little things very few people would even know about, least of all those poor straight noses in the office who never had a suit in their lives that wasn't off the peg. They have better accents, but he has ... THE LIFE ... and a secret place he goes at lunch time – a noonday underground. And nobody is even lapsing into the old pub system either, that business where you work your gourds off all day and then sink into the foaming ooze of it all. You can buy enough pills and other lovelies of the pharmacological arts to stay high for hours. In THE LIFE even the highs are different. The hell with bitter, watercress and old Lard-belly telling you it's TIME ...*

From the start it was obvious that coexistence between mods and rockers wasn't to be. Rockers thought mods were effeminate, wimpish and snobbish. Weedy poofs. Mods thought the rockers were coarse, out-of-date, thicko yobs with no class. 'We thought they were morons,' Barrie Taylor shrugs. With more than a little help from the media, battle lines were drawn up, and, after Fleet Street exaggerated a Clacton

Easter Bank Holiday run-in out of all proportion (CHAOS IN CLACTON), the genteel Southern seaside resorts of Margate, Southend, Hastings, Brighton and Bournemouth all saw genuine clashes between the two cults. On 30 March 1964, the *Daily Mirror* splashed with WILD ONES INVADE SEASIDE – 90 ARRESTS, with the subheading POLICE CHIEF SENDS SOS FOR REINFORCEMENTS. In May that year, the Battle of Brighton Beach was illustrated with dramatic pictures of rockers jumping off a seaside sun terrace to escape the mod hoards. Nik Cohn wrote of 'ecstatic weekends – 72 hours without sleep and all you did was run around, catcall, swallow pills and put the boot in. For the first time in your life, the only time, you were under no limitations and nobody controlled you and you caught sight of Nirvana.'

Mostly, the action was saved for ritualised Bank Holiday battling because the two groups tended to hail from different areas. Mods dominated the cities, especially London, the London suburbs and the Home Counties. Rockers held the countryside and the Northern towns. Where the two groups crossed over, aggro abounded. Hackney's Victoria Park and Leyton Baths were notorious for mods'. and rockers' 'offs'.

Leyton Baths were regularly used as a music venue in the early sixties. The centre's swimming pool would be covered by boards, creating an artificial dance floor. Acts including the Beatles, Rolling Stones, Small Faces and Marianne Faithfull all played the venue. When the Stones played there in 1963, 3,000 fans packed in – with as many outside. But tensions developed between mods and rockers at the venue, exploding in regular bloody battles. In *Buttons: The Making of a President* – the biography of a notorious Islington-born British Hell's Angels leader called Peter 'Buttons' Welsh – Jamie Mandelkau recalls,

*A system of segregation developed at the Leyton Baths between our rockers and the mods. We covered the front near the stage and the mods hung in the dark of the rear of the hall. There used to be a lot of close fighting, sometimes with knives, and people would stumble out of the baths, cut and*

*bleeding. I think this was possibly the main reason why the baths were eventually closed for gigs.*

Buttons, who later became president of the Hell's Angels' first London chapter, also describes a fight between a fellow rocker, named Ritchie, and a mod, saying, 'He attacked Ritchie, who waited for the guy to lunge, let the knife slip by him and hammered the mod on the neck with a pick-axe handle. The squishing sound coupled with the skin splitting was a nice effect.'

Trying to winkle out the reasons for the wildness, agony aunt Marjorie Proops interviewed a young mod girl Teresa ('Terry') Gordon in the *Daily Mirror* on 23 May 1964. Patiently, Terry explained, 'We've got a different attitude to life. Mods enjoy life, they like to dance. Rockers don't dance. Mods like blues and blue beat rhythm music, and they go to clubs and dances. Rockers just listen to pop music. Rockers carry knives, mods don't have weapons. You've got to be a mod or a rocker to mean anything.'

But in between the two extremes there were several groups of unfortunates who just couldn't get it right. Terry talked about 'states' in the *Mirror* – the contemptuous mod handle for kids who thought they were mods but were hopelessly out of touch with the real look and feel of modernism. 'Mockers' were neither one thing nor the other. For example, they might wear a nylon version of a rocker's leather and top it off with a mod haircut. But at least the mockers were consciously mixing up the two fashions. Another subgroup, the 'mids', combined elements of the two opposing styles without sussing that they looked about as cool as the Towering Inferno.

Partly because of the violence, partly because the very essence of mod was change – that constant search for the new, the ultimate look – mod began to decline after 1964, and by 1966 the movement was on the skids with increasing numbers of modernist youths becoming attracted to other areas: pop art, flares, psychedelia and hallucinogenic drugs. They cross-fertilised with students, and the Hippy Underground, with all its attendant follies, blossomed. Tune in, turn on, cop out. What a corny con that turned out to be!

David Lazar, the mod-turned-avenging-columnist hero of Tony Parsons' seminal novel *Limelight Blues*, twigs that the lifestyle is dying when his mates mock his immaculate mohair whistle as 'passé', start earwigging Dylan instead of Motown and dump their pills to puff on joints. In real life, Ronnie Lane's realisation came when he chanced upon Rod 'the mod' Stewart out on the west coast of America – Rod started slating his perfectly pressed 'gangster suit' while flamboyantly modelling a floral blouse from Miss Selfridge.

There were two major reactions against this development – one in the North, the other in the South. By their own admission the Northern mods caught onto the cult later, but held onto it longer. In the North change was slower and different and the Northern scene was still flourishing long after trend-setting London townies were into acid or aggro. Mod DJs everywhere had always prided themselves on their ability to search out new artists and new labels, developing beyond the more mainstream strains of Stax and Tamla. Naturally, Northern DJs continued this trend, and their searching eventually evolved into the distinctive sound of Northern soul – fast, brassy, and often bootlegged. Based on speed-fuelled all-nighters in Wigan and also Cleethorpes and Manchester, Northern soul developed in the early 1970s as a mod offspring with marked differences. The cult made such a fetish of obscurity that musical values went increasingly by the board, while, for practical purposes, suits, collars and ties were replaced by vests and wide baggy trousers – aesthetically unappealing, but all the better to dance in.

Aside from soul music, the other constant in the North's evolution was the staple diet of cross-country scooter runs. These clubs spanned the years from the 1960s to the mod renewal of the late 1970s and, even though at times the clubs' memberships may have been down to five or six enthusiasts, the tradition wasn't allowed to die.

In the South, skinheads evolved.

# ENTER THE ROCKER

By 1958, the Teddy Boy look was becoming dated. The next youth wave wasn't a direct descendent of the Ted, but it was a close relation, for the second youth uniform to appear was based more on the Teddy Boy's delinquent American equivalent. Drapes were swapped for leather jackets, jeans worn tight, open shirts became fashionable, hair was getting longer and was awash with grease, heavy motorbikes were all the rage. By 1959, the media had identified a new youth villain – the 'ton-up boy', who was to father the rocker, a.k.a. the greaser or the biker ('ton-up' was British slang for driving at 100mph).

The American black-leather cowboys predated even the British Teds. The outlaw motorbike club the Booze Fighters had been involved in the Hollister riot in California in 1947 and had inspired Brando's 1953 film *The Wild One*. Like that of his American cousin, the rocker's point wasn't just to ride his bike but to ride it as fast and as recklessly as possible. Bike casualties were British hospitals' biggest boom area in the early sixties.

Because of his wildness and his noise, the development of the rocker overshadowed the parallel appearance of the Italian look as a Ted spin-off. This first appeared in 1958 and was, ironically, the direct ancestor of the rocker's biggest rival, the mod. The Italian look was more arrogant than aggressive, but the vanity and flash were inherited from the Teds. It was characterised by short collarless jackets nicknamed 'bum freezers', narrow ties, trousers without turn-ups, and pointed 'winkle-picker' shoes (which the surviving Teds also adopted around this time). Hair was cropped and the music was modern jazz (Charlie Mingus being a prime example), hence the term 'modernists', hence mods …

Mod was all about change, evolving, aspiring. The rocker was the polar opposite. Rockers didn't change, wouldn't change, have never changed. They have kept pretty much the same look for more than 40 years. Only their motorbikes got bigger and better.

Vic Ashbee, from Tonbridge, Kent, was a dedicated rocker. A train engineer in the early sixties, he lived for bikes, rum and rock'n'roll. 'Mod didn't appeal to me at all,' says Vic. 'For starters, they looked like girls. Their music was girly, all those soppy sentimental Motown lyrics weren't for me, it wasn't a patch on Eddie Cochran or Duane Eddy. Gene Vincent, Chuck Berry, Buddy Holly, Elvis … that was the greatest music ever made. The Supremes couldn't hold a torch to it. And mod scooters were like motorised hairdryers. You didn't get any power out of a Lambretta. It was a sissy bike for sissy boys.'

Like many of his contemporaries, Vic Ashbee bought his motorcycle, then stripped it down, tuned it up and modified it to look like a racing bike.

The dream machine was the Triton, a custom-made bike with a Norton Featherbed frame and a Triumph Bonneville engine. Other popular bikes of the period included BSA, Norton, Triumph and Royal Enfield.

'We'd race on the roads,' Ashbee recalls. 'They didn't like the look of rockers in most pubs, so we tended to get together in cafés.' Famous rocker hangouts in London included the Ace Café on the North Circular Road, the tea hut on Blackheath, the Ace of Spades and the Chelsea Bridge tea stall. Drugs, which were an integral part of the mod scene, were despised by many rockers. 'I couldn't abide none of them,' says Vic. 'Uppers, downers, dope, they were all evil as far as I was concerned. If you took drugs you were morally weak. You didn't need none of that shit.'

There wasn't much contact between rockers and mods to begin with.

'Mod was a London thing,' Vic Ashbee recalls. 'Out our way in Kent we never saw a mod. Same in Sussex and Surrey. That whole mods-and-rockers thing was hyped up by the papers to start with, and it became real because of what they wrote about it. After the first front pages about the so-called riot in Clacton, you got the lunatic fringe from each side seeking each other out for a punch-up. I didn't mind a fight but it wasn't high on my list of priorities on a night out.'

The rocker look was practical. Black leather jackets, leather trousers or Levi's jeans, Lewis Leathers motorcycle boots – all perfect for riding at high speeds on England's rain-soaked A-roads. The only nod to sartorial styling would be the metal studs, pin badges and patches they adorned the jackets with. The rockers weren't dressing to impress: they were dressing to ride, long, hard and fast. But, when they weren't on their bikes, they would go in for brothel-creeper shoes and Daddy-O shirts.

Rockers came to be known contemptuously as 'grease'. But to start with greasers were quite distinct. The look originated in the 1950s among street gangs on the east coast and southern states of the USA, and featured in classic cult films like *The Outsiders*, *The Wanderers*, *American Graffiti* and *Last Exit to Brooklyn*. The name came from their greased-back barnets – hair would be combed back with wax, gel, pomade, creams or tonics; sometimes even olive oil or petroleum jelly. Greasers were a US teen phenomenon. The term caught on in the UK only in the seventies as a dismissive putdown. Skinheads called all varieties of rockers and motorcycle gangs 'grease' – they weren't people; they were dehumanised; they were a slimy substance.

The rockers who squared up to their mod rivals in 1964 didn't look much different from their equivalents 15 years later, except that maybe they'd become scruffier. After all, the earliest rockers, having some affinity with the Teds, were often noted for the elaborate designs on their leathers. Buttons himself acquired his nickname from his distinctive self-made leather jacket covered in pearl buttons. But by the end of the 1960s, the jackets that really stood out belonged not to the ordinary rockers but to an extreme subsection of motorcyclists – an American import called the Hell's Angels.

## CHAPTER THREE

# IN THE BEGINNING:
# SKINHEADS

'I WANT ALL YOU SKINHEADS TO GET UP ON YOUR FEET, PUT YOUR
BRACES TOGETHER AND YOUR BOOTS ON YOUR FEET, AND GIVE ME
SOME OF THAT OLLLL' MOONSTOMPIN"
Symarip 'Skinhead Moonstomp'

'We were coming back from an away game against Walsall. When we pulled up at Newport Pagnell services, we saw Coventry on the other side of the motorway. We spotted their coaches and decided to have it with them. We surged over the bridge, me and the other Middle Park skinheads at the front and the rest of the Charlton mob behind us. We were about five hundred strong.

'The Coventry were eating. When they saw us, they came running out to meet us – skinheads at the front. But the thing was they brought their knives and forks with them. Me, Jim Jarrett, Johnny Kingdom and Dave Waldron were in the vanguard, leading the charge, and we realised immediately that they were tooled up. We steamed in regardless, smashing in with fists and boots, trying to get a good hit in before they could lash out with the iron wear. We were fucked but at least we stood our ground.

'Then a load more Coventry came running over the bridge. We were outnumbered good and proper. So the Charlton mob started to retreat and now our mob was at the back, all taking a wallop. Jim, my best mate, got bashed in the mouth. I got a clump on the right side of my head. Dave and Johnny got cut and clouted. We couldn't let that go. So when we made it back to our side, the South side, we turned, reorganised ourselves and run at them again. This time we did them good and proper – even though they were still using the knives and forks. We just hit them harder. We were much more aggressive, we wanted it more. And they ran back to their coaches with their tails between their legs.

'The police just stood back and watched. They did nothing until it was over, and then they herded us back onto our Lewis coaches. We told them the Coventry started it, but they weren't bothered.

'Some of us took a whack, but we won, that's what counted. The side of my head was dripping blood but Jim had it worse. His mouth was bleeding and his teeth were hanging out. His white Sta-Prest [trousers] had so much claret [blood] on them they could have been an England flag. I noticed a hole in the middle of his Levi jacket. I said, "Jim, they've ripped your Levi, mate." I put a finger into the hole and it just kept going in. He'd been stabbed in the back. He'd also been slashed across his leg – the only thing that had saved the artery was his away football programme.

'When we got off the coach at Tunnel Avenue in Greenwich we went straight to the hospital, St Alfreges. Jim got seen; he had been stabbed. His teeth were hanging out and by this time his lip was too swollen to do anything; and me, I'd been stabbed in the head too, and I never knew. It just felt hot. I still have a lump in the shape of a small bum on the right side of my head to this day, as a permanent reminder of a fantastic day.

'First we'd done Walsall after the game – we chased their mob out the ground and whacked their top boy with a mallet. Then we'd done the Coventry and all, even though they were tooled up and we weren't.

How good was that? On the pitch we may have lost 3–2, but off the pitch it was 2–0 to the Charlton firm. A perfect day out. We got up to loads in our day, and it still seems only like yesterday; I remember it all so clearly. Being a skinhead was the greatest time of my life.'

Chris Weeks became one of the 'top boys' of Charlton Athletic Football Club's skinhead following. He adopted the style in 1969, when he was 14, and was in the thick of the fighting at 15.

1969 was the year the cult went mainstream and skinhead reggae ruled the charts. It was a genuine mass working-class phenomenon – every city, every town in every part of the UK had a cropped contingent. Richard Allen's 1970 novel *Skinhead* sold more than a phenomenal 1 million copies in paperback, and spawned 17 further novels. The back-cover blurb sums it up as 'a book that portrays with horrifying vividness all the terror and brutality that has become the trademark of these vicious teenage malcontents' – words certain to horrify the press and other self-appointed guardians of public morality, but for the nation's young tearaways they were an enticing advert.

So what made Weeks and his gang go skin?

'Skinheads had it all,' he says. 'They had class, music, style. There's no way I could've been a 'grebo' – the greasers were filthy rotten back then and still are. They're nothing but a poor man's Hell's Angels. Give me half-inch braces and a clean Ben Sherman [shirt] any day.'

A 16-year-old skin interviewed at Margate in 1969 echoed that revulsion: 'We hate the grease 'cos they don't wash and they wear all that leather and oily hair. They're just dirty and their girls are even worse. So when you meet them you just want to get in there and do them.'

Chris Weeks's gang were the Middle Park Skins, from the Middle Park council estate (also the home of Boy George), in Eltham, southeast London. These kids went to either Eltham Green or Bloomfield, both comprehensive schools (or they just hopped the wag), and their lives revolved around fighting, fashion, ska and dancing (or, for the luckier ones, fucking). Their allies were the Coombe Avenue Skins from Westcombe Park, Blackheath (who included a young Chris Difford and Glen Tilbrook, later of Squeeze). Their natural enemies were the rival skinhead gang the Eltham Hounds.

'We used to crew up with the Coombe Avenue firm at Charlton, in the Old Covered End, as the old school know it,' Chris Weeks recalls. 'We hated the Eltham Hounds. They thought we were the weaker mob but we gave them a right pasting in Eltham High Street – they used to hang around the old bus sheds there opposite what was then Burton's, the tailors.'

When they weren't fighting, the Middle Park skins would frequent the White Swan pub at Crystal Palace for their Friday reggae night, with DJ Brian Jones, or take their own records to the Castlecombe youth club at Mottingham.

(Me, my friends and cousins went to a club above the Co-op Halls in Catford for our fix.)

Though they loved Stax and Motown, reggae was the soundtrack of their lives. Like me, Weeks would buy his ska imports from Music City in Lewisham Market, run by a Jamaican fella called Lee, who later deejayed at a club called Tites in Beckenham.

Weeks recalls, 'Before every home game we'd go to my best mate Jim's house, and have a reggae hour and drive his sister June mental with tunes. Then we'd lock his bedroom door, and put "Young, Gifted and Black" on the turntable and all jump out of Jim's window to go to the match. It would play and replay all afternoon until we got back.

'Reggae was a religion with us. I still have all my original vinyl. Ninety-four singles and forty-five LPs. Most of them mint condition ...'

The roots of Skinhead stretch back years before 1969. Its development can be traced directly to the 'suits', a Spartan branch of mod first spotted on the London club scene around 1965 and very much a smart working-class alternative to the dubious lure of psychedelia. West Indian culture exerted a major influence on the evolution of skinhead style. Ska, from which skinhead reggae sprouted, was a Jamaican development of American R&B embellished with jazz touches like the omnipresent horn section. Wailers guitarist Ernest Ranglin said that the word 'ska' was cooked up to describe the 'Skat! Skat! Skat!' scratching guitar strum that goes behind.

Emerging as a recognised form in 1956, by 1963 ska dominated the Jamaican music scene and also reflected the optimism of the people who'd just been granted independence under a Jamaican Labour Party government.

Ska arrived in Britain in the early sixties via West Indian immigrants and was accepted as a credible alternative to American soul on the hard-mod scene. In Britain it got called 'bluebeat' because it was Melodisc's Bluebeat label that released the bulk of this new music by groups such as Laurel Aitken and the Carib Beats, Basil Gabbidon's Mellow Larks and Desmond Dekker and the Aces.

The first British bluebeat hit was Millie Small's bouncy bundle of joy 'My Boy Lollipop' (with Rod 'the mod' Stewart on mouth organ). Ska was the music of the first-generation British blacks and the teenage immigrants who also adopted their own look and a name – the rude boys.

The name was assumed by Jamaica's tough and volatile young ghetto hooligans who were noted for their savage gang wars and lawlessness. Ska records often aimed at persuading the rudies to cool it, but perversely the Wailers' first single, 'Simmer Down', and later songs like 'Rude Boy' and 'Jail House' only helped to glorify the cult.

The rude-boy rig-out sported by West Indian youths in south London was a direct ancestor of skinhead style: Crombie-type coats, trousers worn higher than the norm to emphasise white socks and black shoes, and all topped off with pork-pie hats and wraparound shades. Creole brought Desmond Dekker to the UK in 1967 to promote his Top Twenty hit '007 (Shanty Town)'. They gave him a suit; Dekker immediately insisted that the bottom six inches be cut off the trousers. For most of his new, young fans this would be their first exposure to rude-boy sartorial style.

Razor hair partings also originated with the young blacks, and it's highly likely that the skinhead crop, although having roots in the mod crew cut, was accentuated as a means of imitating the rude boys' hairstyle (although its similarity to the hairstyle of GIs and the glamorous, pioneering US astronauts can't be overlooked as contributory factors).

In the beginning these shaven-headed white kids were known by a variety of names (peanuts, cropheads, boiled eggs, no-heads and so on) but became identified as skinheads as early as 1967. In Jamie Mandelkau's *Buttons: The Making of a President*, he talks of battling 'the Walthamstow Skinheads' in late 1967. Of all the names, only 'skinhead' really did justice to the new cult's tough, aggressive and passionately working-class stance.

East End skinhead Alan Mortlock recalls seeing his first skin gang in the spring of 1968. 'It was at the fair at Wanstead Common. I was there with my mum and dad and saw all these guys with cropped hair. I remember Mum saying, "What a lovely smart lot of boys" – and then they started rucking.'

By the summer of 1968, the skinhead look had taken off as the working-class youth look, spawning a new media demon: the bootboy. Ian Writer claimed in *New Society* to have seen 4,000 skinheads running rampage at one soccer match. 'They all wore bleached Levis, Dr Martens, a short scarf tied cravat style, cropped hair,' he wrote, adding, 'They looked like an army and after the game went into action like one.'

By the following summer the cult had reached its peak, and skinhead was 'the look' for young working-class kids. Fighting, dancing, fashion – these were the skins' main preoccupations. Fighting was largely territorial and occurred mostly at or around football grounds, although the mass media were more interested in the shock-horror mileage to be had from stories of skinhead attacks on minorities – homosexuals, squaddies, long-hairs (from my own childhood I can recall 'hippy types' getting off at the next stop on the train rather than risk a beating from the skins off the Ferrier Estate in southeast London) and Pakistanis, although these attacks were more to do with cultural than racial differences – a fine distinction to be made after you'd just been clobbered over the head with a half-brick to be sure, but an important one nonetheless. The new Pakistani immigrants were different: unlike the West Indian kids, they weren't cool, they didn't mix, and in fact they were equally (if not more) disliked by West Indian skinheads, or Afro Boys, as they became known.

A rudie spin-off, the Afro Boys were plentiful in cities such as London and Birmingham, and were equals in skinhead gangs, initially at least; although the skinhead kids from the Collinwood gang, based in Stepney, interviewed in the Paint House (a skinhead co-operative in a decaying Victorian building), testify that sexual rivalry generated ill feeling.

The original skinheads weren't renowned for political activity, but, if asked, the majority would have been Labour voters, like their parents. During the dustmen's strike of 1969, the Collinwood filled market barrows with rubbish and dumped it by the front door of Stepney town hall, shouting, 'We're skinheads and we're doing this for the dustmen.'

Class was a major factor in skinhead thinking. They hated bosses, the rich, and the middle class – middle- and upper-class hippies in particular. The Collinwood mob found them 'plain revolting … you notice that a lot of rich people turn hippy; they have been spoilt … they are reacting against society 'cause their own people are society. Hippies are just lazy no-good dropouts … they look down on us …'

The skins of the Chelsea Shed reacted to the student uprisings of 1968 with a chant of 'Students, students – ha, ha, ha.'

Escalating violence at football matches – which neither began nor ended with skinheads – resulted in the adoption of various weapons or 'tools', possibly the nastiest being homemade kung fu metal filed into star shapes to be chucked like darts (which were also popular) at your opponents. Millwall fans came up with the 'Millwall brick', a cosh made from a simple tabloid newspaper folded until it became lethally hard. Hooligans also fashioned makeshift knuckledusters out of coins wrapped in paper.

The most popular 'helpers' however, were the simple metal comb and steel-capped Dr Martens work boots. It's unlikely that the good 19th-century Bavarian Dr Klaus Martens had the slightest idea of just how seminal his patented Airwair soles (resistant to fat, acid, oil, petrol and alkali, and topped off with handsome leather uppers) were to become for generations of British hooligans. Martens, or DMs, were an essential ingredient of the early skinhead look. Then they were usually brown or cherry red, and just eight-hole affairs as a rule. Girls never wore DMs: they favoured monkey boots.

The very best guide to the evolution of skinhead sartorial style over the golden age of 1968 to 1971 was written by Jim Ferguson and published in Nick Knight's *Skinhead* book (although his essay and Harry Hawke's handsome reggae discography are the only things worth buying the book for, as the rest consists of overgeneralised, underresearched, pseudosociological claptrap about the late-seventies skinhead resurgence). Simplifying, early workday/football wear would be boots, braces (to emphasis working-class origins and loyalties), any unfashionable shirt, an army or RAF great coat, a Levi's or Wrangler jacket, or a donkey jacket. For best, dances and suchlike, all skins aspired to possess a decent suit, preferably a mohair, two-tone or Prince of Wales check affair, worn with brogues, and later loafers. The all-time favourite skinhead coat was a sheepskin – Crombies didn't really catch on until suede-head time. Hair was razor-cropped, but heads were *never* shaved bald. The razors were set to different lengths, one to five, with the number-one crop being the shortest. The favourite shirt was the Ben Sherman with button-down collar and back pleats. Bens were usually checked (*never* white) and worn with the top button undone and the sleeves turned up once. Brutus check shirts and later the humble Fred Perry were also acceptable. Smarter skins replaced Levi's red-tag jeans with Sta-Prest trousers.

Andrew McClelland, a former skinhead from Woolwich, southeast London, says, 'Everything had a name. When you went out at night you went in your Ben Sherman shirt, your Levi's, your Doctor Martens or your Squires. Even when we went down to Margate you could always tell our chaps. We all looked the same, like a uniform, in sheepskins, white jeans and boots.'

For Chris Weeks and his mates, getting the right look was essential but hard for working-class kids on low incomes. He says, 'I couldn't afford a proper Ben Sherman, so my first shirt was a Brutus. They looked just as good and at 39 shillings and 6d [£1.98] you couldn't go wrong. I got that shirt at Harry Fenton's in Eltham High Street.

'After I left school I got a job at Burton's in Bexleyheath and so finally I could afford my first handmade mohair suit and proper Bens. The manager didn't mind me crop because he said it reminded him of his days in the RAF.

'I got my first Crombie overcoat in Burton's, because I got staff discount. I got my two pairs of Sta-Prest strides in Millets, one white and one a dark green pair. My Levi jeans cost 59 shillings and 6d [£2.98]. They had half-inch turn-ups. Levi's ruled in London, but in the Midlands Wranglers were more popular.

'I had half-inch braces, one blue pair and one red pair, at 12 bob [60p] each. My DMs were burgundy with yellow stitching and had to be polished with Kiwi brown polish. Also in my wardrobe was me Squires jacket, made by Harrington, my black Royals [brogues], my black Gibson lace-up basket weave tops, and my cappers with screw-on thick rubber soles – a lot like the boots I had a few years later in the Guards ... To complete the look I had to have a Trilby titfer [hat] which I nicked out of Selfridges up London. I was with a girlfriend from Chislehurst and I just walked in, tried it on and walked out wearing it.'

Older skins with more ready cash pushed the smartness with a mod's attention to detail. Tonic mohair suits were the ultimate in style. They were worn with handkerchiefs in the top pocket. Suit jackets would be single-breasted with as many as five buttons, large (four-inch) pocket flaps with ticket pockets inside.

Black and white skins mixed freely at dancehalls such as the Streatham Locarno and the Croydon Suite. Reggae was the skinhead music, but it was a markedly different reggae from the simple ska that the rudies had introduced mods to earlier on in the decade. Around 1966, ska in Jamaica had developed into rock steady, which was faster and funkier than the original, in much the same way as US R&B had developed into soul. Alton Ellis's definitive dance hit 'Rock Steady' was typical of the new genre, which itself developed, until by 1969 it was producing massive British chart hits like Desmond Dekker's 'Israelites'. This 'reggae of the '69 kind' was a major chart factor for the following few years, with some Jamaican artists quite shamelessly pandering to their British audience (the best example of overtly skinhead-orientated reggae was Symarip's 'Skinhead Moonstop'). Trojan Records released budget-price compilations like the *Tighten Up* and *Reggae Chartbusters* series, which sold for 14s 6d (72½p) and sold in excess of 60,000 units a pop.

In the earlier part of the decade a bluebeat aficionado would have to go to Brixton (where Somerleyton Road and not Railton Road was then the front line) and clubs like the Ram Jam to hear the music, or southeast London pubs like the Three Tuns. We would trek miles for the latest imports. But, as the music moved into pop's mainstream, so reggae nights became regular features of dance halls like the local Palais. Contemporary reggae promoter Tony Cousins recalls, 'The great thing about this kind of music was that the audiences were completely integrated between black and white.'

US soul was still extremely popular too, and artists like Booker T had a large skinhead following, although inevitably the music lived more through DJs in the pubs and clubs than on stage.

The Middle Park Mob were from an all-white council estate, but the skins were mates with Jamaican lads from Brixton who also congregated at the White Swan in Crystal Palace. Chris Weeks recalls one black kid called Tony who would delight the regulars with his impression of Arthur Conley singing 'Sweet Soul Music'. The happy harmony ended only when a big Jamaican DJ called Neville tried to take the venue over, bringing his own massive PA to drown out Brian Jones's sounds.

Says Chris, 'The bloke was massive and Brian was shitting himself. But as far as we were concerned he was ruining our night and he had to go. So we all got stuck in. The police came and lobbed us out. Sadly, that was the end of the White Swan reggae night.'

No youth cult stands still, however. The skinhead look became progressively smarter, with boots and braces dropped in favour of belts and loafers even during the day, evolving into the suede-head style. Suede-heads wore their hair longer – it was combable – and favoured the Crombie coat, preferably with a velvet collar. Some suedes developed a 'city gent' look sporting bowlers and brollies, although the classic suede image was the Harrington jacket – named after Rodney Harrington who wore it in the TV show Peyton Place (like the city gent look, it was originally briefly fashionable with mods) – Sta-Prest trousers (white ones looked best) and ox-blood Royals.

Barrie Taylor (a.k.a. Barrie the mod) from east London recalls, 'By the end of '71, suede-head had developed into the "smoothie" look with the hair even longer, Fair Isle yoke pullovers, polo necks and later tank tops, and shirts with hideous rounded collars. The favoured smoothie shoes were called Norwegians. They were lace-ups and had a basket weave design on the front.'

With the gargantuan growth of glam and glitter between 1971 and 1973, skinhead was finished as a mass movement, although some diehards would dye their Docs rather than ditch 'em.

On the terraces the bootboys returned post-skins but kept themselves to themselves. The first 'droogs' were sighted in 1972, a tiny minority youth cult inspired entirely by the film of Anthony Burgess's novel A Clockwork Orange. A Clockwork Orange was Burgess's nightmare vision of a future of urban decay, where brutal teen tribes terrified the rest of society, gang-banging and battling at will. The antihero was malchick gang leader Alex, who led his marauding mob of droogs in their amoral adventures, and spoke a strange Soviet-tinged slang. The droogs dressed all in white except for their black bowlers, bovver boots and codpieces. They also wore makeup on one eye. The future-shock fun, filmed on south London's celebrated concrete wasteland of the Thamesmead estate, outraged the Establishment but struck a chord with hooligan youth.

Droog 'firms' formed all over the country , the first being spotted on the terraces of the Valley, Charlton Athletic FC's ground in southeast London. Chris Weeks was one of this pioneering firm who made their debut at Charlton's away match at Plymouth Argyle in 1971. All six of the firm were ex-skinheads, from the Middle Park Mob. They were Chris, Jimmy Jarrett, Dave Waldron, Phil Quigley, Johnny Kingdom and Steve 'Mazo' Mason. Shortly after they adopted the droog look, they were making headlines. Weeks recalls, 'We stupidly invaded the pitch only to be grabbed by the local constabulary and ejected from the ground. [Charlton manager] Theo Foley wasn't too impressed.' The look lingers on in small pockets around punk and skin gangs to this day.

Other fashions evolved on various terraces, such as the wearing of painted pit helmets or white butchers' coats, but these were localised and didn't spread outside the grounds. In Lee Green, south London, a group of largely Crystal Palace fans calling themselves 'Gumbies', from the comically cretinous Monty Python characters, started sporting training shoes, cloth caps and white laboratory coats. It never caught on.

Various bands began to attract boot-boy followings. Mott the Hoople were one, Slade another. Slade (formerly Ambrose Slade) emerged as skinheads well after the cult was on the decline but established themselves as the yob kings of glam, with a peerless stream of stomping pop classics. The Wolverhampton band attracted a massive hooligan following, but unlike the unfortunate Sham 69, who followed in their tradition years later, football fighting at their concerts was confined to outside the halls, not inside. Nowhere aside from the football grounds themselves could one encounter such a splendid peacock parade of terrace finery than at a Slade gig. The band developed a look that crossed old bovver-boy sartorial style with bold Music Hall checks and ludicrous platform boots. Lead singer Noddy

Holder actually sported a skinhead girl's feather-cut hairstyle cropped at the top and long at the sides. He still wore braces but replaced his jeans with tartan trousers, worn high to show off the platforms.

For the most part, working-class kids at this time were content to dress fairly normally or 'smoothly'. The next real youth cult development were the soul boys, who emerged in the mid-1970s as a mod update. The elite of the disco kids, they dressed casually but smart. The standard look was Levi's, white socks, moccasins and cap-sleeved T-shirts. US bowling shirts were a popular look, too, and they listened to a contemporary US black soul development called jazz-funk. Pill-popping Essex kids were the elite scene leaders, congregating at Chris Hill's wondrous soul discos at the Chadwell Heath Lacy Lady and the Goldmine on Canvey Island.

Not only were they musically dedicated and adventurous, they also spurned the ordinary soul-boy look, dressing to shock post-Glenn Miller and pre-punk. These trend-setting soul kids were dressing as flamboyantly as the New Romantics of the early 1980s six years before the rise of Spandau Ballet *et al*. And of course when punk exploded on the scene, a sizable proportion of them went on to posing at the Roxy Club.

It's the arrival of punk as an all-purpose teenage enema in 1976 that marks the end of the first era of youth cults and the beginning of a chaotic decade-long cascade of revivals, reinvention, creativity and confrontation.

CHRIS WEEKS RECALLS THE NAMES OF MORE THAN 30 OF THE MIDDLE PARK SKINS. OF THEM, FIVE ARE NOW DEAD, THREE OF NATURAL CAUSES (CANCER, HEART PROBLEMS). JIMMY JARRETT HANGED HIMSELF, AND THE OTHER FORMER SKIN, POPULAR EX-PUBLICAN DUNCAN FRAME, WAS KILLED AT THE CUTTY SARK PUB ON THE THAMESMEAD ESTATE BY A SPURS HOOLIGAN MOB IN 2006. CHARLTON FAN DUNCAN HAD EVEN BEEN RUNNING A CHARITY TO RAISE MONEY TO BUY A KIDNEY DIALYSIS MACHINE FOR THE LOCAL HOSPICE AT THE TIME. HE WAS ATTACKED WITH A CHAIR AND DIED OF A CORONARY THROMBOSIS.

# CHAPTER FOUR

# ANARCHY IN THE UK: PUNK AND THE BATTLE OF LEWISHAM

Lewisham, 13 August 1977. It's supposed to be a peaceful protest against the National Front, but we're not happy about that. A 4,000-strong ragbag alliance of dockers, punks, local black kids and students have followed the SWP's lead and made their way to Clifton Rise – the Front's intended meeting point – and taken it over.

We've left the pacifists, the Communist Party and the churchmen doing their own peaceful protest down the road. We're here, and we're ready to fight. The atmosphere is upbeat.

I feel a momentary twinge of discomfort when I see my future brother-in-law and his brothers, all plasterers, walking past us to join the 500-strong NF march, now assembling in Achilles Street around the corner. I don't grass them up, but neither do I have second thoughts about what is about to happen.

Mounted police try to move us, but we stand firm. Smoke bombs are thrown. At about 3pm, the Front march begins, behind a large banner that proclaims, 'STOP THE MUGGERS'. The cops are here in force – 3,000 were mobilised – and they escort the NF up Pagnell Street and into New Cross Road. Our side immediately begin to pelt the marchers with bricks, bottles, coins and lumps of wood. Some of the black kids are carrying ammonia.

Realising that the artillery won't stop them, Peter Chapel, a 'George Davis is Innocent' campaigner newly recruited to the SWP, runs out on his own and launches himself into the NF honour guard. Seconds later, close friends and comrades, including East End docker Eddie Prevost, follow suit. We see the Front's flags scatter. A huge cheer goes up. A group of SWP manage to split the honour guard from the rest of the marchers. The fighting goes on for about ten minutes, with both sides throwing plenty of punches before the cops regain control and separate the reds – 'the rats' the Front called us – from the outnumbered fascists.

Mounted police clear a path and allow the Front to continue towards Deptford Broadway while the counterdemonstrators set fire to purloined NF banners. Junior Murvin's 'Police & Thieves' comes blaring out of an amp suspended out of a window by an Afro-Caribbean man.

The cops are now three deep on either side of the march. We walk alongside them, hurling abuse. Our elation is only slightly dented when Millwall fans come out from the Old Den. Many of the young white kids join the NF march, leaving their black mates looking confused on the pavement.

We shoot ahead to block Lewisham High Street. The NF hold a quick rally in a car park in Connington Road, before the cops escort them to Lewisham British Rail station.

The fighting continues for a good hour, with the police repeatedly charging us. In the ensuing chaos I get knocked down and almost out by half a house brick lobbed enthusiastically but imprecisely by a young black kid aiming at a copper on a horse.

214 protestors are arrested, and 111 people, including 56 cops, are injured, 11 seriously. One policeman is knocked unconscious and two mounted officers are dragged from their horses. Some officers have ammonia sprayed in their faces. The fierceness of the attack leads to the

police using riot shields for the very first time in mainland Britain.

Metropolitan Commissioner of Police David McNee accurately described the events of the afternoon as 'an orchestrated and violent attempt' by extremists to prevent a legal National Front march taking place.

It was a bad day for the Front. Their turnout was unimpressive, and they needed massive police protection to pass through streets that were largely deserted. Only hardened supporters listened to the speeches at their rally. The anti-Front demonstrators failed to stop the NF march but we did dent their confidence. What was significant was the number of punks involved, including me.

Throughout the afternoon, especially when the police chased us up Belmont Hill, The Clash's 'White Riot' was my mental theme tune.

There were a lot of punks there that day, including punk writers Tony Parsons and Julie Burchill. Parsons told the *Guardian*, 'I gave her a flick knife and my telephone number. I think she threw away the number and kept the knife.'

It was rumoured some of The Clash were here but I didn't see them. Tom Robinson definitely was. But spiky-heads were here in force, many from Deptford and other surrounding areas.

Other events, such as the Anti-Nazi League (ANL) carnivals, were to knit the new punk phenomenon closer to the far Left (see Chapter 16, 'Blowing in the Wind'). But the Battle of Lewisham was historically important. Lewisham was the day punk stopped talking about revolution and took a stand.

No more nihilism. The young white punks had had our riot, a riot of our own.

So what was punk?

Never mind the quality, feel the myth. Punk was glorious, and punk was a con. Above all else it wasn't what it seemed to be at all, not at the start at any rate. Despite the media definition (and self-image) of punk as a poor-white-trash British backlash, the punk look didn't originate on this side of the Atlantic, and its earliest exponents and adherents weren't principally working-class. The only part of the spiky mythology that was 100 per cent authentic was the music – punk's original din.

An aural incendiary device, punk was a reversion to primal rock'n'roll cranked up to new, exhilarating extremes, and it kicked seven shades of shit out of all other contenders.

You only have to look at the charts at the time to realise why punk's energy and anger caught the imagination of a (blank) generation.

After an anorexic period in the early seventies, black American soul had branched out into disco – a genre of brainless, lyrically tame, although occasionally joyous, dance music with nothing much to say. Meanwhile, white rock music had spewed up a species of sanitised stadium stars who spent more money a month on cocaine than most of their young audiences could earn in a year. You could count the artists who really mattered on the fingers of one hand, the honest few: Alex Harvey, Ian Hunter, Bowie, Townshend and solo Lennon. Slade had started to fade and Thin Lizzy were a year away from breaking big. Elsewhere, lumbering monoliths held sway. Glam rock had been a party, but prog rock was the hangover; a depressing comedown, an earache era.

Key words and phrases of the time included 'concept albums', 'champagne receptions' (preferably involving the aristocracy), 'pomp', 'megastars', 'supergroups' (i.e. loose alliances of famous/idle tax exiles) and, of course, 'virtuosity, also known as the sterile art of musical masturbation, which was placed on a pisspot pedestal with the emergence of jazz-rock fusion. This scene featured some superb musicians, such as Al Di Meola and Chick Corea, but not one decent song; some of Weather Report's numbers lasted more than thirty minutezzzz … beam me up, Swotty. It was self-indulgent all the way. Popular music had once more passed out of the hands of the teenager. The music business held the reins again. And, as *Melody Maker* said at the time, there was a cash register at the heart of the rock dream. Older fans left over from the fifties and sixties were still buying records and adult-orientated rock (AOR) became a respected genre. Those trusty tenets of golden age rock'n'roll – sex, style and subversion – suddenly sounded naïve and dated. The rift between the stars and the punters had never been as gaping – or as ugly.

Naturally, there were roots reactions against it. During the mid-seventies, a back-to-basic R&B pub-rock phenomenon fermented in London and Essex. The most exciting exponents were Canvey Island's Dr Feelgood; the most revered, the pioneering Brinsley Schwarz. Also nurtured on the London pub-rock circuit were many artists who went on to be associated with punk and its tamer music-industry-approved twin, New Wave. Names like Elvis Costello, The Clash's Joe Strummer, who duck-walked it like he talked it for the 101-ers (pub rockers who took their name from the number of the fancy Walterton Terrace squat where they lived), Eddie & the Hot Rods, who motored out of Canvey and forgot to lose their flares, and the Stranglers, who first saw the black of night in late 1974 and who, after gaining keyboardist Dave Greenfield in May 1975, pioneered an updated Doors sound with an added dash of distilled Velvet Underground.

If pub rock caught the mood, punk rock caught the imagination. The key motivator and self-styled Svengali behind this spiky explosion was a middle class Jewish former art student from London's Stoke Newington called Malcolm McLaren. McLaren has been called many things, some of them printable. He saw himself as a 'situationist' (art agitators with roots in Marxism, anarchism and the avant-garde, who believed in embracing threats, making them safe and selling them on). Others saw him more simply as an articulate confidence trickster. He was of course a notorious self-publicist. But, above all, he was an entrepreneur, and a very lucky one.

With his partner in grime, former primary school teacher Vivienne Westwood, Malcy opened a King's Road shop called Let It Rock in 1971 selling Teddy Boy threads on the premises of the old Paradise Garage. The shop took off because they shrewdly bought in stocks of old clothes, cut-price brothel creepers and vintage rock records from discount bins. Eventually, they became bored with their Ted clientele and changed the shop name to Too Fast To Live, Too Young To Die, shifting the sartorial emphasis to bikers; but not before Let It Rock had become an essential diary date for such seminal American proto-punks as the MC5, Iggy and the Stooges, and the Flamin' Groovies.

But it was only when the New York Dolls bowled into town in late 1973 and enticed a cynical Malcolm into catching their gig at Biba's that the entrepreneur began to appreciate the moneymaking potential of rock'n'roll of the most wrecked and wasted kind.

The Dolls were the most glorious glam rip-off of the Rolling Stones the world had ever seen – all image and sleazy trash anthems. They'd appeared on *The Old Grey Whistle Test*, much to Bob Harris's disgust, and their live act blew Malcolm away. He played the starry-eyed camp follower on the rest of their European tour.

Back in the King's Road, Malcolm and Viv hit upon yet another angle for their boutique – cash through copulation. They changed the name to SEX and specialised in sexploitation gear such as rubber schmutter and bondage togs, sick Cambridge Rapist masks, plus T-shirts splattered with selected obscenities or politico-shock chic – like the famed 'Anarchy' one and the dumb 'Destroy' one with its massive swastika; and, if you wanted a pair of strides with zips on the arse, hey, this was the place for you.

To the passer-by the place looked terrifying, although possibly not as dangerous as the kebabs on sale in the shop next door. The windows were all blacked out and covered with a wire grill to stop them getting smashed in for the umpteenth time. Inside, it was full of leather drapes, rubber curtains and bright neon signs. The walls were covered with slogans, the carpet as red as horror-movie blood. Former art-student-turned-used-car-salesman (and later, Clash manager) Bernie Rhodes was the man who printed up their tasteless T-shirts, such as the infamous gay cowboys with their hefty sex-shooters on display and upside-down crucifixes.

Pamela Hook (a.k.a. Jordan), famous for her arse-baring plastic leotards, was the shop assistant. She was helped out at weekends by a fresh-faced art student called Glen Matlock, who was soon to become a member of one of the most notorious bands in the country: the Sex Pistols.

The catalyst for the chaos to come was Steve Jones. Boxer's son Steve had never got on with his stepdad. He played truant, dropped out of school and became a teenage kleptomaniac, falling headlong into a life of casual crime. After notching up 14 convictions he got 'popped' and did 18 months at approved school. He was a proper handful. Steve had been a skinhead – he stole all the best clothes – and a regular on the terraces of all three west London clubs, although he freely admitted he never went to watch the football.

'The fighting was what it was all about,' he told me once. 'I loved running rampage.'

His best mate was Paul Cook, a carpenter's son. He'd been a good kid until he fell in with Jones at the Christopher Wren School. From then on it was all downhill.

It was Paul's classmate Wally Nightingale who got the two of them into rock. He had a Les Paul copy, he had an amp – and the rest of the band's equipment was stolen wholesale and shamelessly by Steve.

Already an accomplished tealeaf and enthusiastic joyrider, Jonesy lifted the best part of a set of drums from a BBC studio; and then bass guitars and amps were stolen from vans. Steve even targeted his hero Rod 'the mod' Stewart's mansion home in Windsor, nicking two guitars from the great man. But David Bowie's Hammersmith Odeon gig was the scene of his biggest crime. Steve and his cronies broke in the day before and half-inched the entire PA.

At first they called their band the Strand (taking the name from Roxy Music's 'Do the Strand'). Wally played guitar, Paul, now an electrician's mate, drummed, Steve sang, and Steve Hayes was bassist. For a while a friend called Jimmy Mackin played rudimentary organ. But Steve's singing let the side down and Hayes and Mackin jacked it in.

It was then that they started hanging around Let It Rock. Jonesy kept on and on at McLaren about what a great band they were. Eventually,

Malcolm shelled out for a rehearsal room so he could see them play. They were awful but there was something about them that Malcy liked. He introduced them to another local kid, his part-time shop assistant and ex-grammar-school boy Glen Matlock, who became their bass player. Eventually, the band became the Swankers. Their set in 1974 consisted entirely of cover versions of 1960s standards: everything from credible Who and Small Faces to incredible old tat like the Foundation's 'Build Me Up Buttercup' and Love Affair's 'A Day Without Love'. Kindly Uncle Malcolm's pocket money helped keep them afloat.

A trip to Manhattan for a fashion trade fare later in 1974 changed rock-music history. McLaren sought out the New York Dolls and persuaded the band to let him manage them. It was a disaster. Malcy decked them out in red-leather stage gear and had them perform in front of a hammer-and-sickle backdrop, an image guaranteed not to endear the noxious noise boys to 'Nam-burned Uncle Sam. Later, Johnny Thunders described him as 'the greatest conman I've ever met'.

Nothing came of this red relaunch in the spring of 1975, but Malcolm stuck it out with the band for a further five months and learnt plenty from his sojourn in NYC. The Rotten Apple's club scene was thriving, alive with exciting new bands like Television, Blondie, the Ramones and wild poet Patti Smith. And slippery old McLaren lifted a lot of what are widely seen as English punk ideas from these pioneers.

It was Richard Hell — a.k.a. Richard Myers, a private- (i.e. public-) school chum of Tom Miller, a.k.a. Tom Verlaine, who played bass in their band the Neon Boys — who came up with many of punk's visual ideas such as spiky hair, torn clothes held together with safety pins, studded dog collars, studded leather jackets, not to mention fifties suits with loose ties.

The band, who became Television, also prepared the way for Brit punk's nihilism, playing numbers like 'Blank Generation' and 'I Don't Care' at New York clubs, principally CBGB on the Bowery (at the time, an area about as fashionable as beautiful downtown Deptford), as early as 1975.

## ANARCHY IN THE UK: PUNK AND THE BATTLE OF LEWISHAM

CBGB had been a home from home for Hell's Angels and alcoholics until Television persuaded the gaff's guvnor, Hilly Kristal, to let them put on live music there every Sunday night. Swiftly establishing a following of their own, Television threw open the venue to other bands. One of the first was the newly formed Ramones, who sported tight, ripped jeans, smelly sneakers and bikers' leathers, and who pioneered the art of the two-minute punk pop pearl – souped-up heavy metal with real tunes and lyrics so dumb/inspired ('Now I Wanna Sniff Some Glue', 'Beat on the Brat') that, when the music press finally caught up with them, no one could decide whether they were slumming geniuses or lucky morons.

Almost nobody outside of New York knew about this burgeoning young scene – except, of course, Malcolm McLaren.

When the Dolls finally dissolved, Malcy offered to manage Hell and Verlaine. They knocked him back and he was on the first plane home, where he wasted little time reshaping the Swankers with his pirated images. Bubbling over with enthusiasm, he dedicated himself to recreating them New York rebel style.

Steve Jones was an average vocalist, but he turned out to be a gifted guitarist, allowing Malcolm to sack the eyesore Wally. Malcolm now needed a frontman. He tried many. He was blanked by Midge Ure. Out of desperation he even took singing lessons himself before finally chancing upon a lapsed Catholic speed freak from a Finsbury Park council estate called John Lydon.

Crane driver's son Lydon was a genuine eccentric. He wore a ripped and torn Pink Floyd T-shirt, which he'd customised with a felt-tip pen to read 'I HATE PINK FLOYD'. When he sauntered into SEX, dripping razor-sharp sarcasm, it was love at first slight. The kid was an original whose anti-style mirrored the look that McLaren had seen in New York. But John was no softie. The son of Irish immigrants, Lydon was a working-class Arsenal fan. His older brother Jimmy and his best mate Rambo were proper street fighters; they had worn *Clockwork Orange* boiler suits to the matches. Later, when a mob of Nottingham Forest fans marched down the King's Road chanting 'Kill the cockneys', John single-handedly charged at them screaming 'Arsenal' and, by his own admission, 'frightened the living daylights out of them'.

Plying him with Pils, Malcolm persuaded the pale but fearless youth with his wild, angry eyes to audition over the SEX jukebox playing Alice Cooper's 'Eighteen' ('I've got a baby's brain and an old man's heart ...'). Johnny had everything: charisma, contempt, sulphate cheek ... He also had green teeth, which were to win him a new nickname from Paul Cook's mum: Johnny Rotten.

At first Steve Jones didn't rate him, but Malcolm was convinced he'd hit upon the right formula. He rechristened his dangerous brood the Sex Pistols. It was an uneasy alliance full of tension and mistrust, but it worked. McLaren masterminded strategy, Rotten sneered out angry contempt, Glen Matlock came up with the tunes, Paul Cook beat the drums and Steve Jones supplied the ferocious HM guitar wallop. There was nothing now to stop them. They had all the gear they needed: Cook and Jones, the self-confessed 'working-class tossers', had swiped the lot. They had attitude, defined by their first songs such as 'Seventeen' where John sneered at long hair and flares and boasted that he didn't work, he just took amphetamines.

All they had to do now was gig.

Almost inevitably, their first performance was a disaster. They opened for a Ted combo at St Martin's College of Art in November 1975 and proved about as popular as Oliver Reed at a feminist rally with his dick out.

Students and Teds in the audience chucked bottles and hurled abuse until the student social secretary pulled the plugs. Undeterred, the Sex Pistols soldiered on. The next night they played the Central School of Art, where they actually managed to finish their savage 30-minute set. After that, they hit on the strategy of gatecrashing gigs, posing as the support band and terrorising audiences.

By January 1976, McLaren had all his selling points sussed out.

'I'm gonna change the face of the music scene,' he told Ray

Stevenson, who was to become the Pistols' photographer. 'All the music at the moment is by and for 30-year-old hippies. Boring. The Sex Pistols are fresh and young. They're kids playing music for the kids. Not some property tycoon singing "My Generation". The Sex Pistols are from the streets and the dole queues. They represent most of the kids in this country.'

But the first kids the band attracted weren't like that at all. Malcolm deliberately shunned the pub-rock circuit, preferring to blag the Pistols gigs at colleges, and their first fans were thoroughly middle-class. Dole-queue rockers? Hardly. They were a bunch of self-confessed posers from suburban Bromley in Kent, who became known as the Bromley Contingent. A few of them caught an early Pistols gig at the Ravensbourne College of Art. Among their ranks were Banshees-to-be Susan Ballion (later Siouxsie Sioux) and Steve Havoc (later Severin), Billy Broad (later Idol), Ray Stevenson's brother Nils, Simon Barker, Debbie Juvenile, Philip Salon, Simone Thomas, 'Berlin' (Bertie Marshall), Tracie O'Keefe and Linda Ashby. Associated with them was Soo Lucas, better known as Soo Catwoman, whose self-created hairstyle became punk's most distinctive female look: cropped and bleached at the back and sides, with two black tufts to resemble a cat's ears. The only pop star they'd have given the time of day to back then was that immaculate ex-mod chameleon David Bowie, who, for a while at least, was to share their morbid fascination with 1930s Berlin.

McLaren's next move was to spread the word through the bourgeoisie – something he accomplished by having the Sex Pistols play at loaded socialite and sculptor Andrew Logan's Valentine's Ball on 14 February 1976; one of the blown-away guests was art student Mick Jones. This sent shock waves through the London art world's elite. Malcy also recruited a young artist called Jamie Reid, who was co-founder of an anarchist/situationist outfit called the Suburban Press, and whose radical, eye-catching designs helped inflame the mythology around the band. These were to include the Union Flag torn apart and reassembled with safety pins and the Queen with a safety pin through her nose. Another image, with Her Majesty's eyes replaced by swastikas, would be banned by their record label. Reid saw punk as an extension of the art movement, a way of communicating anti-Establishment ideas to a new generation.

Back on the streets, anarchy of the apolitical kind abounded. The Pistols were barred from London's Marquee (and then the Nashville) after blagging a support slot with Eddie and the Hot Rods and trashing the monitors. 'You can't play,' said a heckler at the Marquee. 'So what?' Matlock retorted.

After the show Lydon sneered, 'We're not into music, we're into chaos.'

To beat the bans they opened their own club, taking over the Maltese-owned El Paradiso strip joint in Soho. By now word had spread and the place was packed. Among the audience was John Ingham of *Sounds*, who wrote the first feature on the band in April 1976. 'I hate hippies and what they stand for,' Johnny scowled. 'I hate long hair. I hate pub bands. I want to change it so there are more bands like us.' It wasn't long before Johnny got what he wanted.

The Pistols progressed to a Tuesday night residency at the 100 Club throughout May and June, followed by dates at the London Lyceum and in Manchester, then the 100 Club Punk Festival in September. They found themselves attracting an ever-growing following. Few open-minded eyewitnesses failed to be thrilled by their killer combination of music fire and lyrical brimstone: post-Stooges, post-Dolls sulphate-charged rock'n'roll coupled to the crude, scorching anger of Rotten's words.

The wrapping paper was new, but what was inside wasn't. It was a red-hot resurrection of primal rock'n'roll.

When the band unleashed what was to become their anthem, 'Anarchy in the UK', the anarchy was in their attitude, not culled from the utopian visions of Proudhon and co. Lydon didn't know exactly what he wanted, he said, but that didn't matter. And neither did the fact that he sounded like Albert Steptoe. His references to the UDA, the IRA and the MPLA, along with John's claim to be the anti-Christ who was out to 'destroy' the passer-by were guaranteed to offend. His raging nihilism demanded attention and even though the single was to peak at 38 in the charts, the song inspired new bands to form (and yet more bands to try and bask in its reflected glory).

However contrived the Sex Pistols' image may have been, they and the bands they spawned played a genuinely exhilarating (and a very varied) brand of hi-energy rock – a vital alternative to the poncy, plastic offerings of the menopausal music biz. That's why punk caught on.

Behind the Sex Pistols, the best of the new breed of bands were The Clash and The Jam. The Clash were the band who turned the heads of thousands of teenage socialists, mine included, who overromanticised them to a ridiculous extent. Suddenly, punk's anger seemed to have a purpose; this was rock played with a clenched fist. They claimed to be working-class yout' from under the shadow of the West Way, and we, like mugs, believed them. But the band were never quite the street-smart rebels of their self-image. Mick Jones (the Keef-lookalike guitarist) and Brixton-bred Paul Simonon (blond bass beefcake) were art students, while Joe Strummer's standing as the Wolfie Smith of punk was slightly dented when it eventually emerged some time later that his father was a British diplomat. Singer/guitarist Strummer had been born John Graham Mellor and had been educated at the City of London Freemen's School at Ashtead, a private boarding school, and then at art college. An all-round good guy, he was faking it too.

Joe's stage name had been Woody Mellor when he sang in the 101-ers. Other early bands members were Keith Levene (short-stay junkie guitarist who ended up in PiL) and Terry Chimes (a.k.a. Tory Crimes, slightly longer-stay drummer).

Along with Generation X's Tony James (a Brunel maths graduate), Jones was a veteran of the capital's leading glam-slam tribute to the New York Dolls, the London SS – who also included in their ranks Brian James and Chris 'Rat Scabies' Miller. Jones, Simonon and Glen Matlock chanced upon Strummer strutting down west London's Portobello Road and asked him, reasonably enough, why such a gifted performer was wasting precious time in a passé pub rock outfit. Strummer, swooning at the sight of their military schmutter, had no better answer other than to join forces with them. Enter Clash manager Bernie Rhodes and the new band was born (although Levene was to last just three gigs). They worked through a lot of monikers – the Mirrors, the Heart-drops, the Psychotic Negatives and the Outsider – until Simonon or Rhodes, depending on whom you believe, suggested The Clash, taking the name from London *Evening Standard* headlines.

They played their first gig on 4 July 1976, supporting the Sex Pistols in Sheffield. 'They're not very good, are they?' sneered Rotten.

The Pistols were first, but The Clash supplied punk's manifesto. They were less heavy-metal (when punk's political threat was defused, Pistols songs were regularly played at HM discos), but instead The Clash served up a tireless tirade of terrace pop singalongs coupled with rabble-rousing political clout (Bernie got them to drop the love songs early on). Their anthem 'White Riot' wasn't anti-black: it was asking why white working-class kids couldn't be more like their black counterparts and unleash a few riots of their own. Black people had problems, said the frustrated Strummer, but they didn't mind fighting back. In contrast, white people seemed to have had all the fight knocked out of them at state schools designed to turn out dumb factory fodder.

When it was released by CBS in late 1976, the B-side, '1977', warned of 'Sten guns in Knightsbridge' and proclaimed, 'No Elvis, Beatles or Rolling Stones in 1977', while the sleeve decreed that the real 'clash' in society wasn't between the young and old, but between the rulers and the ruled.

Bob Dylan, eat ya heart out! To a Left-leaning music press, understandably concerned about punk's negativity and its casual flirtation with Nazi imagery, the explicit socialist stance of The Clash came as a breath of fresh air. Writing in *Socialist Worker* at the time, I seized on them to defend punk from the crustier comrades. Joe was a stale old Stalinist at heart, but back then it didn't seem like it.

Anti-dole, anti-bureaucracy, anti-the-music-establishment, The Clash appeared to stand for a street socialist alternative to Rotten's barbed nihilism. They were genuinely exciting live, with Strummer tearing into his often incomprehensible vocals like a man possessed as the band stoked up a barrage of anger and frustration behind him. And nowhere is that captured better on record than on their epic 1977 Lee Perry-produced single 'Complete Control', with Strummer raging at his record company, CBS, for taking the diabolical liberty of releasing 'Remote Control' as a single without the band's permission.

The Clash also pioneered an individual line in nifty hand-painted shirts and guerrilla chic. How were we to know that beneath the angry words they were just another Rolling Stones struggling to get to the very USA they claimed to be so bored with?

Then there was The Jam, who were different still.

Attracted by punk's energy, the Woking Wonders took their cues from The Who and mod. Refusing to conform to the new anti-fashion dictates, the exhilaratingly talented trio trod the boards in immaculate two-piece mod whistles, celebrating 'the young idea' in a Rickenbacker-powered storm of fiery melodies. The Jam were tight, cool and as sharp as the creases in their trousers. They were far more working-class than The Clash and outraged punk opinion when Paul Weller said he was voting Conservative. Weller, a labourer's son, had been to comprehensive school, not an art college. He was also a royalist. Inevitably, their look and attitude made them 'the black sheep of the New Wave', according to Weller, but they ended up meaning more than all the other bands as Paul's songwriting talents blossomed and his politics crystallised into a kind of mod socialism. (More on the Jam in Chapter 6: 'Days of Change'.)

The very diversity of the original punk bands is startling in retrospect. For comic relief there was The Damned, Concorde-paced clowns led by a low-rent Vincent Price called Dave Letts (a.k.a. Vanium) and including in their ranks ballerina-garbed bassist Ray Burns (a.k.a. Captain Sensible), guitarist and chief songwriter Brian James and demon drummer Chris Millar (a.k.a. Rat Scabies), who claimed to have invented the idiot practice of gobbing (though the late Gary Holton's Heavy Metal Kids used to spit at their crowds and vice versa).

They had no political agenda; indeed they had more in common with Screamin' Lord Sutch than dreamin' Lord Soper. They were fun, likable idiots. They released the first ever British punk single, the furiously superb Nick Lowe-produced 'New Rose', and the first punk album. They were also the first British punk band to play the USA (bombing spectacularly at CBGBs). They threw the Dolls and the Stooges into a mixer with a dash of Hammer Horror, and stood for punk as slapstick fun. The cover of their debut album, featuring the band smeared in beans, cream and jam, pretty much said it all.

The Bromley Contingent spawned Siouxsie and the Banshees, who originally included John 'Sid Vicious' Beverley in their line-up, wore swastikas and sang songs that included outrageous lines like 'too many Jews for my liking'. When it dawned on them that Nazi chic was not only dumb but also a music-biz no-go, they dumped it in the dustbin of history and set their sights on a one-thousand-hits Reich of more marketable pretentiousness.

The Stranglers paid homage to The Doors and Leon Trotsky, although the ice-pick-allergic Lev's views on strippers were never made clear. The band used busty broads to perk up their live shows. They paid lip service to punk and appealed right across the board, pulling in Hell's Angels and mainstream rock fans. Largely, they were old-school. To the horror of the rock press they got busted for drugs, caused a riot in Nice, and, in between references to the poet Shelley, lusted shamelessly after hot women – 'peaches' – sunbathing on beaches ('Peaches'). Bassist J J Burnel, a karate black belt, spelt out the band's determinedly different vision to the *NME*: 'Rock'n'roll is about cocks and jiving and the odd bloody nose,' he said, 'and about people like us talking seriously about the social order.' *NME* predictably hated them.

In Manchester, intellectual Howard Devoto and romantic Pete Shelley were inspired by early whispers about the Pistols. They made the pilgrimage to London in February 1976, caught two early gigs and formed the Buzzcocks, adopting their name from a review of *Rock Follies* in *Time Out* that ended, 'It's the buzz, cock.' Devoto booked the first of the Pistols' two seminal gigs at the Manchester Lesser Free Trade Hall that summer, spreading the word North and having a cathartic effect on Manchester's own soon-come new musical explosion. The Buzzcocks' *Spiral Scratch* EP, released on their own New Hormones label, wasn't only a masterpiece of simple infectious pop, but also the direct launching pad for the glut of independent releases that coloured the late 1970s and early 1980s.

The explosion of so much talent justified the Pistols' stance of outraged bor-dum. Adding to the excitement, the Ramones blitzkrieg-bopped into Blighty in July 1976, the same month as their debut LP (called *Ramones*, what else?) was released by Sire. In the process they inspired a young Deptford bank clerk called Mark Perry to become Mark P and launch punk's seminal fanzine *Sniffin' Glue* that very same month. Other great, distinctive punk 'zines followed, including Lucy Toothpaste's *Jolt* and Sandra Short's *Hangin' Around*.

Bands, attitude, anger, a look – the music press soon sussed there was a movement raising its spiky head here. The name 'punk' stuck but the bands weren't called that originally, and indeed there was some resistance to this unsavoury epithet to start with.

'Punk' can first be found in Shakespeare's *Measure for Measure*, where it meant whore. It travelled to America with the Pilgrim Fathers, where, as well as retaining its prostitute meaning, it also came to mean worthless, of poor quality, or weak in spirit or health.

By the 1930s it had acquired new US slang meanings, becoming synonymous with a passive homosexual or a catamite (a boy kept by an adult male for sexual pleasure). Here too it acquired the meaning gangster-film aficionados will know best – becoming another word for streetwise juvenile delinquent, an angel with a dirty face. Thirty years later, in the sixties, it had taken on yet another new connotation as a description of music churned out by the first generation of US garage bands, suburban boys trying to imitate Brit invaders such as Them and the Yardbirds with the aid of two good chords and a truckload of acid tabs (Lenny Kaye's *Nuggets* compilation illustrates the growth of these bands into full-blown psychedelia).

Although these garage outfits bear precious little musical resemblance to the sonic ravishes of the Pistols *et al.*, the pre-Brit-punk New Yorkers were more obviously influenced by their predecessors. Early Television admitted their debt to the 1960s punks (as well as the seminal Them/Stones/Yardbirds/Velvets), and, of course, Lenny Kaye performed with Patti Smith.

The Ramones were using the word 'punk' in their early songs in its gutter tyke meaning ('Judy Is a Punk'). The cover of their debut album was a Roberta Bayley picture lifted from *Punk* – a fanzine devoted to garage guerrillas past and present created by the artist John Holmstrom in 1975 New York. Needless to say, Malcolm discovered it there and sold it in SEX.

When people started referring to the British scene as punk in mid-1976, Mark P observed in *Sniffin' Glue*, 'You get the feeling at Pistols' gigs that everyone's posing so they can't really be punk, can they? Punks are carefree, and I mean completely … you know, like a football fan who kicks in someone's head and don't care a shit. Yeah, the Pistols crowd are not punk, they're too vain. But what's wrong with that? So am I!'

In the October 1976 *Sounds*' punk roundup (again written by Ingham) only The Jam referred to the 'punk rock scene', with Rotten favouring 'anarchy rock', Siouxsie 'rock' and long-haired Mancunian-bore Paul Morley of *Out There* 'zine advocating 's' – for 'surge rock'.

But with repetition came approval, and punk became all-encompassing and all-accepted within months.

By the time a drunken Bill Grundy had provoked the Pistols into swearing at him live on TV, on 1 December 1976, no other word would do. 'THE FILTH AND THE FURY' screamed the *Daily Mirror*; an Essex lorry driver called Jim Holmes kicked in his TV set, and punk was reborn as Public Enemy Number One. Bernard Brook Partridge, a Conservative councillor, called the band 'the antithesis of humankind', adding that 'the whole world would be improved by their total and utter nonexistence'. But by now it was far too late to halt the deluge.

At the time, even most music-press staff writers regarded the phenomenon as violent, ugly and dangerous. Their doubts seemed confirmed when a young girl lost the sight of one eye during The Damned's set at the two-day 100 Club Punk Rock Festival in September 1976 (also featuring the Pistols, Clash, Subway Sect, Siouxsie and the Banshees, Chris Spedding and the Vibrators, Buzzcocks and French band Stinky Toys). As a result the club banned punk. It didn't matter a damn. Six hundred punters had queued outside waiting for the festival to start and that fast-growing demand was impossible to deny.

The new music continued unabated as the London scene shifted to Covent Garden's Roxy Club. Andy Czezowski, one-time manager of nonstarter band Chelsea, opened up the Roxy (formerly Chaguaramas Club) for punk in late December 1976. The Clash played on 1 January 1977, and for the next few months it became *the* punk venue, the only place to be. This soon soured, however. Punk's burgeoning notoriety and the club's reputation meant that it quickly became polluted with plastic posers, gee-wow-look-at-the-freaks sightseers and miscellaneous music-biz vultures. The best punk writers of the day, the 'verbal gunslingers' Tony Parsons and Julie Burchill, charted its decline in the *NME* that spring (Parsons and Burchill weren't so much journalists writing about punk as the first punk journalists – although in truth Julie was never at all keen on the actual music: for her it was all in the attitude). In April 1977, Czezowski got turfed out by the owner Rene Albert and the place deteriorated rapidly. Not that the real punks cared. They'd already moved on to the Vortex in Wardour Street.

As the word spread, so more and more kids were attracted by the colour, chaos and high momentum of the new scene. Great bands were still aligning themselves to the cause: Penetration from Ferryhill, County Durham, with their sweeping pop vision; London schoolboy punks Eater; and the Adverts from Devon, who debuted at the Roxy in January 1977 and had early chart success with 'Gary Gilmore's Eyes' the following August.

One of the best new bands was X-Ray Spex, led by mixed-race waif Marion Elliot (a.k.a. Poly Styrene) from Brixton, south London, with their searing sax embroidery, titanic tunes, asexual stage presence and incisive insights into the consumer society.

Fresh-faced pop princelings Generation X (named after a 1960s paperback novel) were a breakaway from Gene October's Chelsea. Led by pretty-boy plastic pin-up Billy Idol and including Tony James, ex of the London SS, Gen X played their first gig at the Roxy in December 1976 and released their debut anthem, 'Your Generation', the following September. It was an obvious swipe at The Who, referring to both 'My Generation' and 'Substitute'; although clearly in terms of both pop prowess and youth-culture impact the words were just an Idol threat. And Townshend mattered far more than bimbo Billy ever would.

The birth of Rock Against Racism, in the Winter of 1976, was to open up a large number of clubs and college venues to punk bands. Unlike the ANL, which was a front organisation formed by the Socialist Workers' Party, RAR was founded by grassroots revolutionary socialists like Red Saunders and print worker Roger Huddle – both ex-mods – as a reaction against Eric Clapton's pro-Enoch Powell comments at a Midlands concert and David Bowie's apparent flirtation with fascist imagery. Pub rockers Carol Grimes and Vinegar Joe were the first recruits to the cause; but, later, bands like the brilliant Ruts, reggae outfit Musical Youth and the posh and endearingly naïve Tom Robinson's Tom Robinson Band became most associated with RAR. Recruiting Lucy Toothpaste, RAR launched the fanzine *Temporary Hoarding*, which I wrote for.

As punk's audiences swelled, there were noticeably fewer posers and more working-class kids. Many of them were the tower-block tearaways of Malcy's wet-dream mythology. Punk was moving out of the art schools and into the council-estate concrete jungles (with middle-class adherents inventing working-class backgrounds to keep their credibility). Bored teenagers everywhere were stirred into action by the lure of new energy.

And, as the movement grew, so did the opposition.

Fleet Street did their shit-stirring best to blow up the punk/Ted skirmishes into a full-blown teen war, like the mods and rockers a generation earlier.

To reinforce the view of punk as just another off-the-peg youth uniform (which is what it eventually became), Grub Street eagerly leapt onto the bandwagon of tribal belligerence after a group of Hammersmith Teddy Boys, put out by the media attention the punks were attracting, decided to prove they were still number one and duffed up a crew of spiky-tops outside Hammersmith Tube in west London. Sporadic clashes spread to the King's Road. Most early punks gravitated here to hang around outside the SEX boutique, but their presence annoyed the Teds, who saw this part of Chelsea as their stomping ground and set about bashing the newcomers – until the younger punks called in the cavalry.

Tom McCourt and his teenage mates from Hoxton in east London were veterans of the scene, having been attracted to punk early doors. Tom recalls, 'We were up the Music Machine in Camden one night and this punk – can't remember his name – in a boiler suit and orange hair, came up to us and said we should come down the King's Road on Saturday. The plan was the punks were going to meet in the Roebuck pub at 12 noon and start fighting back against the Teds. We used to go down the King's Road now and then, anyway, but this was different.

'At the time, the Teds were much older than us and were jumping individual punks or small groups. On the Saturday, me and John O'Connor went down there. There was quite a mob of us at the Roebuck. We had a few beers and a good laugh, and then we all went down to Sloane Square, where we caught hold of a couple of Teds and gave 'em some of their own medicine.

'On the way back, some of us got jumped by plain-clothes Old Bill (not me and John) and then went up to the World's End and on to the estate where a couple of local blokes had told us that the Teds were jumping punks, but no one was there. It went on like that for a few weeks and we brought a few more of our mates from Hoxton down. There were a few skirmishes, but mostly there was a growing sense of camaraderie. It was a bit of a laugh. Then, naturally, it got blown up out of all proportion by the press.'

Another flashpoint for the punk-versus-Ted scuffles was Liverpool Street Station and especially the Wimpy bar outside (which used to be opposite the Dirty Dick pub).

Johnny Rotten did his bit to defuse the situation by appearing in full Teddy Boy regalia, but inevitably this served only to wind up the Teds even more. Despite the shock-horror newspaper coverage, the clashes soon drained away to nothing, and in reality, Punks had more to fear from 'smoothies', soul boys and skinheads than they ever did from Teds.

Pictures of the young street-fighting-class King's Road punks – including Tom McCourt and John O'Connor – were used on the Clash's 'Clash City Rockers' single of March 1978. These photos really represent what most punks looked like in the late summer of '76 as the music began to spawn a youth movement: straight jeans, boots or Jam shoes, black T-shirts with hand-sewn zips in them, stripy T-shirts, black blazers, fluffy mohair jumpers, combat trousers, Harrington or jean jackets; black leather jackets or black combats with zips became more common a bit later.

The standard punk look for the less heavy kids encompassed safety pins (through clothes or mouth, nose or ears), zips, dog collars, cheap plastic shades and any old clothes that looked the part – you built up your own look from Oxfam shops, jumble sales and street markets. Only the mugs or slumming rich patronised the rip-off boutiques like SEX and BOY, paying £200 for bondage suits. Punk logic meant DIY: your own 'zines, your own clothes, your own bands. It wasn't really until well into 1977 that the look became a uniform, the 'zines started worshipping instead of rubbishing, and too many new groups were just crude copyists.

But there was another, harder, wave of punk incubating. They came from the football terraces and they didn't need to invent their backgrounds. First up were rabid, cranked-up R&B boys Slaughter & the Dogs, hailing from Manchester's Wythenshawe estate (once the skinhead capital of the North), who pumped out furious, speed-fuelled singles like 'Cranked Up Really High' (Rabid) and 'Where Have All the Boot-Boys Gone' (Decca). Sham, and to a lesser extent Menace, became beacons for the newly revived skinhead cult (see Chapter 5, 'Comeback of the Boot'). From the East End of London came the equally thrilling Cock Sparrer. Slaughter had been a Glam band; Sparrer adopted a *Clockwork Orange* look and turned down Malcolm McLaren's management interest 'because when we met him he didn't buy his round', they claimed. Their hard-knuckled debut single on Decca was 'Running Riot'. But, when Decca dropped them in 1978, they disbanded, not re-forming until after the new Oi! bands had started making an impact two years later.

Throughout 1977, terrace hooligans and other mobs of dangerous-class yobs were increasingly drawn to punk, and more usually to just one band. The Stranglers were the first punk band to have a 'crew', in the shape of the Finchley Boys. They latched onto The Stranglers after they played the Torrington pub in Finchley, north London, in early 1977 and the band adopted them as their legion of honour. Hugh Cornwell recalls, 'Twenty-odd guys with short hair trooped in. I thought we were going to get bashed but when we started playing they went crazy.' The Finchley Boys followed the Stranglers all over the UK. The band repaid the compliment by talking about the gang and their place in the Stranglers psyche in interviews; they even had Finchley Boys T-shirts manufactured.

Cock Sparrer attracted the support of the Poplar Boys who were (largely) West Ham United fans. Skinheads began gathering around Sham 69 (see Chapter 5, 'Comeback of the Boot'). Punk's working-class pose was becoming reality.

As you can see, there were many parallels between punk and the mod of over a decade previously. Like mod, punk was about doing, about activity. Like mod, punk had mixed-class roots but became predominantly a street cult. Like mod, punk was (originally) about an individual/distinct style of dress (albeit a deliberately anti-fashion one). Like mod, punk cleared the way for a new generation of talent right across the board – from musicians to fashion designers and from novelists to TV personalities and DJs. As with mod, there was a tremendous feeling of new possibilities. And like mod, punk aligned itself with black music, although obviously not to the same degree. After all, mod music (and skinhead music) was black music.

Punk was white, but an influential element among the punks (principally Paul Simonon and Joe Strummer of The Clash and Johnny Rotten) adopted contemporary reggae. Reggae DJ Don Letts was interviewed in *Sniffin' Glue* with Mark P recommending his readers to check out Eric Fuller's definitive reggae column in the short-lived *National Rock Star*. King Dread Bob Marley toasted the spirit of it all with his 'Punky Reggae Party'. The killjoys of the Young National Front were horrified, branding Johnny Rotten 'no better than a white nigger'.

Unfortunately, also as with mod, the positive aspects of punk – its radicalism, its commitment to change and to questioning everything – ran out of time. It's hard to pin down an exact date, or indeed point to one factor, for the decline of the first waves of punk, but you can see the way it fell apart.

Let's start with the Pistols.

Towards the end of 1976, they hit newspaper headlines as they publicly made mugs of EMI and A&M Records by conning them out of £125,000. In between they brightened up Bill Grundy's *Today* TV programme. When Grundy tried to chat up Siouxsie Sioux, he got showered in abuse and then goaded more instant outrage out of the band.

'You dirty sod,' said Steve Jones. 'You dirty old man.'

Grundy replied, 'Well keep going, chief, keep going. Go on, you've got another five seconds. Say something outrageous.'

Steve: 'You dirty bastard!'

Grundy: 'Go on, again.'

Steve: 'You dirty fucker!'

Grundy: 'What a clever boy!'

Steve: 'What a fucking rotter.'

It was the end of Grundy's career and the start of a new one for the Pistols, who found themselves on the front page of every tabloid in the land. Under the Fleet Street spotlight for good, the band began to split at the seams. In March 1977 they sacked melody man Glen Matlock and brought in Sid Vicious, more for his mindless image than his minimal musical skills. Sid's previous claims to fame had been debuting with the swastika-swathed Banshees, inventing the pogo, and chain-whipping *NME* writer Nick Kent at the Nashville. In May they released their second single 'God Save the Queen' (on Virgin), which had the distinction of becoming Number 1 in every honest chart at the same time as the Queen's Silver Jubilee celebrations reached their zenith, selling in excess of 2 million copies in the process.

But their anti-royalty, anti-Establishment message outraged the public. Johnny Rotten got his face callously carved up by blade-wielding thugs unknown in a Highbury car park, getting glassed up at Dingwall's a week later. (Later, John said his attackers were West Ham and had used the controversy as a handy excuse to bash and cut a high-profile Arsenal fan. 'We got them back, though,' he says. 'We got them back lovely.') Going for the treble, a gang of six heavies attacked Paul Cook with coshes and iron bars as he sauntered out of Shepherd's Bush Tube soon afterwards.

Being a punk in 1977 was truly asking for it. The Sex Pistols were banned from playing on land, so McLaren hired a boat and sailed up the Thames blaring out subversively anti-monarchist sentiments in a frenzied cacophony. Enter the River Police, who drove the boat back to Charing Cross, where they were all nicked.

Weathering the storm of cops and the would-be vigilantes, the Sex Pistols finally made it onto *Top of the Pops* with 'Pretty Vacant' on 14 July. Eager to turn his protégés into longer-lasting superstars (and keep their names in the headlines), Malcy arranged their first UK tour, and began work on their very own *Hard Day's Night* – a movie to be directed by soft-porn legend Russ 'King of the Nudies' Meyer. But already the rot had set in and the legend was to fall apart as swiftly as it had attained prominence.

'Holidays in the Sun', the band's fourth single, blatantly ripped off the riff to The Jam's 'In the City' (later, Weller told me that only The Jam's commitment to the spirit of Punk unity stopped them taking the Pistols to the cleaners for that). The controversial album *Never Mind the Bollocks* fell well short of the blistering bootleg *Spunk* LP. Sid hooked up with an American groupie, a punk parasite called Nancy Spungen, who introduced him to sex and smack.

The US tour was a fiasco. Rotten rebelled when Malcy ordered him down to Rio to film with Great Train Robber Ronnie Biggs. He quit, and from that moment on the Sex Pistols adventure was over.

From being one of the most subversive forces ever to cock a leg at the British Establishment, the Sex Pistols became a Carry On (carrion) cash-in. The hilarious *Great Rock'n'roll Swindle* movie (finally directed by Julien Temple) came out, siring singles from both Sid and Biggs.

Sid got banged up in Rykers, New York's toughest chokey, on a murder rap. Nancy Spungen played the tragic corpse. Released on bail, he OD'd on smack. It was sad, sordid and funny all at the same time. But it wasn't punk. It was pantomime.

Some images linger from the Sex Pistols' death agony: the band recording Sid's sick 'Belsen Was a Gas' with its punchline 'Be a man, kill yourself' (Sid did!); and the sorry spectacle of the Sex Pistols with Sham's Jimmy Pursey at the helm for one gig only at the Glasgow Apollo.

What a way to die!

Other myths crumbled equally fast. Fumbling with the less than sublime 'Clash City Rockers' single (which nicked the riff from the Who's 'I Can't Explain'), The Clash pulled the masterly 'White Man in Hammersmith Palais' out of the bag before disappearing to the USA and the arms of big-shot producer Sandy Pearlman. When they eventually shed their excess Am-Ex bulk, it was obvious to all but the most starry-eyed believer that all their images of insurrection were as genuine as an Arthur Daley antique, and we'd have to settle for just another gifted, good ol' rock'n'roll band – see 'London Calling', a great single album stretched out over four sides of vinyl (but far better than 1980's sprawling, self-indulgent, six-sided triple album *Sandinista!*). Inevitably, *Rolling Stone* magazine loved it.

Meanwhile, the industry had worked out the punk profit margins and thrown its weight behind that double-edged sword, the New Wave.

On the one hand, the New Wave meant punk opening closed doors for the superior pop of Blondie, Costello and Ian Dury. On the other, every two-bob loser on the circuit cut their barnet and tried to hitch a ride to riches on the bandwagon. Hindsight shows us only too vividly the way the new-wave establishment became just as rotten as the old-wave one.

Elsewhere, Zandra Rhodes was designing 'punk' clothes and the tabloids were running gormless guides on HOW TO BE A PUNK. On the streets the punk look became one-dimensional and cloned, while nine out of ten bands settled for an identikit three-chord thrash sound. The first wave of punk was dead by 1978, and nowhere are its death throes better documented than in Parsons and Burchill's *The Boy Looked at Johnny*, a brilliantly flawed, savagely entertaining account of the decline of a movement into another all-purpose consumer palliative. What they didn't realise was that the flames lit by the class of 1976 would go on to ignite and excite genuinely explosive bands all over the country (in the shape of the Ruts, Skids, Rezillos, the UK Subs, Stiff Little Fingers and all) and indeed the world.

Most punks refused to be drawn. After all, 1977 was the punk year.

It's difficult to articulate the spirit of the times. Punk was on the offensive and we really did feel that we had the world to win. 'God Save the Queen' was at Number 1, The Clash and The Jam released killer albums, punks sided with blacks and the Left for the Battle of Lewisham. Plus, the opposition of narrow-minded local councils and the birth of Rock Against Racism gave punk something to fight for.

(The small neo-Nazi punk scene that built up in Leeds around bands like the Dentists and the Ventz was to prove small beer in comparison; and the coming ANL carnival of 1978 planted punk's flag firmly in the anti-Nazi camp; see Chapter 5, 'Comeback of the Boot').

But, for all the optimism of 1977, it was also the year that class divisions began to show through the fragile unity of punk style. As punk crumbled in 1978, the class divisions became more and more important, and in its wake tendencies were evolving that were still called punk but were in fact very different phenomena. There were 'post-punk' university neo-Marxist bands like the Gang of Four, a dark punk-funk outfit from Leeds (named after hardline mass-murdering Maoists), whose lyrics ranged from sloganeering to themes of alienation, and who took the music from the streets and back to the campuses.

There were Crass and their 'classless' (i.e. middle-class) empire, hippy ideals dressed in nihilist black.

There were the lumpen sons of Sid who evolved the Apocalypse bands and finally congregated around a bunch of pretend bikers called the Anti-Nowhere League, thus illustrating that they were little more than an updated version of greasers (to the cynical, their music was cranked-up heavy metal with little of interest to say to anyone outside of the Obscene Publications Squad; their leather-and-chains look was increasingly similar).

And there was the tough, working-class alternative that became Oi! ...

# CHAPTER FIVE

# COMEBACK OF THE BOOT: SKINHEADS AND THE RAINBOW RIOT

'WHAT HAVE WE GOT? FUCK ALL! WHAT HAVE WE GOT? SHAM 69!'
SKINHEAD CHANT ADOPTED FROM 'SONG OF THE STREETS'
by Sham 69

'I CAN'T STAND THE PEACE AND QUIET/
ALL I WANT IS A RUNNIN' RIOT'.
'Runnin' Riot', Cock Sparrer

No British youth cult has been as consistently misrepresented in the press as skinheads, especially the second-generation skinheads who reached the peak of their popularity between 1978 and 1980. But were they really as bad as the papers made out? Really just a bunch of thick fascist thugs and mugs destined for the jug? Gutter-press treatment of other youth cults should lead us to suspect otherwise. And, OK, the rock press did their bit to perpetrate the bullshit, but what else could you expect? A lot of the new skins were violent, some were extremely Right-wing, and almost all of them were working-class. In contrast, music journalists were (and are) overwhelmingly middle-class; and in the late 1970s they were largely ex-hippies. They tended to paint all skins with the same brush and were either ignorant of, or wilfully dismissive of, the positive aspects of the cult.

Just as the bulk of the music press sneered at punk until the New Wave gave them bands they could comfortably champion (Verlaine's new, improved, intellectual Television, art rockers Talking Heads, easy-listening Dire Straits and the vapid pretend-reggae of The Police), so their hostility towards the new skinheads began to cool only when the 2-Tone bands started to brighten up the charts; but their basic deep-rooted distaste for the skinhead way of life remained unchanged.

Skinhead evolved into suede-head in 1971 and so perished as a mass youth cult (see Chapter 3, 'In the Beginning: Skinheads'), but it never died out completely. Small pockets of skins, and the odd few dedicated individuals, were untouched by the lure of fashion. The Shipley Skins in West Yorkshire, for example, claimed to have kept the faith throughout the dark years of the early seventies, while others were succumbing to the colourful pull of Rupert the Bear trousers, Fair Isle yoke pullovers or bright, crêpe-soled shoes. In London, too, a hardcore few stuck to their boots while all around them switched styles to suede-head, smoothies or glam. Garry Hitchcock, one-time manager of the infamous 4-Skins, recalls, 'There were always skins somewhere. For instance, in the early seventies there was this geezer at Arsenal who had cropped hair – an inch crop, so it laid down – and wore a Crombie while us young 'uns were wearing Budgie jackets or later going for the college-boy look.'

Hitchcock was one of the first of the second generation of skinheads who had caught the tail end of the cult at school. He says, 'We always said that if it ever came back we'd be skins again. Nothing else was really us.' In 1976, Hitchcock was wearing a Harrington jacket, DM boots and straight jeans; the only thing he lacked was a crop. Seeing other kids his own age who had gone all the way was all the push he needed.

The earliest 1976 skins were from different parts of London, but, once they'd established contact with each other, they kept closely in touch. Garry Hitchcock and his mate, Tony 'Panther' Cummins (who went on to sing with the 4-Skins), were from Shepherd's Bush in west London. Panther supported Chelsea and from football he knew a kid from Camden called Graham McPherson (Hastings-born McPherson was later to find fame and fortune as Suggsy, the singer with Madness – see Chapter 7, 'Rude Boys Outta Jail') and Terry Madden from Kilburn, who had been a skinhead since his early teens. On the Clock End terraces, Garry Hitchcock befriended Arsenal Binnsy, who came from Hampstead and had also been a skin since school. This small group were the nucleus of the skinhead revival. As you can see, contrary to popular belief, it didn't start in London's East End.

The first skin to emerge at Upton Park was Steve Harmer, known as H, who went on to roadie for the Cockney Rejects and play guitar for the 4-Skins. He was followed quickly by Gary Hodges, who was to be the first singer with the 4-Skins. West Ham Binnsy, who acquired a degree of notoriety as a roadie for Sham and then the Cockney Rejects, was still a punk with a ring through his nose in 1977. Garry Hitchcock recalls, 'Glen Bennett and Kevin Wells were others from that side of London who were skins real early on, but west and north London was where the skinhead revival started.' Wellsy became the Cockney Rejects' road manager; Bennett became an activist with the neo-Nazi British Movement (BM).

Terry Madden remembers how it was in the early days of the revival: 'I used to have to go from Kilburn to Boreham Wood just to have a drink with other skinheads,' he says. 'There were only a few of us but we all kept in touch.'

Hitchcock: 'In those days, whenever you saw a skinhead you didn't know, you'd talk to him. There was a feeling of almost comradeship. There were very few of us about.'

The return of the skinheads ran parallel to the birth and the growth of punk. It wasn't punk-inspired, but it was boosted into a mass movement by punk.

'When we became skins again,' says Terry Madden, 'you've got to understand that the only other things to be were soul boys, which was dull and mostly a black thing, anyway, or Teds – Showaddywaddy. To us, they were a joke.'

Hitchcock: 'When punk came along we didn't relate to it at all. We didn't like punks: they were too untidy. And another thing: I'd always associated skinheads with the working class and, despite all they said, the punks I met were all middle-class plastics.'

Although they didn't appreciate punk style, the new skins grew in its shadow for the simple reason that, back then, nightlife options were limited to discos and punk clubs, and the discos wouldn't let them in. The revivalists remained true to the first skins' sartorial standards. None of them were impressed with the DIY scruffiness that surrounded them. Like their predecessors, they prided themselves on being smart and clean, searching out obscure shops to buy authentic skinhead clothes: Ben Sherman shirts, Sta-Prest strides, narrow braces, DM boots or brogues, tonic suits for best, sheepskin coats, Crombies or Navy coats.

Hitchcock: 'I remember Suggsy used to get his Sta-Prest from this little shop in Kilburn. Me and Panther found a place in Earls Court, which had all the old gear left over from the first days. The bloke was dusting off boxes for us, he thought he'd had a right result. We got Ben Sherman's for thirty bob [£1.50], tonic suits for £2.50, DM boots for two quid. It was the bargain of the century. But of course, when other people heard about the shop, he sussed on and his prices rocketed.'

The new skinheads never shaved their heads bald, as later boneheads did. They'd have number-two crops, and wear Levi's red-tags or jungle greens – smart ones that fitted, not the scruffy baggy ones that caught on in the eighties. This generation would look on in disgust when, a few years down the line, the skinhead name became associated with bald punks with ludicrously high boots, torn jeans and face tattoos.

Hitchcock adds, 'And needless to say we never sniffed glue, either. What a disgusting habit that was. The first people on the scene that I remember sniffing glue were the filthy punk squatters at King's Cross. We used to batter 'em.'

By 1977, this group of skinheads had emerged as the vanguard of the revival, meeting regularly in the top bar of the Vortex. They weren't the only new skin mobs in town, though. The Ladbroke Grove Skins, known as the LGS, had also been around their west London manor since 1976. Like Hitchcock's mob, they were largely London Irish, but they also included many West Indian teenagers in their ranks. The LGS were led by a character called Chrissie Harwood and were notorious among Right-wing skins for their 'Lefty' – i.e. nonracist – leanings. As a historical footnote, it was the LGS who pioneered the original 2-Tone badges: black-and-white buttons boasting the legend 'SKINHEAD REGGAE', over two years before the actual 2-Tone explosion.

Tom McCourt (a.k.a. Hoxton Tom), who became the bassist with the 4-Skins and is recognised as an authority on the cult, also recalls early skinhead gangs from Archway in north London who had a lot of black members too, as well as Toks and Chalky, who roadied for Menace and Madness. Other early skin gangs emerged from Becontree in Essex and from Packington in north London. The Packington lot were first spotted in 1976 and were noted for their look of crops, boots and Adidas T-shirts.

Unlike the LGS, several of Garry Hitchcock's firm had far-Right sympathies – Hitchcock included. 'We were political, a few of us,' he recalls. 'But we never tried to bring our politics into the scene, not at first, anyway, because the rest were just into fashion, the look. I wouldn't even have said we were troublemakers especially. We had fights because people started on us. We didn't use to go around smashing up gigs.'

One historic ruck took place in the Angel pub in St Giles Street near Denmark Street in Central London. Early on in 1977, the skinheads chanced upon a group of older football nutters who supported Charlton Athletic (Charlton had quite a firm in the mid-seventies). It didn't take long for things to kick off. 'The Charlton mob got the hump because we were dressed like skinheads and they'd been skins the first time round,' Hitchcock recalls. 'And also, ironically, because one of our number was a black kid. There was a lot of eyeballing, things were said and before long they steamed into us and battered us. The following week there were only half of us left, but that was a good thing because the ones who stayed were hardcore.'

Six months later there were still very few skinheads about. Hoxton Tom recalls, 'I was a punk in 1976 and it was quite a shock to me when in the autumn of 1977 I bumped into a bloke in full skin regalia: Sta-Prest, Ben Sherman, Crombie and loafers. The last proper skins I remembered were my uncles and cousins in sixty-nine/seventy. Should I stay a punk or go skinhead? To me it was no contest. The skin was different and sharper. At first being a skin was class. Everyone who got into it went looking for the right gear, visiting every old tailor and army-surplus shop hoping to get Ben Shermans in the "wooden boxes". Me and my mates in Hoxton preferred loafers and brogues to boots. They looked smarter and were just as hard. Hair was a number-two crop with a classic razor parting. I raided my uncle's old room for records and original Shermans. He had the lot, *Tighten Up Volume 2*, Tamla and Stax.

'At first it didn't matter where you were from. We met the Archway skins, Suggs and Toks, Joel McBride from Kilburn and the Becontree lot – Nelson and Lawrence. We met the Croydon, the East End skins – H and Hodges. Away from the grounds, football rivalries and political differences didn't matter. We were skins. It was us against the world – and there weren't many of us.'

The thing that transformed the new skinheads from a minor cult into a mass one was the band Sham 69, led by their gangly and engaging singer Jimmy Pursey.

Pursey has told so many tall tales it's hard to know what to believe, but it's likely that the band derived their name either from old graffiti on a toilet wall in their Surrey home town of Hersham – 'Hersham 69' with the 'Her' eroded by wear, tear and time. However, it was widely believed in 1977 that they'd taken their name from a notorious skinhead riot in Kent: Skinheads at Margate, 1969. Either way, they hailed from a tranquil village, and Pursey – who is usually viewed as either a lovable ham or a loudmouthed buffoon – was their spokesman and soon-to-be-self-appointed voice of a generation.

James Timothy Pursey was an immensely likable and generous 'Jack the Lad' who would have sold his soul to have been born within the sound of the Bow Bells (he missed by about 20 miles). He was never quite the innocent victim that he likes to be seen as, but he was generally well intentioned. Jimmy was born on a humble farm in Turners Lane, Hersham, on 9 February 1955. His dad was in the army, his mum was a cinema usherette. He was a skinhead at 14, the first time round, and was adopted by an older gang as a kind of mascot. They used to take him to their fights and leave him watching the action from their van. At 15, Pursey was expelled from Rydens comprehensive school for organising a pupils' strike and blowing all the power in the school in the process – he got the other kids to wrap silver paper round every plug. After school, by day, he slugged through more than 30 dead-end jobs – everything from factory hand to washer-up in a Wimpy bar.

But by night Jimmy came alive. His musical career began at his local disco, the Walton Hop in Walton-on-Thames. Here, aged 17, he led a bunch of mates on stage and, dressed in finest Bay City Roller tartan, drunkenly mimed his way through the Rolling Stones' 'Satisfaction'. They called themselves Jimmy & the Ferrets and their spot miming to all manner of chart records became an established facet of Hop bacchanalia. Encouraged by the Hop's proprietor, the Ferrets developed into a real band. They included bassist Albert 'Albie' Maskell, who lived on a local pig farm (Sham 69's first rehearsals were to be in Albie's dad's pigsty). The Ferrets were a fairly ordinary pub-rock band to begin with, playing rock'n'roll standards and setting a few of Jimmy's own early lyrics such as 'Let's Rob a Bank' to basic 12-bar formats.

The Sex Pistols made all the difference. Jimmy caught one of their earliest gigs at Weybridge Food College and was converted on the spot. By the summer of 1976, and newly christened Sham 69, the band played their first ever show as a punk band, supporting Albertos y Lost Trios Paranoias at Brooklands Technical College. The resulting shower of eggs, spit, tomatoes, beer and metal bolts made half the band immediately question the change of musical direction, so Jim sacked them. In January 1977, he and Albie recruited local guitarist Dave Parsons, who was playing Beatles and Stones covers in a band of schoolmates called Excalibur.

The last member was drummer Mark Cain (a.k.a. Doidie Cacker), who they met at the Hop and who auditioned for them in his mum's kitchen.

After a session of songwriting and pigsty rehearsals (wearing gloves, overcoats and balaclavas because there was no heating in the place), Sham 69 were ready to face the world again. Their first gig was at Guilford University. After that there was no stopping them. They headed into London regularly, gatecrashing West End punk clubs such as the Roxy, blagging gigs and building up a following. They recorded a demo tape and Jimmy put his motormouth to good use, dropping off a copy at Miles Copeland's office and telling all who'd listen that Sham were the best punk band around. Copeland was intrigued enough to give them a bottom-of-the-bill slot at the Acklam Hall supporting Chelsea, the Lurkers and the Cortinas. Miles brought a friend along, John Cale of the Velvet Underground, who was so impressed by the band's clout and Jim's big gob that he talked Copeland into signing them for a one-off single.

That Step Forward three-track, released in July 1977, comprised 'Ulster Boy', 'Red London' and 'I Don't Wanna': raw bursts of brick-wall punk with a Right-wing populist message. 'Red London' was specifically anti-socialist, equating London streets turning red with the absence of democracy and concluding that individuals rule. This boisterous conservatism played well with Copeland, whose dad worked for the CIA (Miles's brother Stewart played drums for the Police).

Other numbers in Sham's set targeted exploitative punk boutiques like SEX and BOY with Jimmy righteously branding their tatty but over-priced products a rip-off.

'Hey Little Rich Boy' hit out at snobs and the middle classes ('I'll never believe you're better than me') while 'The Song of the Streets' – which was given away as a free disc at gigs and better known as 'What Have We Got' – banged the anti-politicians drum, condemning Conservatives and Communists as being two sides of the same coin.

The band hit a nerve. Mark P of *Sniffin' Glue* called them 'the first true punk band ... with cleverly constructed working-class anthems. Sham were the very essence of punk ... the true successors to the Sex Pistols.'

Danny Baker and I were early fans. So were the new skinheads.

According to Jimmy, he just happened to notice a mob of skins at an early Sham gig in west London and perchance remarked, 'Oh skinheads, I used to be a skin.' Tony Cummins remembers it differently. 'Pursey used to wear jungle greens and have his hair cropped and go around saying "Skinheads are back",' he recalls. 'That's why we used to follow Sham everywhere.'

'Sham 69 was the first band we followed,' agrees Garry Hitchcock. 'I can remember getting on stage with Pursey and he used to sing "What have we got?" And we'd all go "*Fuck all*" because what did we have? Nothing. We were working-class kids out of school who no one gave a shit about. We really didn't have a future.'

Sham were in the right place at the right time. A focal point for the new skins, they also appealed to working-class punk rockers disillusioned by the high dilettante and debutante count diluting and polluting the self-styled street movement. Many of these punks became skinheads, recognising the skin style as a genuine repository of proletarian values. Sham also seduced a lot of football hooligans into adopting the cult, kids who at other times would have been content to confine their leisure time to tear-ups on the terraces.

Crossing the raucous chants of the soccer crowds with the energy of punk, Sham rapidly built a massive street following. Although usually confused, Pursey's lyrics were always anti-pose, anti-middle-class and anti-system. Their general message was clear: we may not have much but no one is better than us. Pure populism.

'Borstal Breakout' summed up the mood of guttersnipe bravado perfectly.

For Jim it was a song lyric, but a lot of his early audience had actually spent months of their teenage years sitting in cells. Sham's angry protest hit the spot. They went Top Forty with 'Borstal Breakout' (their first single on Polydor), penetrated the Top Twenty with the follow-up 'Angels With Dirty Faces' and went on to have three Top Ten hits before 1979 was over: 'If the Kids are United', 'Hurry Up Harry' and 'Hersham Boys'. But, as we shall see, the kids weren't united and that was to prove Sham 69's undoing.

Meeting and growing around punk clubs, the new skins became increasingly associated with Sham; but there were other bands around at the time who also appealed to skins and terrace regulars. Of these, Cock Sparrer were the most exciting. Forming at school in East Ham, by 1976 the band were gigging locally in east London, sprinkling their set of souped-up rock'n'roll with choice covers from the Small Faces, Humble Pie and T.Rex song books and generally kicking mike-stands about the stage a bit.

Early reports about the Sex Pistols filtered through to them. To Sparrer they sounded like kindred spirits, so they contacted Malcolm McLaren about management. Malcy turned up at their rehearsal room above the Roding pub in East Ham and left a trail of merriment in his wake. He'd come to the East End wearing spurs.

The band ran through their set and Malcy was bowled over. They adjourned to the public bar, where McLaren declared them 'the next big thing'. He made it clear that he wanted to manage them and offered them a support slot on the Pistols' next shows. Insanely, Sparrer turned him down, saying they'd never support anyone. What happened next beggars belief. Miserly Malcolm refused to buy a round. The band were so disgusted that they kicked him out and that was that. Drummer Steve Bruce later admitted, 'It was the biggest mistake of our lives.' Undeterred, Sparrer went on to build up a sizable

East End following, winning the particular attention and affection of a group of (largely) West Ham nutters known as the Poplar Boys, who had chanced upon the band at an early gig at the Roxy. They had a reputation for heaviness, but the Poplar Boys' presence at every subsequent gig put paid to crowd trouble.

Favouring a skinhead and boot-boy image rather than a standard punk one, Cock Sparrer revived Doc Martens and Sta-Prest years before they became fashionable, and, as the video to their 'We Luv You' single shows, singer Colin McFaul also picked up on *Clockwork Orange* imagery ahead of the herd. This single, and its scorching predecessor 'Running Riot' (both released by Decca), show just how fine a raw rock band Cock Sparrer were, and give you some idea why Jimmy Pursey once remarked that Sparrer were 'too good to be a punk band'. They should have been massive, but managerial hassles put paid to the band's career. 'We just signed a lot of dodgy contracts,' bassist Steve Burgess explains. 'And then we went to the States and no one wanted to know. It all added up and we got pretty disheartened. To top it off Decca offered us a two-grand advance for a five-year deal, which worked out to about thruppence a day ... and we just fizzled out really.' This was in April 1978 – just a year or so before bands like The Ruts, the UK Subs (who had been a Sparrer support band) and the Angelic Upstarts were hitting *Top of the Pops* with a similar strand of street fire. Bad timing was the story of Cock Sparrer's career.

Menace were another bunch of could-have-been contenders who broke up too early and re-formed too late. Never quite as dynamic as Sparrer, this north London quartet got together in early 1977 and were fronted by 'Mad' Morgan Webster. With their armoury of brick-wall guttersnipe anthems, Menace were tailor-made for the job of Sham support band. They soon built up a solid following of their own, separate from the Sham crowd – Hoxton Tom McCourt and Millwall Roy Pearce (a.k.a. Roi the Boi, who went on to sing for the Last Resort) were both Menace roadies. The band proved their prowess on plastic with 1977's 'Screwed Up' (on Illegal) and 1978's essential

'GLC' (Small Wonder). But the music press were unwilling to accommodate a second Sham, and, in the face of constant press hostility, Menace petered out with more singles released after they disbanded than before.

Then there were Skrewdriver. Famed for their notoriety rather than their ability, the band formed in Blackpool, Lancashire, around vocalist Ian Stuart (real name Ian Stuart Donaldson), a factory manager's son from nearby Poulton-le-Flyde. Originally a Rolling Stones cover band called Tumblin' Dice, they moved to London to become a punk band and were given the name Skrewdriver by their record label Chiswick. They were still punks when they appeared on Janet Street-Porter's London Weekend Television show *20th Century Box*, and on the sleeve of their first single, the so-so 'You're So Dumb'. Their second single was better – a cover of the Stones' '19th Nervous Breakdown' coupled with their own good and anthemic 'Anti-Social' which professed to hate the world. They weren't political at this point, other than being vaguely against society, but they had cropped their hair and adopted an unshaven skinhead look augmented strangely by a penchant for lumberjack jackets.

No one took Skrewdriver seriously as a punk band, but Stuart was shrewd enough to realise that the skin revival was the next big thing and acted accordingly. 'Ian Stuart approached us at a Sham gig at the Roxy,' Garry Hitchcock remembers. 'He told us about Skrewdriver and said that they weren't like Sham, that they were real skins.'

The word spread and, come Skrewdriver Mark II's gig at the Vortex, there was a massive turnout of skins, which surprised even Hitchcock. 'We never knew there were so many around,' he says. 'And no one there looked under twenty-five.' Stuart told the skins that he wouldn't slag off their violence, as Sham had started to do. Unfortunately, they took him at his word. After a disco warm-up of classic Trojan reggae, Skrewdriver hit the stage and the majority of the crowd went nuts, smashing up everything in sight. Skrewdriver were immediately banned from the Vortex, the Roxy and even the 100 Club. They also lost the support slot on the Travers tour that Chiswick had bought them onto.

Unable to follow Sham into the charts, Skrewdriver eventually dropped the skinhead look and tried again as a punk band, once again failing to attract either interest or record sales. Pretty soon Stuart was a skin again and the band had gone through more line-up changes than a Death Row inmates' football team. He began flirting with various far-Right groupings – the band had cropped their hair and adopted an unshaven image – and wound up agreeing to play a National Front-organised Rock Against Communism gig at London's Conway Hall in August 1979. At the death, though, Stuart bottled out of the show and before long he'd called it a day and disappeared back to Lancashire. But not for long. Returning to London in 1980, Stuart joined the Manor Park Royals (who never played a gig) with neo-Nazi Glen Bennett before re-forming Skrewdriver again with himself as the only original member. Every other month or so he'd materialise in the offices of *Sounds* and *Melody Maker* telling anyone who'd listen that he was just a misunderstood patriot – a stance he could keep up until about the sixth pint – before breaking up the band once more.

He re-formed Skrewdriver for the final time in 1983, and, after a brief attempt at being accepted as an 'apolitical skinhead band', Stuart pinned his true colours to the mast and aligned the band to the rump of the decaying National Front, declaring me to be the movement's natural enemy. Stuart produced leaflets saying 'BEAT THE BAN, BEAT BUSHELL', as if I were responsible for their being banned from any self-respecting London venue.

Flattering, I suppose, although if I'd had that power I would have used it against Soft Cell too.

Back in 1977, as the skinhead cult grew, it became increasingly aggressive. Defensive violence was no longer enough. Inevitably, the skins were drawn into the punk-versus-Teds battles on the punk side, although, earlier on, veteran skins like Terry Madden and Arsenal Binnsy had hung about with rockabillies. With the street clashes escalating, such collaboration became impossible. Tensions had already been building up between skins and Teds down east London's Brick Lane, where the rival cults coexisted uneasily. The Teds had frequented the Black Raven pub and the Wimpy bar there for years, while skins drank in the Green Gate. Petticoat Lane was always a popular hangout for skins because of the clothes shops in the area (decent loafers and brogues could always be found in Blackman's in Brick Lane). It was only after they'd beaten off the Teds that far-Right activists followed the Right-wing skins into the area, and pubs such as the Crown & Shuttle and The Bladebone became notorious neo-Nazi drinking dens. As street violence flared between the cults, the trouble spread to a punk stall in the market run by a long-time rag-trade character called Mickey French and his missus Margaret, who later left him for a Rastafarian. The Teds tried to trash it, so the skins defended it. The stall finally took up permanent residence as a punk boutique called the Last Resort in Goulston Street before switching to a largely skin fashion emporium in 1978, which is how it stayed; although it always sold punk schmutter too, and, after the 1979 mod revival, French started to stock mod gear there as well for a while.

Fashionable with later skinheads, back in 1978 the shop was regarded as a bit of a joke. Garry Hitchcock says, 'No serious skinhead would buy anything at the Last Resort, except the braces.'

The skins didn't hate the Teds in particular: they just hated anyone who wasn't a skin. Not even punks were safe. Tom McCourt remembers punks getting moronically hit over the head with hammers for their tickets outside the Roundhouse when Sham played with the Adverts in 1977; although they probably suffered less than other cults simply because many of the new skins had been punks and the two tribes still went to the same gigs and followed some of the same bands. Skinhead gangs began to fight other skinhead gangs too. The ongoing war between the Packington and Hoxton mobs could be seen as the first example of internecine skinhead rivalry this time round. The motivation was purely territorial, however, with soul-boy mates fighting on both sides too. Elsewhere, football rivalry was the biggest source of skin-versus-skin aggro.

Inevitably, there was a lot of trouble with bikers – the Becontree mob rowed with local motorcycle gangs all the time. Two Hell's Angels were beheaded by skinheads in Wickford. The warnings were all there for Jimmy Pursey when Sham 69 played the Reading Festival in August 1978. Jimmy fled the stage in tears as his Sham Army steamed into bikers, hippies and other festivalgoers.

The most serious aggro, however, came from a group who were just as hard, just as working-class and far more numerous than the skins – soul boys. Tension between the two cults culminated in a small war around the Angel, Islington, from November 1977 onwards. For Tom McCourt this ended when he was jumped by a gang of 'soulies' on his way home from a Menace gig in 1978 and severely stabbed. Similar territorial clashes erupted all over London. In Stepney, a Right-wing skin firm led by Ian Hettinger were turned over by a soul-boy crew led by Jay Williams in the Black Boy pub. Out in Becontree, the skins encountered serious and sustained opposition from a mob of straights and soul-boys who called themselves the CAL, which stood for Chelsea Arsenal Liverpool. Yet, ironically, the many brutal clashes between skins and soul boys attracted far less attention in the media than other skinhead-related violence. Certainly, it generated far fewer column inches than the trouble between skins and Pakistanis in Brick Lane.

'Hard as it may be to believe, that really did start by accident,' testifies Hoxton Tom. 'In fact, ironically, one of the first skins down the Lane was Asian. I remember him appearing at the start of all the fighting with the Teds, and he was dead smart. He used to wear a Crombie, and a shirt and tie with a tiepin. But then one Sunday we went down there after the Teds and the Asians had put up a barricade. They were going mad. I suppose they didn't like us fighting each other in what they saw as their area. But, when they got stroppy, it was like a red rag to a bull.' Garry Hitchcock concurs, 'They got the hump,' he says, 'because we were always down their ghetto.'

Although football rivalry was the biggest source of gig violence, politics occasionally entered the equation. For example, the violence at Sham's Kingston Poly gig was between Right-wing skins and the Croydon Boys, who were largely Left-wing.

Sham 69 suffered from all sorts of grief, but how innocent was Jimmy Pursey? To this day, veteran far-Right skins insist that the Sham frontman encouraged them. 'Pursey used us,' says Garry Hitchcock. 'He dressed like us and encouraged us to come to his gigs, but as soon as he started getting famous he didn't want to know.'

In truth it was only ever the Right-wing skinheads who Pursey turned against. He says he never encouraged the racist element. They disagree. Essex boy Kevin Wells, who was one of the first of the second-generation skins, used to roadie for Sham in 1977. He says, 'I remember driving Pursey in a van down Oxford Street and when he saw a white girl with a black bloke he started calling her a slag and wanting to get out and roll the bloke.' Jimmy denies this categorically, and certainly from the time I first knew him as a fan, and a fanzine writer in late 1977, in front of me at least he always argued against racist ideas and the growing Nazi tendency.

Some confusion was evident in the lyrics of the Step Forward EP. 'I Don't Wanna' was standard anti-system fare, but 'Ulster Boy' was immediately adopted as an anthem by Loyalist elements in the London skins; and there was no denying the message of 'Red London'. Was he playing a dicey game?

If Pursey had flirted with hard-Right elements early doors it would help to explain the vehemence of their backlash against the band.

There was no ambiguity in Pursey's public actions or statements, however. He aligned himself with the newly formed Anti-Nazi League (see Chapter 16, 'Blowing in the Wind') and told me, 'Every gig I do is a Rock Against Racism.' This infuriated the small but committed far-Right element among his fans. Terry Madden then had the rare distinction of being both an Irish Republican and a neo-Nazi (single-handedly inspiring a dubious *News of the World* report on the 'Nazi wing of the IRA'), although he later shed the Nazi side of his politics. Madden pulled a blade on Pursey and demanded he agree to lead a National Front march.

So how did these odious politics come in to a youth cult that owed so much to black music and West Indian culture (see Chapter 3, 'In the Beginning: Skinheads')? Many commentators assumed, not unreasonably, that the far-Right groups consciously infiltrated the punk scene having been attracted by punk's confused political symbolism. This was not the case, not at first at any rate. True, the National Front did make propaganda plays for white rock fans, with a whispering campaign spuriously claiming support from stars such as David Bowie and Rod Stewart. Later, members of Spandau Ballet were the subject of equally unfounded whispers. But on the streets in 1976–77, the NF were viewed as the soft option, and the hardcore ultra-Right minority among the early London skins were attracted to the less astute, but more extreme, BM.

Crucially, their Nazi elders did not approve.

'The British Movement thought we were degenerate for going to gigs,' recalls Hitchcock. 'They considered the music business to be completely Jewish-controlled. They thought the Jews were trying to corrupt white youth through punk. Their disapproval was the reason we brought politics into it and started leafleting at gigs and steaming people. We wanted to prove to the BM that we weren't softening up and that we were there to spread their word.'

The Nazis, known colloquially as 'the right-arm mob' or contemptuously as the German Movement – and later the 'boneheads' – were only ever a tiny minority of skinheads. But, just as a small cog can move a much larger one, so they were able to create an impact far in excess of their actual strength. In 1977, their numbers were swelled by the notorious bullyboy Matty Morgan (a.k.a. 'Mad Matty'), who was to become a leading element and whose brother, Steve Morgan, was already an established name on the West Ham terraces. These were the people later bands would have to face and defeat.

Sham and the Lurkers suffered most from ultra-Right violence. In London, the organisation the racist skins supported tended to be determined by which part of town they were from. Chelsea, for example, were more likely to be National Front. The BM, who were stronger at West Ham and Charlton, were more of a disruptive force at gigs. And, as the BM skins cranked up the action, the older Nazis mellowed in their attitude to the cult.

'The Right wing was courting the skins during the summer of seventy-seven,' recalls Hoxton Tom, who was never a Nazi. 'They would hang about in Brick Lane especially, buying drinks, trying to get people on side. Meanwhile, the Left tended to ignore us.'

In fact, the Left-wing skinhead tradition goes back just as far as the Right-wing one, and, countrywide, the Left probably attracted more skin support (although the bulk of skins were either apolitical or vaguely Labour by tradition). The LGS and the Archway with their black skins were there from 1976. Skins in Croydon and Oxford were renowned for their socialist sympathies. Sharon Spike, a skinhead, contributed to Rock Against Racism's *Temporary Hoarding* magazine. And, when Jimmy Pursey put in an appearance at the Brixton ANL Carnival in September 1978, it was heartening to see scores of Afro boys come out of the woodwork – over a year before 2-Tone erupted and enticed thousands of black kids to resurrect the rude-boy style.

Revolutionary socialist band Crisis, from south London, had a skinhead following and a skinhead bassist in Tony Wakefield, who edited the Socialist Workers' Party youth mag *Rebel*. And there was also a short-lived Skins Against the Nazis (SAN) group formed by four East End skins in Hackney in August 1978. A mention of the group's creation in *Temporary Hoarding* brought in more than 60 letters from skins all over the country requesting membership forms, with Acton skins proving a hotbed of support. Both Pursey and Menace's Noel Martin gave the SAN their blessing. I interviewed founder member

Laurence Newis, a young Clock End skin, in *Sounds*, but, after his photo appeared, he got so much stick from Nazis that he later claimed (falsely) to have been an NF mole all along – just to save himself from hidings. Two years on, Joe McAvoy, a stoical ex-Stalinist skinhead from Chelsea, launched the League of Labour Skins. A mention in *Sounds* brought hundreds of positive letters flooding in, but the League was frustratingly inactive.

Outside the capital, socialist skinheads could be found in abundance. Left-wing skins organised around political issues in Sheffield and Glasgow – the Glasgow branch of the Sham Army was featured positively in the Trotskyist *Socialist Worker* and they contributed much muscle and manpower to summer 1978's Right to Work march. There was significant skinhead involvement in Rock Against Racism around the country too. The far Right were stronger in the Midlands but they weren't unopposed. In May 1978, a multiracial group of West Bromwich skinheads led an anti-Nazi demo against the NF. Some of the white ones infiltrated the NF meeting and heckled so enthusiastically that it had to be abandoned after just 11 minutes. It would be fair to surmise that whichever political side ruled the streets in any area also ruled the skins.

From the very start, Sham 69's existence was marred by violence, most of it football-related rather than politically motivated. At first Jimmy had been optimistic about his following. In 1977, he had told me, 'See, skinheads are not acceptable because they represent violence, but you can channel that violence, that energy and excitement, into something good and show you can be a rebel with a cause.' He was right. It was just unfortunate for Jimmy Sham and the innocent bystanders in his audience that he wasn't to be the person to achieve that noble aim.

At the start, the bulk of Sham's London following came from Ladbroke Grove and Lewisham, but before long the hardcore were aggressively West Ham. They included such notorious claret-and-blue street fighters as Binnsy, Gary Dickle, Johnny Butler and Vince

Riordan, who became a Sham roadie alongside Albie Maskell (Albie had been kicked out of the band in late 1977 and replaced on bass by the more competent Kermit, a.k.a. Dave Treganna). Vince was later to play bass in the Cockney Rejects (see Chapter 8, 'White Riot? The True Story of Oi!'). By 1978, West Ham's Grant Fleming (who was to be the first of the new mods at Upton Park) had become Jimmy Pursey's right-hand man, and the neatly turned out Dean of QPR was the only LGS regular left.

Football clashes plagued innumerable Sham gigs. The bloodiest was the brutal Arsenal-versus-West Ham battle at their Hendon College gig in January 1979. The violence at Hendon was awful. Jimmy was so horrified that he took an overdose of sleeping tablets. If it wasn't for the prompt action of his girlfriend's mum, Jim would have died.

The riot prompted Pursey to make the first of several 'That's the last gig we'll ever play' proclamations. Unfortunately, he never stuck to them. Small wonder some observers began to see him as a garrulous Dr Frankenstein, unable to control the lurching monster he'd created. At first he tried to soothe the savage beast through his lyrics. 'If the Kids Are United' was a powerful plea for youth unity over football rivalry: 'If the kids are united, they will never be divided.' The chorus was lifted and modified from the chants of the previous year's Grunwick picket line: 'The workers united will never be defeated,' which made more sense; but, no matter, the song became Sham's first Top Five hit. It didn't stop the violence, though, so Jimmy tried another tack, directing Sham towards the sort of goodtime rowdy pop that Slade had pioneered and turning out singalong terrace gems like 'Hurry Up Harry' and 'Hersham Boys'.

If he'd stopped playing gigs and stuck to churning out hits, Sham would almost certainly have thrived and survived. As it was, it was Pursey's attempts to combat the far Right head on that sowed the seeds of his downfall.

Again, at first, Jimmy had been optimistic about his chances. In 1977 he said, 'It's not true that all skins are Nazis, but I'd rather have an NF skinhead come to my gig so I can turn around and say, "I'm an anti-Nazi – what do you think of that?" than some robot who agrees with my every word.'

Good as his public statements, Pursey would argue for hours with racist fans. In 1978, he made personal appearances at both the massive ANL carnivals, memorably joining The Clash on stage at Victoria Park to sing 'White Riot'. No doubt he did reach and influence a hell of a lot of kids, but the tiny Nazi rump were significantly pissed off by his actions. They felt betrayed. Slogans such as 'SHAM ARE RED CUNTS' were sprayed on east London walls and, at the end of their 1978 tour, trouble flared at the Electric Ballroom gig in Camden when BM Skins turned on the rest of the audience. The reggae band the Cimarons, whose single at the time was 'Rock Against Racism', were the tour support, but they had been mysteriously dropped from the Ballroom bill after an apparent altercation with the bouncers. Given the atmosphere at the gig, it was probably just as well. It was evil. Poisonous gangs of BM skins prowled around picking on individuals asking them if they liked Sham. If they said yes they were called 'red cunts' and occasionally belted.

The BM skins couldn't get at the band because of the massed ranks of West Ham heavies (all wearing crossed-hammers T-shirts) at the front of the stage, but the audience were terrified. The next night there was no trouble and a defiant Pursey changed the words of 'Song of the Streets' to include the lines, 'Conservatives and National Front / They're all a shower of shit.'

Throughout 1978, however, especially in London and the Midlands, supporting the NF, or saying you did at least, was becoming a natural sidebar to being a skinhead. It was a trend the national press went out of their way to encourage, rarely writing about skins without linking them unthinkingly to the Front. Why was this? Part of the problem was lazy, irresponsible journalism, but a greater part was the failure of the traditional working-class parties to relate to white working-class teenagers who felt rejected by society and ignored by politicians. It could have been a bumper period for the neo-Nazi British Movement, but the Master Race dumbly shot themselves in the foot by demanding that every member prove their loyalty by having a BM symbol tattooed on their arm. As a result, scores left the sect – one of them Garry Hitchcock, who said that the tattoo decree coincided with his own personal realisation that Nazism was no good.

For Jimmy Pursey the pressure was to prove too much. After surviving his post-Hendon suicide attempt, Jimmy bounced back, launching his own JP label through Polydor, and then shot off to France to record the 'Hersham Boys' single and album. Both were hits. This was the apex of Sham's commercial success, and out of the blue the chance of a lifetime, the chance to leave Sham and its troubled legacy behind for good, presented itself. Pursey was offered the opportunity to replace Johnny Rotten in the Sex Pistols. The new line-up was to be Jimmy (vox), Steve Jones (guitar), Paul Cook (drums) and Kermit on bass.

Leaking half-truths to the press, jubilant Jim announced that Sham were over, killed by the uncontrollable element among their fans. A farewell gig was announced for 29 June 1979 at the Glasgow Apollo. None of us in the audience knew what was about to happen, but maybe we should have guessed when we spotted Virgin Records boss Richard Branson in the crowd. For the encore, Sham were joined by the pair of self-styled 'working-class tossers' Cook and Jones. Covers of 'Pretty Vacant', 'White Riot' and Sham's own 'If the Kids are United' followed. It was a vision of a future that was not to be. After the show, the plan for the new Pistols was unveiled.

In the party atmosphere that surrounded the whole affair, only two voices of sanity were heard, and sadly ignored. John Lydon said the enterprise 'smacked of desperation', while the deposed Dave Parsons observed, 'I don't think it's gonna last long because Jim always likes to be 100 per cent in control.' Nostradamus, eat yer heart out!

Overcome with emotion, Jimmy Pursey enthused about his future in the new Pistols and decided to play a farewell gig in London as well.

'It would break my heart if we couldn't say goodbye to London,' he said.

Oh, dear!

The Rainbow was booked for 18 July 1979. It was the day Sham 69 died. From the minute I stepped off the Tube at Finsbury Park I just knew it was going to end in tears. The first thing I saw was the late Matty Morgan smash a pint glass into a teenage boy's face because he had a ticket and Matty didn't. The British Movement had mobilised in force for the farewell show. They congregated in the George Robey pub opposite the venue, *sieg-heil*ing at passers-by. Black and mixed-race skinheads were attacked and passing immigrants subjected to sick, gory singsongs about the 'showers of Belsen'.

The atmosphere was pure evil, their intentions were crystal clear. Young Nazi London was united in one aim, united like a pack of animals under a whip: they were going to destroy Sham 69.

I don't suppose there were more than 40 actual BM members, but, as always, the hardcore headcases exerted an influence far greater than their numbers. The support bands, the Little Roosters and the Low Numbers, played to a barrage of abuse and hurled coins. In between sets, a gang of around 200 skins ran amok through the unseated venue.

Pursey had new personal security: a scruffy mob of Road Rats and barrel-chested bikers from Surrey had replaced his West Ham minders. They kept well out of the way.

When the safety curtain finally rose to the strains of '2001 – A Space Odyssey', Jimmy looked understandably brown around the trouser department. Fuelled by an instinct for self-preservation, the band stormed into 'Song of the Streets'. They sounded savage, vital, harder than they'd ever been, but by the fourth number, 'Angels with Dirty Faces', all pretence of normality was over. One by one hulking neo-Nazis and other embittered ex-fans invaded the stage. The safety curtain dropped and Sham retreated. The Nazi-led mob *sieg-heil*ed in triumph. They were still a minority, but, with no organised force to confront them, they were unbeatable.

After about 20 minutes the stage area was cleared. Insanely, the band returned and smashed into 'Angels' again. The mood of the non-Nazi element of the crowd lifted. Could it be that, now they'd had their protest, the boneheads would let the band finish in style? Some hope! Seven stunning numbers followed. Then the second stage invasion started. Pursey finally cracked. He hurled the drum kit across the stage, grabbed a microphone and shouted, 'I fucking loved you! I fuckin' did everything for you! And all you wanna do is fight!' A tear rolled down his cheek. It was all over. Robbi Millar wrote in *Sounds*, 'Jimmy said goodbye to London, and London kicked him in the teeth.'

Celebrating their victory, the BM went on a beano. The next night, they hit a Jobs for Youth benefit gig organised by the Young Socialists in Brent's Gladstone Park with Misty and the Ruts playing. Just under a hundred Nazi-led skins stormed the stage, tore down the red flags and *sieg-heil*ed their defiance at the helpless crowd. The gig was abandoned. This summer was the zenith of neo-Nazi strength on the street. Paradoxically, it was also their undoing, as it rapidly became clear to the unconverted that all the BM stood for was the destruction of bands, gigs and therefore skinhead culture.

The Movement never grew any bigger and the new breed of skinhead-orientated bands never repeated Sham's many mistakes, or showed that kind of weakness in the face of far-Right aggression.

The BM's campaign of violence also led directly to the growth of a new, hard, street-level Trotskyist hit squad called Red Action, a 'workerist' spin-off from the Socialist Workers' Party, who were determined to meet fire with fire – and were arguably just as suspect.

As for Jimmy Pursey, his bid to turn Johnny Rotten into Johnny Forgotten petered out. By the end of August the new Pistols had split without ever playing a proper gig. Dave Parsons was right: they just couldn't work together. And besides, who'd want to risk that kind of tour mayhem?

In September, Jimmy re-formed Sham, but the band were never the same. Deeply fucked up by all he'd been through, Pursey seemed to have lost the knack of writing decent songs. The *Hersham Boys* album went silver but it had as much bite as a toothless pensioner. It wasn't until the follow-up album, *The Game*, in May 1980 that Sham came anywhere near finding their old form and by then they'd been surpassed by the Cockney Rejects and the Angelic Upstarts. The rest of Sham's releases document the decline of a band who were once the ultimate in street-punk aggression.

The next time I saw Jimmy Pursey on TV he was performing some kind of bizarre ballet-dancing routine. He appeared to have gone nuts. It was a sad end for someone who had been a great performer, a decent man and a friend.

Jimmy once told Danny Baker, 'My attitude might seem thick to you 'cos I was brought up to be thick to keep rich cunts in money.'

I think it probably seemed thick because he was. Just a bit. Jimmy was articulate, but the crux of what he said often made little or no sense at all. His words came straight from his heart and into his mouth without ever connecting with his brain. He was out of his depth and he paid a terrible price for it. But it's sadder still that scenes of that sorry riot at the Rainbow have been tattooed in to the public memory as the lasting image of the late-seventies skinhead scene.

## CHAPTER SIX

# DAYS OF CHANGE: GLORY BOYS AND THE MOD REVIVAL

The idea was simple. Disillusioned with the music business and 'the punk elite' at a tender age, Dave Cairns and Ian Page formed a band that was going to be determinedly underground; it would be anti-biz and anti-hype, strictly street level. It was supposed to be a 'secret affair', and so that was the name they chose for the band.

Singer Page had envisaged their following as, 'This group of kids called Glory Boys, a new kind of kid walking up and down Wardour Street, taking the place over. And what they were was kids with suss – they knew about the inside of the music business, which made them cynics, but it was because they knew so much that they could be optimistic. That's why they could change things. The original idea was that we'd go out and do so well live that we'd built up a really big following, so we literally had to be signed up – like Siouxsie and the Banshees ...'

Instead, the band became enmeshed with the late-1970s mod Renewal, and some of the Glory Boys became a monster to Page's immaculately tailored Frankenstein.

East London mods, many of them former skinheads, got in on the secret early and, adopting Page's name for themselves, these real-life Glory Boys briefly became the fighting elite of new mod.

Prominent among them were faces like Dave Lawrence from Dagenham, Tommy Russell, a.k.a. Boris the Spider, Steve Borg, a.k.a. the Crank, Ricky and Danny Meakins and Danny Harrison. The early and harder Glory Boys were a mix of the Becontree ex-skins and regulars from the Barge Aground in Barking such as Kenny and Frank Tierney, Barney Rubble, Bob Baisden, Tom McCourt, John O'Connor and Kevin Wells. Most of them were bright as buttons and many were like junior Del Boys dabbling in various dubious cons, stings and mild dishonesties. Many were so committed that they tattooed the name of the band, the keyhole logo and 'Glory Boys', on their biceps. Crank had the logo tattooed inside his lower lip. Dave Lawrence had 'mod' inside his.

'Most of them were as good as gold,' guitarist Dave Cairns recalls. 'Ninety-nine per cent of them were great blokes and we were very happy to have such a dedicated following. But a few of them – Crank and a couple of the others – were just in it for the rucks. There were a few nasty fights early on. Punks mainly would try to attack the young mods in the audience and the Glory Boys stopped them. We could understand that and we were grateful for that. But what we didn't envisage was the Glory Boys, and Southern mods in general, having a problem with Northern mods in places like Sheffield and Huddersfield.

'Unfortunately, trouble followed them around and they loved it. They were hooligans, a gang of guys from the East End who liked fighting. That was their lifestyle. And I guess that a few of them didn't realise that this wasn't just a bit of fun. It was our living, our vocation.'

A Secret Affair gig on 16 June 1979 at Huddersfield Poly was a turning point. The bill included the Killermeters, the Specials, the Teenbeats and the Scene. Tom McCourt recalls, 'The reason why me, Bernie, Bob, Rubble, John O'Connor and the rest of our mob stopped following the Affair was down to Huddersfield. The atmosphere was good during the day, but it got heated afterwards. The scooter boys started, a few (and I mean a few) of us did them and Page was on the coach back saying that it was all out of order, there shouldn't be violence at gigs blah, blah, blah. Then on the Monday at the

Bridgehouse, on stage, he said something along the lines of we played Huddersfield and this is what we gave them and went into "Time for Action" – to the cheers of people who hadn't been there! The fucking hypocrite! That was it for us and Secret Affair. The rest of the Glory Boys shifted to the Rejects later, mainly as a West Ham thing.'

The Glory Boys weren't always innocent, though. At Canterbury University that same month, a student who was taking the piss out of the band while they were playing was smacked around the head with a hammer by Crank. Police and an ambulance were called. There were no arrests but the bloodied hammer was discarded on the dashboard of Secret Affair's van.

'It was this kind of incident that eventually led us to hiring our own security,' says Dave Cairns. 'Most bands at that level would have done the same. We were letting fans into our shows for nothing who were more often than not winding up in fights or worse. No promoter would stand for that. We were warned by our agent and promoters that, if we didn't contain the situation at the gigs, we wouldn't play.'

The Affair filmed the promo video for their debut single 'Time for Action' at the Acklam Hall in Notting Hill, west London. The Glory Boys made up the audience (with a very youthful Eddie Piller standing in the shadows). The Ladbroke Grove Skins, led by Chris Harwood, got wind of it and turned up in force. In the fighting that followed cars were overturned in the roads outside and set alight.

Dave Cairns recalls, 'We were on stage finishing off the filming, doing retakes and so on, doing our job. We were aware of a fracas outside but didn't know the extent of it. It was a full-scale riot. When we left the club it was like stepping into a war zone. There were burnt-out cars immediately outside and the smell of burning rubber in the air.'

One west London eyewitness noted, 'The Glory Boys got sprung on by the LGS. They didn't see it coming. The LGS kicked the shit out of them.'

By then the Glory Boys were already past their best. But, although the hardcore had fallen out with Page over Huddersfield, those who remained were still game for 'action'. There was more trouble on the March of the Mods tour, which featured Secret Affair, the Purple Hearts and Back to Zero. Trouble flared at the Newcastle Mayfair gig on 31 August. Purple Hearts singer Rob Manton recalls, 'We were a few numbers into our set when we started to get pint glasses of beer, some still full, thrown at us. They appeared to be coming from some older guys in their late twenties at the back of the hall. I said something like, "There are some people here who want to wreck the gig, you know what to do." '

At that point, although outnumbered, the Glory Boys went in to action and attacked the local troublemakers. Manton remembers it as being 'like a barroom brawl in a Western'. He goes on, 'I believe the bouncers must have joined in on our side, because it was all over pretty quickly and the gig carried on without further interruptions.'

As hits like 'Time for Action', 'Let Your Heart Dance' and 'My World' were swelling their live audience, Secret Affair knew they had to take drastic action to distance themselves from violence. They still employed a couple of the hardcore fans – Dave Lawrence and Chris Stratton – to sell merchandise on tour, but they also brought in an ex-Para called Mick and later a former SAS man Dave as security guards to keep the likes of Crank out. When a fan was knifed at their Portsmouth Pier gig that September, the band could at least say that no one on their guest list was responsible.

'Most of the Glory Boys understood,' says Cairns. 'But one or two thought we were getting too big for our boots.'

The trouble persisted, however. At Secret Affair's gig at Torquay Town Hall, Cairns was repeatedly threatened by someone in the crowd with a hammer that he was producing periodically from inside his coat while mouthing the words 'This is for you.' The nut was removed by ex-SAS Dave but even he had to sleep and that night 'fans' ran amok at the band's hotel, causing chaos with fire extinguishers. They stole beer and dumped broken glasses in the swimming pool. Secret Affair were saddled with a £500 bill for damages.

At least the band felt relatively secure when they played Barbarella's in Birmingham. The club was two floors off the ground, with good security.

Cairns recalls, 'The windows in the dressing room were all boarded up, too. So we thought at least this gig would be no problem … We were sitting backstage relaxing pre-show when I heard a banging sound outside the dressing room, which was two storeys up. I said, "What the fuck's that?" The banging continued followed by a tearing and a ripping sound. I said, "Jesus, there's somebody out there." We all looked at each other. Then a fist punched its way through one of the boards – it was like a horror movie. The whole board was ripped off the window and Crank appeared, grinning from ear to ear. "You can't keep me away," he said. You had to admire him. He'd shimmied up a drainpipe like Spider-Man, got on a ledge and smashed his way in. He was eighteen or nineteen and he was like an unstoppable force. He was beyond control and beyond our comprehension.

'He didn't think he was doing anything wrong. Fighting was just what he did. He followed the band in his own unique way. He didn't consider that he might be causing us problems, but he was.'

By April 1980, Secret Affair had not only parted company with their Glory Boys, they had also shed the sharp-dressed look they had so vociferously championed. They posed for pictures with Ian wearing a nondescript brown jacket and Dave Cairns sporting cowboy boots!

The time for slacks-on seemed just days away.

Page had probably popped too many pills. It was the beginning of the end. The flame of new mod had already started to burn out, the bands were outsold and rapidly surpassed by 2-Tone. It was all over very quickly – in little over a year.

It had all seemed so different the previous August, as my review of the night shows:

*Bank Holiday Sunday, the Lyceum, London. Legs astride, but immaculately trousered, Ian Page punches the air and sings. Yeah, sings. No need to shout when you've got a nifty, Jess Roden reincarnate, nasal whine of a voice as confident and full-throated as this well-tailored eighteen-year-old, with his burning belief in his band and in his message ...*

*The band is Secret Affair, the message is mod and the medium a clarion call of a number called 'Days of Change'.*

*Soaking up the stirring sentiments this Sunday night at London's Lyceum are scores of sharp-dressed Glory Boys, even more mods, mobs of raucous rude boys, a significant scattering of skins, and the odd out-of-place punk. The overwhelming feeling is an amphetamine rush of excitement, of energy, optimism and hope. 'Gangsters' by the Specials has just broken into the Top Ten, and tonight a new ska band called the Selecter has shown plenty of pulse-quickening promise. Above them on the bill are a feisty mod outfit with a neat line in post-punk populist pop called the Purple Hearts. There's a tasty new bluebeat and belly laughs band called Madness. And headlining over the lot of 'em are this new Arista signing, Secret Affair, who are soon scheduled to shake some action on Top of the Pops themselves.*

*August 1979 is a rare old time to be young, free and single in London town.*

*Throughout the sweltering summer there have been mod do's every night, a new band every week, and more mods on the streets every day. There's something happening here and we're all caught up in it.*

*Tonight the guv'nors of 'new mod' and the rising stars of the newly emergent 2-Tone delight us with a barrage of diamond (non-disco) dance delights. Tomorrow most of the punters here plan on running free and terrorising a few bikers down Southend way. Tonight the only trouble is in the bogs. The bouncers catch a kid pushing pills and promptly crush ten quid's worth of little blue liveners underfoot. Criminal. One kid was gonna lick 'em up. He was nearly crying ...*

*This 'new mod' scene is all action and don't (most of) the jaded music press hate it. Elsewhere Grub Street is up to its slimy neck in misrepresentation, trying to put it all down to Quadrophenia. But most sussed mods suspect that the Who's new movie will mean the kiss of death rather than the kiss of life for their lovingly revitalised second-hand style ...*

History lesson time. Original mod was topped by its own logic – that tireless commitment to change transmuted the ultimate in teenage flash into swinging-London trendiness, chased down by the criminal naïveté of flower power, psychedelia and the corny con of the 'revolutionary' Hippy Underground.

Ronnie Lane knew Mod was over when he bumped into Rod Stewart wearing a floral blouse (see Chapter Two). Jack Lyons, a.k.a. Irish Jack, the pill-popping Goldhawk Club face who Pete Townshend based his Jimmy character on in the 1973 album of *Quadrophenia*, experienced a similar shock when he wandered into a West End club suited up, only to confront Townshend sporting a psychedelic dicky-dirt [shirt], beads and an Afghan coat four sizes too big for him. Soon after, Jack packed his bags and fled home to Cork. In the circumstances it was the best anyone could have done.

As mentioned elsewhere, the suits – the stubborn few who resisted the impetus of change for the sake of change – evolved the skinhead style in the South. Their equivalents in the North bequeathed the Northern soul scene. It's true to say that, by the early seventies, mod, as any sort of group activity, existed (albeit in a distorted form) only around the likes of Northern scooter clubs.

In the South, the classic mod look was carried on by scattered individuals – for instance, Surrey schoolboy Paul Weller. The Beatles were his first love (he said he became infatuated with them after seeing them on TV at the Royal Command Performance of 1963, when he was just five), but he fell head over heels for mod via an obsession with the Who. The Face-favoured DJ Jay Strongman also championed mod style for years in his native Crowthorne, Berkshire. His younger brother Phil achieved a degree of fame in an April 1976 *Sounds* report on a Southern mod revival. Phil reckoned there were around 50 mods in his locality, sustained by the contemporary short-lived Small Faces revival and sixties soul discos, like the local one at the Hawley Hotel in Camberley and the Crackers club in Wardour Street (which was to become the Vortex).

In those days, mods went far and wide to find their gear, and, although Sta-Prest were hard to get hold of at the time, much sharp schmutter could be had down the King's Road (mostly from Marx's in the Common Trading Centre and Acme Attractions in the basement of Antiquarius). In the *Sounds* picture Phil was scandalously sporting flares and advocating the wearing of peg-leg trousers – but then we all make mistakes.

Of course, nothing was to become of mod in 1976. Any hints of localised revivals were firmly swamped by the spiky explosion all around it. The overwhelming pull of punk was to attract and distract would-be modernist youth like Strongman and Weller. Chickenfeed developments like that *Sounds* piece are worth mentioning, though, if only to rub home the point that there was 'Life Before *Quadrophenia*'. Nothing against the film; the 'Oo's action-replay account of the life and times of London's teenage tickets back in 1964 was a great grin. But so many half-baked hacks put 1979's mod renewal down to the movie that the truth got lost somewhere along the way.

In fact the one thing 'new mod' was *not* was a media/marketing invention. If you need someone to blame, blame the Jam who blazed onto the primal punk scene with their mixed-up anthems, Rickenbacker wallop and tasty suits and gave the whole to-do a touch of teenage blue class.

Weller was a 14-year-old Who obsessive when he formed the band with older Sheerwater Secondary School pupils Steve Brookes (guitar), Bruce Foxton (bass) and Rick Buckler (drums). Their earliest songs were ripped off from *The Beatles Complete* songbook. Brookes had quit by the time the band got caught up in the gob-'n'-spew energy explosion of 1976. Self-penned fireballs of R&B frustration like 'In the City' and 'Art School' quickly confirmed their importance and potential. The Jam were signed by Polydor and hit the Top Twenty with the 'In the City' single and album in early 1977. The follow-up second album later that year, *This Is the Modern World*, was rushed and relatively weak. But the band justified all the early critical praise with their glorious third album.

Released in November 1978, *All Mod Cons* wiped the floor with everything the trio had committed to vinyl beforehand, while at the same time seeing Weller concentrate on his pet mod themes. It wasn't just the album's name that made the connection: it was the ska album and the Vespa outline on the inner bag, the Op Art target design on the label and, of course, the schmutter Surrey's most famous sons elected to wear on the sleeve …

Tom McCourt recalls, 'The inner sleeve of *Modern World* had a mod feel, but it was *All Mod Cons* that really kicked it off. That's when I got my Vespa 200e to go with my Hush Puppies, 501s, crewneck jumpers, ben and tonic jacket …'

The Jam weren't the only punk band to be inspired by mod, however. Another were The Jolt, who were Scotland's first punk band, emerging in the Glasgow area towards the end of 1976. They played Glasgow regularly until the punk ban, and the small industrial town of Wishaw, building up a strong local following with their souped-up brand of raw R&B. In September 1977 they hit London to play the Marquee, only to be shot down in flames by a plethora of bored poseurs who predictably, albeit unfairly, wrote them off as Jam copyists. Obviously there were overlaps. Guitarist/vocalist Robbie Collins shared Weller's love for sixties mod England, except that, whereas Weller took his cue from The Who, Collins was more inspired by the Small Faces and the early Kinks. They both modelled mod suits (the Jolt picking theirs up in 1978, but tarnishing the image by wearing T-shirts and sneakers with jackets). And both were signed by Polydor, the Jolt getting off to a weak start with the poorly produced 'You're Cold' single (November 1977) and its inconsequential follow-up, a cover of the Small Faces' 'Watcha Gonna Do About It', before proving their potential with the July 1978 released debut album. Called simply *The Jolt*, it was a tastily tough turn-up for the books, suffused with energy and anger that manifested itself in lyrics about the decline of punk's promise. For Collins, punk's 'revolution' was an illusion, and its leading bands had become just another institution. But the Jolt were destined never to rise above local-hero status and broke up at the height of the mod renewal in 1979 after bravely refusing to jump on the one bandwagon that could have brought them the success they deserved.

Back in southeast England, The Jam's success was giving the mod idea fertile new ground to grow in. The idea spread as Jam fans and punk bands became infected. One of the first were a Romford-based Essex band called the Purple Hearts, who I first saw support the Buzzcocks as a schoolboy punk combo called the Sockets. That was in June 1977 at Northeast London Poly in Barking. The Sockets were a trifle shambolic to say the least. Included in their set were such moving originals as 'Down the Roxy' and a punk-opera penned by singer Rob Manton by the unlikely name of *Reg*, an excessively undernourished distant cousin of Townshend's *Tommy*. But even then they were including choice sixties covers like the classic 'Stepping Stone', 'My Generation' and 'Can't Explain', not to mention the more-wrecked-than-restless 'Born to Lose'. In May 1978 the band, whose disillusionment with punk was growing in equal proportion to their attachment to the Jam, changed their name to Purple Hearts, a decision instantly apparent to the good citizens of Romford, thanks to an immediate outbreak of fresh graffiti on every available subway wall and tenement hall.

Rob Manton, the band's main mouth, had been into the mod look at school but was seduced by the sudden arrival of Anarchy, 1976 style, and then inspired into forming a punk bank with his mates by the Jam at the start of 1977. The mates included Hearts-to-be guitarist Si Stebbing and bassist Jeff Shadbolt; drummer Gary Sparks came later. Increasingly pissed off with punk, Manton and co. finally settled on a mod image. In October 1978 I saw them at the Iron Bridge Tavern in Canning Town. They were supporting the Tickets (an East End 'power pop' group, power pop being an industry hype that failed, at the start of 1978, to revive 'beat groups' in the Mersey Beat vein – none of them were a patch on the Rutles). And I was suitably impressed by their Jam/Who/Small Faces-influenced, unmistakably post-punk set (see *Sounds* review 21.10.78).

By the time they were supporting the Inmates at the West Hampstead Moonlight Club in late November, there were 30 mods in the crowd.

Within three months there would be close on a hundred. I saw them again play the Bridge House in Canning Town in late February 1979. By now, there were even more mods in attendance and the band were considerably tighter. Tatty, photocopied handbills were all over the place proudly proclaiming PURPLE HEARTS – THE SOUND OF THE EIGHTIES. Underneath in semi-punk lettering came the roar YOUTH EXPLOSION hovering over the heads of mods on the march – a classic sixties snapshot embellished by a Liechtenstein pistol-in-the-fist design, the words 'Pop Art' and the details of a forthcoming gig.

Mod was happening again right there on the streets, manifest in the parka-packing punters with their Jam badges, Union Flags, neat haircuts, collars and ties and wild talk of other bands in faraway places – the Jolt, the Ricky Tics from Nottingham, the Teenbeats from 'rockers paradise' Hastings and the Fixations from the other side of London.

Like Manton, the majority of faces on the London mod scene in 1979 had been fanatical Jam fans for the two previous years (although there were also a sizable number of re-forming skins involved, mostly skins sick of the large numbers of weeny-teenies and plastics adopting that style). Also like Manton, most spoke of going through a schizophrenic period, harbouring confused feelings about punk's deterioration, before they gradually began to dress and think of themselves as mods. One of the first was Grant Fleming, Jimmy Pursey's 'batman', who was known to wear his parka on the terraces of Upton Park as early as the spring of 1978, standing out like a bridegroom's expectations among that currently larger mob of disillusioned punks, the burgeoning Sham Army. By autumn, a lot of other Jam fans and a few of the older East End and Essex skins were dressing the same way. The first clue was at the Great British Music Festival of December 1978. The Jam headlined, and Tom McCourt recalls, 'That was where we all started to bump into each other as ex-skins, -suedes and -mods. Grant Fleming was there.'

Tony Morrison (a.k.a. Tony Perfect), who went on to form Long Tall Shorty, recalls, 'I was wearing a Union Jack jacket which I'd bought off Bruce Foxton for £35. I had no idea that there were any other mods in the UK. But that night I bumped into about forty. Bruce Foxton recognised the jacket and invited me backstage, where I met Grant Fleming. I ended up watching the Jam from the side of the stage, which was a real thrill.'

Of the Jam fans, two of the earliest faces were Alan Suchley and Large Al from Hayes. Around the same time in other parts of London other Jam fans were going through the same process, unaware of the parallel development in the East End. Among the most active/important were Billy Hassett in Deptford and Brian Betteridge and Goffa Gladding in north London. These pioneer modernists first became aware of each other's existence as mods at the Jam's Paris gigs in February 1979. Grant Fleming had printed up leaflets advertising the exodus as 'The mod Pilgrimage', and no one was more surprised than the West Ham wide boy when around 50 mods turned up.

From then on the mods got together as often as possible and Purple Hearts gigs were the main rallying point.

The next new band to surface on the mod scene – which had rapidly grown to three or four hundred kids – was Billy Hassett's Chords from southeast London. I caught their third ever gig at the Kings Head in Deptford in March 1979, with the placed packed out with parka-clad punters, and was well impressed by the quartet's clout. They had a powerful two-guitar punch (provided by singer Billy and lead guitarist Chris Pope) and a tight rhythm section (courtesy of Martin Mason on bass and Buddy Ascott on drums). The Jam might have been an obvious frame of reference for their muscular melodies but original songs like 'Maybe Tomorrow' proved their potential as a band who, in Chris Pope's words, could 'couple punk attack with pop sensibility'. Their cover of 'Hold On I'm Coming' was pretty neat as well.

In February, Brian Betteridge's Back to Zero – who were somewhat softer than their colleagues – were the only other band on the immediate circuit, although, parallel to the three main bands developing a scene, a brace of tunesmiths by the names of Ian Page and Dave Cairns had formed what they described as a 'new-wave soul band'. Previously the backbone of power-pop flops the New Hearts (1977–78), they had been left significantly embittered by close contact with the music biz, so much so that the ads for their rhythm section read, 'Drummer and bassist wanted – must have grudge against the business.' Originally the band planned to build up a 'secret', i.e. cult, following by the word-of-mouth gigs and so on, until they had so many supporters that the music business would be forced to come to them cap in hand. The following would, as we have seen, be called Glory Boys – a smart youth elite, a breed Page recognised in the East End of London towards the end of 1978 and who he poetically painted thus: 'Young man, sharp look, street corner, a cold stare from old eyes in a young face. Pride/dignity – self respect.' The look of the band and their intended following was based on south London gangsters featured in the film *Performance*, starring James Fox and Mick Jagger, which Ian Page and Dave Cairns had watched 'countless' times at late-night screenings at the Electric Cinema in Notting Hill.

They appealed to ex-skinheads who hated the way their smart, stylish cult had been watered down by scruffs, 'boneheads' and bald punks who didn't get it. Skinheads had to be sharp to mean anything.

By May, Secret Affair had emerged as the premiere 'new mod' band, and certainly the least obviously post-punk ones, as they took their inspiration from the big wheels of sixties Motown, adding angry guitar and modern lyrics to that genre of glorious Holland–Dozier–Holland masterpieces. Their rise provided mod with a bona fide spokesman in Page and was the focus for a new emphasis on fashion. Parkas and Jam T-shirts were decidedly out, although Harringtons were all the rage that summer. Camel-hair suits, Harry Fenton jackets, checked Madras and seersucker jackets, studs and tiepins were some of the gear the better-dressed punters voted for with their wages. Johnson's in the King's

Road, Flips in Kensington High Street, Hot in Kensington Church Street and (for the less flush) the Last Resort in Goulston Street were just some of the emporiums modernists and stylists checked.

All of London's remaining old tailors and army-surplus stores were also targeted, from Brick Lane to Dagenham Heathway, to Earl's Court to Well Street in Hackney.

As ever, whenever a new movement breaks, the pace was initially very fast. Pretty soon *Sounds* was giving major coverage to the mod movement. My editor, the sagelike Alan Lewis, a former mod himself, encouraged my interest in the scene, which had already thrown up soapboxes of its own and established its first real venues. The first and best soapbox was mod's equivalent of *Sniffin' Glue*, a lively and hyperactive mod 'zine called *Maximum Speed*. In January, three north London mods, Clive Reams, Kim Gault and Goffa Gladding (a.k.a. 'the three baboons'), put out the first issue of what was to become their movement's main mouthpiece, a humble affair featuring only the Chords, the Purple Hearts and the Fixations, which they believed merited a print run of just 45. The second issue took over two months to appear, but by the end of June and issue five they'd gone fortnightly and were printing – and selling – one thousand a time. When Secret Affair set up their I-Spy label through Arista, they pumped funds into the 'zine and it began to attract record company ads. Despite the brief appearance of an anti-'zine (piss-takingly called *Minimum Sloth*), and the baboons' own somewhat 'cotton wool' approach to criticism, *Maximum Speed* flourished. It covered sixties soul and scooter rallies as well as all the bands that deserved exposure, and was generally acknowledged to be the best of a surprisingly professional breed.

The main point that they and the real sussed mod bands were making was that 'new mod' wasn't a mere revival; it was a 'renewal'. They weren't attempting to recreate the sixties, but rather take the best of those former glories as the basis on which to build something of their own, something new. It may sound like I'm playing with words, but it was an important distinction.

Before long the Bridge House in Canning Town, which had been hosting the likes of the Purple Hearts in 1978, had emerged as the mod venue. Revived as a live gig by Terry Murphy when he took over the tenancy in 1975, the Bridge soon established itself as a strong local draw with a string of lucrative if unfashionable punter-pulling pub-rock bands. But Terry Murphy was bright enough to suss that East End talent didn't begin and end with rhythm and blues. With – or perhaps despite – the advice of former Tickets bassist John 'The Chin' McGeady, the Bridge began opening its doors to local punk, skin and mod bands. In early 1979, Monday was established as 'mod night' and was soon attracting a regular 400-plus punters, proving Terry had been right to gamble. A vinyl documentation of those energetic early days, a compilation called *Mods Mayday* (with Robert Lee from Grays on the front cover) was released that July and sold out its first 2,000 pressing within a week. Sadly, there were no Chords, Back to Zero, or Purple Hearts on it, but there were strongly representative toe-tappers from Secret Affair and the very soulful Small Hours, as well as a host of lesser combos. Amazingly, the Bridge attracted more than 300 punters on the May night the album was recorded, despite clashing with the Music Machine Mod Night, which attracted some 900 mods – giving you some idea of how fast the scene had expanded. Another early venue, albeit one that lacked the warmth and camaraderie of the Bridge House, was the Wellington in Waterloo, south London. Then there was Acklam Hall in Ladbroke Grove, west London. Before long, mod would move away from these pubs and onto the club circuit – the Marquee, the 100 Club and the Music Machine, with the old Global Village at Charing Cross (now gay disco Heaven) opening up as a mod club called Vespa's.

In November 1979, Richard Barnes's definitive book *Mods!* was released and played a significant part in improving the movement's fashion sense (as much for the original photos as for his short, outsider's-view text).

Back in April 1979, star names were attracted by mod's flash appeal.

Paul Weller turned up at the Wellington to check out his followers' creations. He was so bowled over by the Chords that he offered them a support slot at the Rainbow. Not to be outdone, Jimmy Pursey announced that he was going to sign the Chords to his JP label. Ageing punks Billy Idol and Tony James put in an appearance at the Chords/Purple Hearts/Back to Zero gig at the Cambridge Hotel in Edmonton, with James dubbing the scene quite accurately as 'entertaining but safe'. This gig, incidentally, was reviewed for *Sounds* by Dave McCullough, who slagged it resoundingly on the basis of one Purple Hearts number and several playings of 'Strange Town' in the other bar, thus setting a precedent for the many months of ignorant criticism to come. For example, Chris Westwood in *Record Mirror* repeatedly slated the movement for being 'Big Business backed', which it patently wasn't, while *NME* scribes Charles Shaar Murray (a.k.a. Sheer Murder) and Danny Baker attacked mod for being non-revolutionary (not that Dan's fave raves, Earth, Wind & Fire, were exactly Singalonga-Trotsky). The most infuriating thing, however, was that these critics were never once seen at the Bridgehouse and so had absolutely no idea of what the scene was really like.

Away from the gigs, the Barge Aground in Barking was one of the key mod meeting places, attracting people from all over, not just the East End and Essex. Tom McCourt recalls, 'There was no football aggro, it was always a laugh and it was banged out on Friday, Saturday and Sunday nights with mods and proper skins.' Soul nights in the Bedford's Head in Covent Garden were also popular.

The Bridge recognised Mod Monday officially in April. Many of the old skins and bootboys had got caught up in the fervour. Faces like 'Hoxton' Tom – a veteran of the scene since 1978 – Bovril Bob Baisden, Barney Rubble and Si Spanner numbered among the Glory Boys, although they never let their hair or dress sense stray past suede-head. Garrie Lammin, former ferocious axe man for boot-boy favourites Cock Sparrer, was another convert, swapping his boots and braces for an Italian suit and his street punk for the late-mod strains of the Little Roosters (a very Stonesy combo who got nowhere but who did feature Alison 'Alf' Moyet as backing vocalist).

By May, the TV had caught onto the grass-roots groove, with that horrendous, pretend-cockney Janet Street-Porter making a mod documentary. This featured live footage of the Chords, the Purple Hearts, the Jam and the Who, as well as the mods themselves, their sixties predecessors and, inevitably, clips from the coming *Quadrophenia*. It was surprisingly good.

The general election saw the first hint of politics on the scene. 'We're voting Labour,' announced Billy Hassett, 'cos we're fun-loving and love drinking'. Perhaps as a reward for such political insight, the Chords won themselves a support slot on the Undertones' tour – after only 11 gigs in their whole existence!

Paul Weller pretty much declined to be spokesman for the new movement, allowing that dubious honour to pass to Ian Page by default. Weller was under pressure from people like the *NME*'s Neil Spencer to disown mod, but at the start he seemed fairly chuffed by all the obviously Jam-inspired excitement and was surprisingly accurate in his pronouncements. In May he told me, 'The spirit seems good at the moment, but I don't think the unity will last. Same as punk, once the record companies get involved and then they're all competing, then no one will speak to each other. The general consensus is that it'll be dead by August … I'll still be wearing me mohair suite in ten years' time.'

Around 30 Glory Boys were accompanying the band on the tour, living up to their Arfur Daley-esque reputation by sneaking into hotels behind the night porters' backs and blagging empty rooms. Obviously, their ruffian good humour was rubbing off on Paul because, when the Jam reached the Rainbow, Weller indicated the rows of seats and said, 'It cost too much to have 'em removed, but you know what you can do about it,' resulting in many of the front-row seats ending up on the stage.

At street level, there were around 500 on the May Bank Holiday Brighton Run, a great day out that culminated in a tremendous gig from Secret Affair in the Buccaneer, supported by cushty local band

Chicane. But the Run resulted in real shocks for the Southern mods — their first encounter with their Northern equivalents, creatures from another tradition with their Northern soul stickers (in one case, a Stranglers patch) and massive flares, instantly christened 'The Trouser Problem' by the Southern belles. The painted scooters and the beer mats on the backs of their parkas were also a rich source of amusement. In fairness to the Northern mods, it was the scooter boys who made the sartorial errors and, as was to become even more obvious as the years went on, the two were quite separate.

Actual mods in the North were resurrected by the Killermeters, a Huddersfield group who'd started life as a punk band in mid-1977, breaking up disillusioned in January 1978 and re-forming ten months later as a mod band largely thanks to their friendship with Paul Nicholson, an unrepentant sixties mod with a fund of fond memories from that original era. According to Nicholson, mod lasted up North until 1969, whereupon it was superseded in the affections of the masses by Northern soul, baggy strides and such like. The Killermeters played their first gig as a mod band in December 1978 — completely independent and unaware of developments down South. Their music was more lightweight than that of their Southern contemporaries and their best song was 'Twisted Wheel', a hymn to Manchester's famous sixties mod Mecca. Gigging locally, the band attracted a following who became mods themselves and who were eventually to style themselves the Jolly Boys as a plastered and peaceful piss-take of their more ruck-inclined Southern counterparts. The Northern scooter boys didn't pick up on this 'new mod' scene until May 1979 when the Killermeters supported Secret Affair in Huddersfield. Unfortunately, their arrival coincided with that of a coachload of London Glory Boys, confirming Southern prejudices about trouser problems and all, resulting in tension and aggravation betwixt North and South and wounds that never healed.

Tom McCourt recalls, 'They had flares, painted scooters and beer towels sewn on to their parkas. It was a bit of a shock to see, especially as we were wearing straight jeans and Sta-Prest, or suits and Shermans.' He adds, laughing, 'A couple of the Northern lads said we looked like poofs.'

The growth of 'new mod' had a healthy effect on the scooter clubs and by October there were 2,000 scooter boys north of Birmingham organised in clubs like the Yorkshire Roadrunners, the Preston Wildcats, the Fugitives from Huddersfield, the Red Lion Club in Heckmondwike, and many more. Some scooter boys succumbed to mod fashions (though many didn't) while many of the Northern mods got into scooters – despite the fact that scooters seemed to attract police harassment. And that's how it remained for a while, with Northern soul on one side, new Northern mod on the other, and scooters linking the two. But the alliance was destined not to last – the Northern mod scene burning out first despite a whole host of bands (like the Name in Peterborough, the Scene in Bradford and the Moving Targets in Leeds) springing up in the Killermeters' wake. As mod declined, the fashion sense died with it. Scooter boys became openly contemptuous of mod and by 1984 mods were organising their runs entirely separately to the scooter boys.

'Dahn' South, the first hints of trouble were brewing by June. The Chords split with Pursey after Jimmy Sham and his two new mates, Paul Cook and Steve Jones, made nuisances of themselves by invading the stage uninvited as the band supported the Undertones at Guildford City Hall. Disillusioned by the way Polydor was handling his label, Pursey took JP to Warner's and announced that he was producing singles by three bands: (1) the Low Numbers, a beefy mod/punk cross; (2) the Purple Hearts, although Rob Manton was too much like Pursey in the motormouth department for their union to survive long, and their debut single 'Millions Like Us' finally came out and charted in August on Chris Parry's Fiction label instead; and (3) Tony Perfect's Long Tall Shorty, a band who Jimmy Pursey discovered as the Indicators supporting the Angelic Upstarts that February, rechristened, and then produced their single 'By Your Love', which was finally issued by Warner's and withdrawn a week later after selling a mere 200 copies.

Tony explains, 'We were supposed to sign to Polydor but the Upstarts had a ruck with a security guard after throwing an aborted foetus out of a top-floor window, so, amid much delay, we finally signed, along with the whole Pursey's Package label, to WEA. The single was scheduled for release, but then A&R man Dave Dee got the sack, the whole of Pursey's label was dropped and all the singles withdrawn – an unfortunate set of circumstances, I think anyone would agree, but, then, if I'd have become a megastar then, would I be in the Gonads now? What a lucky escape, eh?'

Meantime the Merton Parkas (featuring current Style Councillor Mick Talbot and his chipmunk-faced brother Danny) surfaced at the Wellington. A cheerful band with a very poppy singalong set including many a cover version, they were swiftly signed by Beggars Banquet, who attempted to launch them as 'the' mod band, completely destroying their credibility in the process. Beggars attracted the interest of the *Sun*, which devoted almost a page to the Parkas and the Specials in its 29 June issue, with the Parkas getting the lion's share of copy under cringeworthy headlines like FAB! THE MODS ARE BACK! PARKAS LEAD A SIXTIES REVIVAL!

To the average mod it was outrageous that these Johnny-come-latelys, who were a good laugh live but nothing special, could be rocketed into such a commanding position. Trading on the publicity, Beggars rush-released their first single, which tragically was also their first mod single. Called 'You Need Wheels', it was a piss-poor power-pop plod, totally embarrassing and hardly the flyer the new movement needed. Buddy Ascott said, 'I don't blame the Merton Parks: I blame the people who bought it. I mean, "You Need Wheels" ... was that really our "Anarchy in the UK"?'

An anti-Merton Parkas campaign called KAMP – Kill All Merton Parkas – sprang up with the Glory Boys issuing a piss-take mock-up of the single with the 'Wheels' cover suitably desecrated. A character called Mid-Kent was widely suspected to be the instigator. The spoof single was a hoot. The band's name was replaced by 'Bay City Rollers', their faces by Pursey, Rod Stewart and Beano characters and the title became 'You Need Your Brains Tested If You Like Merton Parkas'. The single inside was titled 'We Need Songs' by ShowModdyModdy, which was devastatingly accurate, the Parkas being the plastic equivalents for mod of those camp and corny teeny-bop Teds. Leading mods sneered that the Parkas were just Butlin's redcoats. An insult to show reds if you ask me.

'You Need Wheels' was a one-hit wonder, peaking at Number 40, although keyboardist Mick Talbot was to find fame, and credibility, later in Paul Weller's Style Council.

With the Merton Parkas debacle hinting of the nonsense to come, it was obvious by August that mod had reached a crossroads in its short existence.

Weller was right: disunity and distrust had set in. Session men and power poppers had started donning parkas and coming on as mod bands. Even David Essex brought out a single called 'M.O.D.' The price of clothes was sky-rocketing and Lyndall Hobbs was known to be importing poseurs for her 'mod documentary' B-movie *Steppin' Out*. As mod attracted more and more media attention you kept coming across semi-punk would-be mods, crazed craze-hungry casualties popularly known as 'pods' and 'munks', while the imminent release of *Quadrophenia* was stoking fears that the movement would soon be overrun with 'Quad-mods'.

To a certain extent this did happen, although in fact the film was actually pretty good in so far as it managed to capture the attitudes and the lifestyle of the original kids brilliantly. 'It could've been us,' an excited Grant Fleming could be heard gibbering. Just to be an awkward bastard, however, I'm forced to point out that *Quadrophenia* was actually littered with minor errors that detracted from Franc Roddam's goal of historical authenticity. Clangers included: rockers with Motörhead patches and a mod with the Jam on his parka; the ABC cinema showing *Heaven Can Wait*; the newly opened Brighton Marina in the background shot of Jimmy near Palace Pier; Escorts and Cortinas motoring about; 'NF' sprayed on a scrapyard gate; Chalky's scooter being an 'M' reg; the Old Bill having Transit van meatwagons; an Inter City 125 speeding past Jimmy's window ... and on and on the litany of goofs goes. Still, a fine film though.

Already the Bridgehouse crowd had started saying mod was dead. Grant Fleming fired the first salvo, saying that the movement had been commercialised. 'Our crowd are still the same, we're still mods,' he said, 'but we don't feel part of the mass movement.' Tom McCourt and Bob Baisden also attacked the poseur count at places like Vespa's, where inveterate wallies like Steve Strange could be spotted putting themselves about and Billy Idol and co. were playing 'mod' sets. Others, like Goffa Gladding and Dave Laurence, accepted the faults but were still optimistic that the movement could survive and flourish. They held that events like that month's March of the Mods tour were proof that the grassroots were still healthy. But, before it started, the tour, which was to have included the Affair, the Hearts and the Little Roosters, was the subject of controversy when the Roosters were booted off in favour of the more mod-credible Back to Zero (who just happened to be managed by *Maximum Speed*). 'Ian Page has turned out to be the Maggie Thatcher of rock' was the petulant accusation from Roosters' drummer Graeme Potter. 'He's acting like a Tory. Mod unity means sticking together like workers, not shitting on people like mill owners.' (Trouble at t'mill! What kind o' trouble? T'band's been sacked an' replaced wi' whippets ...)

To the disillusioned, a *Daily Mirror* piece published in its 23 August issue was the final nail in the coffin. Laughingly describing the Who as the 'vanguard of the new revival', the *Mirror* revealed that Townshend's crew had teamed up with Suuchi's of Wellington Street (WC2) to turn out purple suede parkas (a snip at a mere £125). The next month, top London models could be seen prancing around the Lyceum stage in overpriced parkas and zoot-suits.

There were still great laughs and handsome highs to be had – and not only at live shows. Secret Affair got their own I-Spy label through Arista and put out 'Time for Action' – a Top Twenty smash that got to Number 13 in the chart. It went on to sell 198,000 copies.

I-Spy's subsequent releases did less well. They included an underwhelming single from the over-sixties-sounding Squire, another pressing of *Mods Mayday* and ska beauts by the great Laurel Aitken.

The Chords and the Purple Hearts followed the Affair's success with 'Now It's Gone' (Polydor) and 'Millions Like Us' (Fiction) respectively. However, without a doubt it was the Jam who provided the single of the late summer in the sage and sizzling shape of 'When You're Young', their finest three-minute opus to date.

August Bank Holiday was probably the last time all the disparate wings of the original 'new modsters' united with the unholy aim of running amok down Southend way. Apart from the odd spectacular run-in (see 'Notes from a Teenage Rampage'), most of the trouble was with the police. The uneasy alliance between mods and skins on that day was to be short-lived and mod-versus-skin battles were to become a sad and ironic part of street life thereafter – exacerbated by Scottish punk band the Exploited, whose 1980 song 'Fuck a Mod' was a tirade of mindless violence to the tune of 'Jingle Bells'.

Cynicism and disillusionment may have set in at the roots, but some startlingly good records – the proof in plastic, as we said at the time – were still to come out, not least being the Affair's awesome album *Glory Boys*, a soul-soaked dance album sparkling with ire, fire and live-wire tunes. And, for the perfect mod night out, Tony Rounce's recently arrived sixties soul nights were beyond fault. But mod as a whole was never to recover from the death wish that appeared to grip street mods on the brink of what should have been the scene's mass breakthrough. It was something like a collective speed comedown.

Artistically as well, mod was overtaken by the 2-Tone revolution that it had nurtured at its bosom. The bands started on the mod circuit and an elite group of mods picked up on 2-Tone at the expense of the mod bands, adopting the rude-boy look. Meanwhile, Weller, who'd always kept his distance, led the Jam away from the imagery and pop appeal of 'All Mod Cons' in favour of the harder, less obviously sixties-influenced and more politicised sound, which preceded his complete disowning of guitar-orientated rock to embrace stylised white soul in 1983.

The 'new mod' bands themselves floundered. Secret Affair did attract a new audience, a short-term teeny-bop one that soon burnt out. Neither the Purple Hearts nor the Chords proved capable of equalling the Affair's chart achievements, even though the Chords' Top Forty cracker 'Maybe Tomorrow' was moderately magnificent. The Chords eventually ran out of time at Polydor and split – as did the Affair – while the Purple Hearts went on to dabble with late-Small-Faces-style psychedelia before breaking up themselves, only to frequently re-form for 'one-off' gigs. Both their albums smacked of too-much-too-soon, underproduction and underfinance, although their potential was never in doubt.

The final blow came soon after. As the charts exploded with 2-Tone acts, mod was outdone at street level by other soul-based live bands who either revived sixties soul better than the mod revivalists (e.g. the Q-Tips) or renewed it better than the mod renewalists (e.g. Dexys Midnight Runners). The Q-Tips attracted a measure of Glory Boy interest, although most of them went on to congregate around the Cockney Rejects, the uncompromising Canning Town-based street-punk band, either becoming (clean) skinheads again or adopting 'straight' terrace fashions and becoming the forerunners of the 'casual' movement to come.

Ian Page observed, 'All those kids, they basically won't support a band beyond a certain level of success. I mean Sham 69 first, then us, now they go with the Cockney Rejects. That roots following, they can't tolerate having to share their band with anyone else.' This was April 1980 and the explanation was plausible but wrong. The Bridgehouse crew's one real and lasting loyalty was to West Ham United FC in general, the West Side and the West Ham Inter City Firm, or ICF, in particular. They related to their bands for as long as their bands related to them. When superstar-itis set in, and/or when they, the fans, became an embarrassment to the bands' newfound success (something that never happened with the Rejects), the fans ditched them without a second thought.

When the Biz and the teeny-boppers lost interest in Secret Affair, there weren't many mods left. The early eighties were certainly deadly dull by 1979 standards, and one by one the bands split up disillusioned, the bandwagon jumpers among them finding new wagons to leap onto. Billy Hassett 'did a *Roots*' and went 'home' to Ireland. Apart from small dedicated local scenes, mostly in the Home Counties, the only place to really find mods was at Jam gigs. Then, in 1983, Weller courageously/frustratingly broke up the band to launch his new project, the Style Council, with Mick 'Mr Piano' Talbot, which, despite much initial pretentiousness, was certainly to prove responsible for more worthwhile tunes than Weller's wretched Respond label. Ironically, as the Jam became toast, an exciting new-mod-influenced band emerged: the Truth. Formed in 1982 by former pub rocker Dennis Greaves (of 9 Below Zero fame), the Truth for Dennis just meant widening his influences from New Orleans to include the Detroit sound of Motown too. I first became aware of the band in early 1983, when I came across a mob of Truth fans outside the Marquee who really looked the business. A million miles from the parka-clad teenies who'd diluted mod and the glue-sniffing, face-tattooed scruffs who'd polluted skinhead, these kids were wearing button-downs and Fred Perrys, polished brogues, neatly pressed tonic trousers and socks whiter than your granddad's shaving foam. The thing is, they obviously cared about their appearance and, as it turned out, the Truth were good enough to do the kids justice. Bloated on gutsy black stompers, with an obvious debt to mid-period Jam, the Truth's live set was a raging inferno of populist punch-the-air soul, strong on singsongs, high on energy and embellished by a handsome Hammond organ.

They started gigging in October 1982. By January 1983 WEA had beaten Stiff in a two-horse race to get their autographs on recording contracts. The first vinyl fruit of the pairing was the single 'Confusion Hits Us Every Time', a fine thing indeed. However, the Jam split led WEA to think the Truth could take over the Woking Wonders' crowd overnight. 'Confusion' was hyped like crazy, but didn't make the Top Ten. Thereafter, the label pressurised the band into making ever more wimpy and lightweight singles which did sod all for their street cred. Eighteen months later and they'd parted company. Their IRS-released live mini-album *Five Live* gives a taste of how good they were in concert.

As a sidebar, it's worth pointing out that two of the assumed-to-be significant bands of the mid-eighties began as mod groups, namely Seventeen, who became the Alarm, and Graduate, who mutated into Tears for Fears, the former changing their image but not their sound, the latter totally shaking off their mod roots. Seventeen formed in Rhyl, North Wales, in 1978. They had a pop-mod sound, released an indie single called 'Don't Let Go', and were kicked off a Dexys tour support slot after just one show. At one stage the band, led by singer Mike Peters, came to the offices of *Sounds* in Covent Garden and attempted to kidnap me to drum up rock press coverage. I was with Hoxton Tom at the time, who suggested pleasantly but firmly that the four of them fucked right off, which was enough to kill the abduction plan stone dead. We invited them round the White Lion for a few beers instead. In 1981, they changed their name to Alarm Alarm, which they swiftly shortened to the Alarm. They moved to London, released their debut single 'Unsafe Building' and developed unsettling mullets. IRS signed them in 1982 and they supported U2 on tour in the US. The U2 influence was easy to detect on their 1983 album *Declaration* and the superbly anthemic Top Twenty single '68 Guns'.

By 1984 the legacy of 'Quad-mods', teeny-mods and all the other dumb mutations had long gone and only the truly dedicated were left. On the way a lot of people had fallen by the wayside. Ian Page had resurfaced on CBS with a flop project called Bop. Chris Pope, Buddy Ascott and Grant Fleming could now be found doing the rounds in a Big Country-style guitar band called Tin Soldiers, and the three baboons from *Maximum Speed* had disappeared off the face of the earth. Most of the Glory Boys now dressed casual and their contact with the music biz seemed confined to ticket forging, ticket touting, schnide merchandising and other dubious activities. Some ended up in a Swiss slammer for shoplifting pricey label-name clobber.

The advantage the surviving mods and the new recruits had was the ability to learn from past mistakes. What they were doing was fairly unparalleled in youth-cult history – they were consciously attempting to safeguard their ideals and organise their activities. In 1984, serious mods weren't content with merely going to gigs. They'd organised themselves into a scattered network of dedicated modernist societies working almost like regional councils to cultivate the mod cause and protect it from, for example, the sort of shallow press overkill that boiled the 1979 Renewal down to a cheap throwaway fad. There was the Fellowship of Style in Oxfordshire, the Inner Circle in Guernsey, the 24th Hour Mod Society in Leeds, the Emerald Society in Eire and most influential of the lot, the Phoenix Society in London. The faces behind the Phoenix Society were bods like rhythm-and-soul DJ Tony Class; dashing Dagenham activist Eddie Piller, editor of the best contemporary mod 'zine *Extraordinary Sensations* and later to start the Acid Jazz label; and the American-accented but London-born gay mod Mark Johnson, the 31-year-old brains behind the *Phoenix List*, a weekly news sheet of mod events, developments and debate.

In November 1984, the Phoenix Society took the unprecedented step of organising a National Mod Conference, they hoped the first of many, in the Boston Club in Tufnell Park. The day started with a chaotic, cop-disrupted scooter run to Buck House with 500 scootering participants. And in the afternoon 300 mods from all over the country gathered for the conference, where the unwanted attendance by a bunch of scruffily turned-out scooter boys full of beer and abuse served only to emphasise how great the divide had become between them and the mods – precisely why that afternoon saw 1985's mod runs decided separately from the scooter clubs' runs, why mod dos banned scruffy scooter boys and why many of the speakers could be heard condemning 'scooter thugs'. The afternoon also heard a message of support from Ronnie Lane and a well-received diatribe from Irish Jack, the Goldhawk mod turned guru who spoke with Gaelic poetic licence of 'floating in a honeycomb of mod purity'. With the audience eating out of his hands, Jack concluded, 'Peter Meaden would have been proud of you. Jimmy Cooper would never have believed it.' And then Mark Johnson defiantly filled in the facts about new mod's history.

In the evening, the mod DJs took over and around 500 more turned up, including mods, suede-heads and stylists from all over London and the Home Counties – 800 faces testifying to the enduring lure of mod ideals. Live on stage were Fast Eddie, who specialised in reasonable, albeit uninspired, covers. My one overwhelming memory from the night was Irish Jack coming over all misty as Prince Buster's 'Madness' echoed from the downstairs PA. 'I haven't heard this for years,' he said, grinning like a pillhead who's found the back door to his local chemist open after hours.

I don't think he stopped smiling till the music stopped at 2am the next day.


POSTSCRIPT: Of course, it was all wish fulfilment. By the fag end of 1986, the mod revival had fizzled out.

London DJs Paul Hallam (a.k.a. 'the Stalin of Style') and Richard 'Shirley' Early kept the scene alive at a local level. Their Shepherd's Bush club nights were packed with well-tailored enthusiasts grooving to pure soul and rare R&B sounds. Tony Class ran Club Mod at the Bush Hotel until 1986, when the venue changed to an O'Neill's. Hallam moved his Sneakers Club to the Hammersmith Clarendon and the 79 Club, which added the best 1979 songs to the mix, to Oxford Street, but lost interest in June 1987 due to the lure of the Beastie Boys. No standout bands emerged after the Prisoners and Making Time.

Eddie Piller and a few of the other faces grooved stylishly over to the jazz scene; other mods followed their sixties predecessors by moving on into psychedelia. Those who remained went even further underground, picking up on the white psyche/R&B sound of the UK 1967–69. This they called freakbeat. Others drifted off into Northern soul. The scene was not heard of again until the acid-jazz-inspired, mod-influenced club scene of the early nineties, which was soon overwhelmed by Britpop – and that was even more of a mod baby.

On the one hand, Britpop was a welcome reaction against the grimness of grunge. On the other, it was a throwback that underlined the mounting suspicion that modern rock would spend more time looking back at the past than carving out a fresh future. Britpop broke through in 1994, although the term was first used by John Robb in *Sounds* in the late eighties. The bands had catchy tunes, played loud with no thrills and no real point of view.

But at least pop was upbeat and exciting again. The new British bands-with-attitude ranged from the lairy Manchester Herberts Oasis to the arty Blur, via Suede, Pulp, Ocean Colour Scene, Elastica, Supergrass and the Verve. Their heroes included the Kinks, the Who, Weller and the Small Faces. Their debt to mod, along with glam and punk and post-punk Manchester, is hard to miss. Blur's video for their hit single 'Parklife' memorably used actor Phil Daniels of *Quadrophenia* fame, and there's no escaping the echoes of the Small Faces and the Kinks in the song's larky Music Hall feel.

Britpop led to a massive revival of interest in mod, sixties beat groups and classic soul and R&B. The mod events team the New Untouchables, or NUTs – set up by Rob Bailey and Jason Ringgold in 1997 – capitalised on it with newsletters and club nights, national and international weekenders, scooter runs, clothes and record markets and the relatively new phenomenon of the Internet.

From 1997 on, London club nights such as Purple Pussycat, Hipsters and the Mousetrap inspired a new generation of mods and sixties enthusiasts. New bands and DJs were and are actively encouraged. In 2004, more than 4,000 attended their London event, held at the Rocket, celebrating 'Forty Years of Mod' – 'Not from its birth,' explains Rob, 'but from a pinnacle year in its history.' NUTs events were and remain good-humoured – 500 attended Bailey's super-mod do at Christmas 2008 without a single punch being thrown.

Britpop's own influence can be seen clearly in today's third-generation bands such as Kaiser Chiefs, Dirty Pretty Things and Arctic Monkeys.

Abroad, the 1979 mod renewal sparked copycat scene in the US in the 1980s, which thrived in southern California, with bands such as the Untouchables. The 2-Tone bands proved to be more influential on the LA and Orange County scenes.

Just like the old punks, most of the 1979 school of mod bands are still going to this day, finding enthusiastic audiences from Florence to Moscow. Pope, the band formed by Chris Pope of the Chords, and self-styled 'giffer punks' Long Tall Shorty are the most creative although commercial success has so far eluded both of them.

Many of the late-seventies revival mods – and skins – got involved in the scooterist scene, bequeathing the scooter-boy subculture, which flourishes to this day with club nights and rallies where you are just as likely to see Bad Manners or the Cockney Rejects as an old mod band.

Today, hundreds of small bands and tens of thousands of would-be mods and scooter boys all around the world identify with mod and use its symbols, although the gulf between them, their attitude to clothes, life and culture, and those of the freethinking mod pioneers featured in 1962's *Town* magazine is wide enough to park a thousand Vespas.

Once again, a street movement denounced as 'hype' by the snooty UK rock press in 1979 has gone on to pass the test of time.

## CHAPTER SEVEN

# RUDE BOYS OUTTA JAIL: THIS ARE 2-TONE

H ey, you! Don't read that, read this …

October 27 1979. The 2-Tone tour, featuring Madness, the Specials and the Selecter, rolled in to Hatfield Polytechnic. Disaster ensued. The audience, a mix of students, straights, mods and skinheads, had been good-natured and upbeat. But, when the Selecter started their set, a tooled-up mob calling themselves the Hatfield Anti-Nazi League burst into the venue through a plate-glass fire-exit door and started to indiscriminately attack and stab blameless skinheads in the audience.

It was the worst violence ever seen at a UK ska gig.

The anti-fascists – in fact, members of the far-Left Socialist Workers' Party – claimed that there were National Front members present. Madness fan Nikki Clark was just one of the many innocent bystanders who remember it differently: 'There had been no trouble; everyone was in a good mood. Then this lot just broke in and started cutting any bloke who had short hair. It was awful.'

Another eyewitness was mod ace face Grant Fleming. 'There were about thirty of them,' he recalls. 'And they were really tooled up. They smashed in at the side of the hall level with the front half of the audience, who were mostly skins, and started properly slicing people up. It was nasty. The doors flew open, the windows smashed in – it was a proper attack. It was also dark and the band was playing so it took everyone completely by surprise. People were panicking. They couldn't work out what was going on, or why it was happening.

'They were after skinheads, specifically NF skinheads, but how they could tell what someone's politics were by their clothes escapes me. Obviously they couldn't and people were getting stabbed and hurt just for being skins.

'Before the gig, me and about five mates had gone into a pub near the station which turned out to be their pub. They saw me in my red Harrington with the Union Jack and flew through the bar at us. Luckily, one of the local kids knew us and said, "They're all right, they're mod boys." We drank our pints pretty sharpish.

'A few of them were older than us. They were an odd-looking group – they weren't mods or punks. They weren't anything. But they were game.

'We weren't expecting the attack on the gig; no one was. It was the worst violence I had ever seen at a gig ... until the Battle of Birmingham [see Chapter 9] with the Cockney Rejects, which was worse but in a different way. There were a lot of things being thrown at us in Birmingham. Here it was a tooled-up gang attacking individuals, and because of the savagery and the severity of the attack people kept away from them; they didn't want to know. It was a nasty night, vicious and pretty horrible.'

Ten people were hospitalised, there were eleven arrests, and £1,000 worth of damage was caused. Madness's tour manager, a likable character called Kellogg's, was sacked by Stiff Records for having taken the night off, although it's difficult to know what he could have done to stop the premeditated carnage that unfolded.

The SWP later expelled the men behind the attack, denouncing them as 'squadists'. They went on to form Red Action (see Chapter 17, 'Blowing in the Wind').

The far-Right had every reason to hate 2-Tone – it was the antidote to their poisonous message of racial hatred. At a Bad Manners gig at the Electric Ballroom in Camden the following year, a notorious neo-Nazi (a BM member later heavily involved with Combat 18 – see Chapter 17 again) leapt on stage and tried to stab Buster Bloodvessel; mercifully, Louis 'Alphonso' Cook smashed him off stage with his guitar. But at Hatfield the far-Left had been completely in the wrong; their brutal approach was wildly misjudged and utterly counterproductive, having the effect of attracting real neo-Nazis to future gigs.

More flick-blades were flashing on 1 December 1979, but mercifully not at the Specials' gig. Trouble flared up by Lewisham station when mob-handed Bushwhackers tracked down West Ham fans who'd lingered south of the river too long after the afternoon's West Ham–Charlton fixture. Tony Barker, singer with Oi! band Angela Rippon's Bum, and Tilbury skin Kieran White were just two of the claret-and-blue casualties. By their own admission, it had been their fault. As drunk as a thousand sailors, they, and four mates, had decided to 'start slapping Millwall heads' instead of heading straight to Lewisham Odeon. 'If I hadn't picked up a wastepaper bin and smashed one of them over the canister with it, Kieran would have been dead,' recalls Barker ruefully.

At the Odeon, just a goal kick away, tearaway teenage energy was being expended less antisocially in response to the Special AKA's glorious ack-ack attack of ska-spangled rhythms.

It was a magnificent show. Rubber-legged revellers drunk on enjoyment were skanking in the aisles, the rudies right out there on the window ledge of fun, tottering precariously close to plunging into total ecstasy as the band worked up to a rowdy pre-encore climax with their debut summer smash, 'Gangsters'.

This venue was no small draw for ska authentics when most of tonight's tickets were busy cutting milk teeth. But this time around the bluebeat was different, rock-backboned and beefed up by caring upstarts who had picked up the memory dirt cheap in backstreet bargain bins and reshaped its red-hot rhythms for the modern dance.

Mere months before, the Specials had been paying their dues at dives like the Nashville and the Hope. Now they had two Top Ten singles under their belts via their 2-Tone label, a launching pad that seemed unable to put a loafer out of place, and they were headlining a tour that spelled full houses nationwide to kids like this night's draw: the expected array of tonics, mohairs and Harringtons, pimply schoolkids and young workers, podgy birds, scowling, prowling skins, sharp-to-suspect mods, and cushty cool, chequerboard, black-and-white rudies – kids who don't need the disapproving lectures of wincing highbrow puritans or arse-licking assembly-line yes-men's old flannel *one bit*, 'cos they've slogged their balls off all week and coughed up three hard-earned sovs for the best seats, even though they desert them as soon as the sounds start, anyway, 'cos they've come to *dance*, and 2-Tone is currently the best dance music on offer.

Ladies and gentleman, dudes and dames, *these are 2-Tone*, the greatest show on earth – 'Your last chance to dance before World War Three', Specials singer Terry Hall called it – and the most perfect pop music since Trojan reggae ruled the chartland heartlands a decade before, providing the class of '79's prime source of inspiration in the process.

Among its many attributes, 2-Tone was responsible for putting character(s) back into the charts, real larger-than-life lunatics like:

- BUSTER BLOODVESSEL, a moonstomping Michelin Man skin with boots, braces and a belly that quivers like a Quatermass mutation and who pumps out a 13-inch conger eel of a tongue, an awesome organ Soho's saddo mack-flashers could only dream of possessing
- NEVILLE STAPLE, a Jamaican-born chancer with a roguish smile and boxer's physique, who bounces around every stage in the land raucously roaring: '*Hush now, rude booiizzze!*'
- CHAS SMASH, a crazed cockney kid in shades and a pork-pie hat

who dances like he's all elbows, fronts a human train of his Madness cohorts and hollers hoarse commands like '*Hey, you!* Don't watch that, watch *this!*'

- PAULINE BLACK, a hyperactive, heart-meltingly gorgeous mixed-race rude girl running on pure adrenalin with a voice, like her big bouncing breasts, that is an instrument of wonder
- and in Pop Dream imagery, out there fronting the lot, JERRY DAMMERS, the 2-Tone ringmaster theatrically tipping his topper to Joe Public, unleashing a big toothless grin, and hammering at his Wurlitzer with the same insane nonchalance as the naked Terry Jones in *Monty Python's Flying Circus*

2-Tone couldn't have happened without punk and didn't have the space to happen until after the 1976 school of spiky outrage had burnt out. At street level, mod and a new wave of punk bands, exemplified excitingly by the Ruts and the Skids, were keeping things cooking. But from the fag-end of 1978 onwards the music scene as a whole started looking very stale and boring again. Very self-important and pompous. Old concepts were rearing up on young shoulders with bands raiding Pink Floyd and Doors back-catalogues quite shamelessly in the interests of their Art (capital A of course and sod-all to do with such base concepts as pop or rock'n'roll). Correspondingly, the music press became top heavy with tedious turds, solemn youngsters, very serious and quite pious, who tried their damnedest to speak like dictionaries and who wore the sort of dowdy clobber that only the children of the wealthy or the middling wealthy would dream of wearing. It was grim scenarios all round and a glum time was had by all.

Ian Page's diagnosis was spot on of course. It was all deadly dull and the time was right for a new dance music. Sadly for him, and new mod, the nation's youth chose a different remedy – 2-Tone. A breath of fresh (moh)air.

In retrospect, the amazing thing about 2-Tone was its simplicity. The music was basic. As an epithet 'punk ska' doesn't encompass all of 2-

Tone's permutations, but it's a good starting point and one that captures the early feel, of the Specials in particular, bang to rights. It really was a punky reggae party. Punk in feel and bite, ska in the beat. The punk made danceable, the ska intensified. The image was simple, too, black and white because that was what the music was: a mix of black ska and white punk. Going to an early Specials gig was like walking into a world where all colour had been banned. Black-and-white threads were the only things fit to wear during the winter of '79. And the message was simple. On the surface it may have appeared to have all been purely physical – a case of, as the famous Madness slogan had it, 'Fuck Art, Let's Dance' – but the intrinsic message ran deeper. 2-Tone stood for youth unity, black and white kids living it up together as equals without all the middle-class social-worker patronising.

In the Midlands especially, 2-Tone was a vibrantly human, street-level realisation of Rock Against Racism's wildest wet dreams – which is why real Nazis hated it so.

Incubating largely on the mod circuit, within months the 2-Tone bands were vying with the then ebbing tide of disco as the mass dance music of the nation's youth, its attributes plain to see. It was unselfconsciously pop. It was overwhelmingly teenage – despite Jon Savage's rarefied theory that punk had spelt the end of teenage. It was for girls as well as boys, whereas most punk before it and Oi! after it was all-lads-together, jolly-boys stuff. It had fashions and identity, and as a bonus it had a strong intrinsic morality.

Arriving without the benefit of industry hype and totally bereft of pretensions, 2-Tone was the last musical genre to come up from the streets of England and capture, albeit temporarily, the commanding heights of the pop charts. It all seemed to happen overnight, although of course it didn't. It was just that most of the build-up was going on off camera.

The main motivator behind this multitalented monochrome muster-roll was Dammers, a shy, tongue-tied vicar's son. Despite the outward appearance of a simpleton, accentuated by his reticence, his multiple eccentricities, such as kipping under dressing room tables, and his lamentable lack of front teeth (the result of careless cycling and 'mates' brushing his incisors with pint glasses), Jerry Dammers was actually a character as complicated as he was talented.

Born in India, the son of an Anglican dean, Dammers grew up in the Midlands, where his teenage years were turbulent. He rebelled repeatedly against his parents' expectations and their restrictive respectability. At 13 he was a mod. At 15 he'd run away to join a hippy commune. At 16 he was a skinhead. And at 17 he was drinking and vandalising heavily, smashing phone boxes, booting in shop windows and tearing the aerials off cars: dumb, bog-standard, bored-teen excesses. Jerry's antisocial activities came to an abrupt halt only after he'd been dragged before a beak and fined 250 notes for kicking in the roof of a family's motor. Scared of 'prison next time', he calmed down and directed his energies into music.

The sight of the Who demolishing 'My Generation' on TV's *Ready Steady Go* had inspired him first, and by the end of the sixties the skinhead moonstomp had captured his imagination.

Even as young as 15, Dammers had dreamt of creating a new musical dimension by merging elements of rock and reggae. But it wasn't until after punk that he had the chance of taking his musical mixed marriage on stage. The intervening years were a time of experimentation and frustration.

After he left school with one A-level – in art – his mum talked him into attending art school. He did a pre-diploma year at Nottingham before a three-year fine-arts course at what was then Lancaster Poly, where he first met Specials bassist-to-be Horace Panter (a.k.a. Sir Horace Gentleman).

Dammers's first band was Peggy Penguin & the Southside Greeks, who played chart reggae and rock'n'roll numbers but resisted his temptation to try to mix the two. Throughout his college years he was stuck in working men's-club and pub bands, playing anything from country to funk as long as it was a cover version – punters and proprietors would accept nothing less until the trail-blazing tirades of the Sex Pistols exploded away cobwebbed attitudes and kicked open the doors for bands to play their own music. Until that time, the fledgling 2-Tone sound existed only on demo tapes that Dammers had knocked out in his Coventry garret with like-minded pioneer Neol Davies, who was to go on to become the songwriting mainstay of the Selecter. On the basis of these early songs Dammers was to recruit a band called the Coventry Automatics post-Pistols in 1977. The first line-up featured Dammers on keyboards, Panter (ex of soul band the Breakers) on loping bass, West Indian Lynval Golding on guitar, a sticksman called Silverton and a Lou Reed lookalike warbler, Tim, who was soon elbowed in favour of Terry Hall, late of local punk combo Squad and at the time a clerk at a local stamp-and-coin dealer's. After recruiting Roddy Radiation on second guitar from the Wild Boys, and making a second singer/percussionist of former roadie Neville Staple – the only band member anything like an original JA Rude Boy, having done a year's borstal in his teens for causing an affray – Dammers now had the line-up of the band he was to rechristen the Specials at the start of 1978.

Coming to the Smoke to try, cheekily, to recruit ex-Pistol John Lydon too, Jerry chanced upon would-be wide boy and Clash manager Bernie Rhodes, who was intrigued enough to offer them the opening dates of that summer's Clash tour. Which is how came to chance upon their first ever gig as the Specials that June at Aylesbury Friars – and I recall being impressed if not entirely seduced by their raw synthesis of ska and spiky energy. Strummer and Rhodes were, too, Joe offering them the rest of the tour, Bernie offering his services as a manager, which they accepted (although they were smart enough never to actually sign his contract). The result was a five-month disappearing act. Rhodes reckoned the band weren't ready to record or gig, and locked them away for almost half a year. He stuck them in the Clash's rehearsal studios in Chalk Farm, where they worked out four times a week in accordance with his masterplan: to wait until punk was waning and 'people were looking for something new'.

This incarceration spelt mounting frustration for the band, who reacted by tearing the phones out and generally smashing the place up. Silverton actually quit and had to be replaced by John 'Brad' Bradbury (who was instantly rechristened Prince Rimshot). After a disastrous Paris gig, the Specials sussed out that Rhodes wasn't as smart as he thought he was and got shot of him. They scraped enough dough together to record a single on their own label under the nom-de-studio of the Special AKA. That single was 'Gangsters', Prince Buster's 'Al Capone' taken and shaken and given a rock backbone along with lyrics rewritten to lambaste the departed Rhodes. Jerry thought of the 2-Tone label name and Horace dreamt up the smartly suited rude-boy logo man, known to his fans as Walt or Walter Jabsco. Jerry had spent his time at college productively sketching cartoons, so designing Walt was no problem. The only hitch was they didn't have the cash to record a B-side, so they stuck on a two-year-old tape by Neol Davies called 'The Selecter' – it was a neat instrumental recorded in a garage.

And that in turn gave Dammers the idea of making 2-Tone into a label in the mould of Motown and Stax with other acts, a sound and an identity.

In March 1979, Rough Trade agreed to distribute the single and persuaded the band to press up 5,000 copies. Out of his depth, Dammers approached Rick Rogers of Trigger Publicity to help drum up some press reaction. Rogers saw them play in Coventry, was bowled over, and took over the management reins, sensibly plunging the band immediately onto the London gigging circuit. By May, their buzz was packing out the Fulham Greyhound with A&R types. Even lovable rock relic Mick Jagger turned up to take notes. Record companies were flashing chequebooks from all directions – and who could blame them? Live, the Specials were animation itself, mixing energetic originals (replete with decidedly post-punk bleak/bitter social-comment lyrics) with such essential evergreens as 'Skinhead Moonstomp', 'Long Shot Kick De Bucket' and 'Guns of Navarone'. Hall adopted a glowering Son of Rotten persona live, his burning owlish eyes perfectly complementing Dammers's alternately amusing and acid lyrics.

Sometimes he'd dance on the spot, but mostly he was static, looking like the eye of a hurricane with his comrades a whirling powerhouse behind him. Chief rivals for the eyeballs were the man himself, organ-grinder Dammers, who was transformed into General Donkey, a merrily manic Mr Hyde figure onstage, and the ultra-athletic Staple, who would hurtle round the stage like an Olympic gymnast, leaping off speakers, cartwheeling and dancing like a man possessed. He'd sport a sharp 2-Tone whistle or dress up to the nines as Judge Roughneck for 'Too Much Too Young', and half the time he'd end up stripped down to his Y-fronts – it just got *too hot*. Later, veteran Jamaican trombonist Rico Rodriguez became another vital part of the act.

In the end, the Specials signed their label deal with Chrysalis, who were willing to chance their arm and let 2-Tone sign bands and release their singles – CBS for one had found that idea preposterous. 'Gangsters' was reissued and surprised everyone, not least Messrs Dammers and Rhodes, by soaring up to Number 6 that September, a success 2-Tone were to replicate with their first 10 releases, which all dented the Top Twenty, most making single figures.

First recruits for one-off-single honours were Camden's Madness. London skinheads had tipped the Specials off about the fledging Nutty Boys combo when they'd first played the capital. It made sense. Madness were working along similar lines to their own. Originally known as the North London Invaders, the band began gigging in a recognisable form in 1978, although their musical roots stretched back two years prior to that. In April 1979 they changed their name to Madness, the title of one of the tastier tunes from the pen of Prince Buster, who'd become the bluebeat figurehead for English mods and whose reputation carried him on to pride of place in the record collections of all discerning skins. It was doubly appropriate since, like the Specials, Madness took their original inspiration from pre-natty reggae, and because dancer and chanter Carl 'Chas Smash' Smyth and singer Graham 'Suggs' McPherson had kept the skinhead faith for years.

Equally influential were the ripe cockney vignettes of Ian Dury's Kilburn & the High Road, all the band being fans and Lee Thompson in particular becoming great mates with the Grand Old Raspberry. Fusing their influences with their own anarchic teenage humour, mainman Mike 'Monsieur Barso' Barson's fairground organ sound, and Lee's farting sax as fat and greasy as a motorway caff waitress, Madness cooked up their own highly distinctive musical muesli, which they defined as 'the Nutty Sound' and likened it to the carefree cacophony of circus organs and summer-holiday fairs. This they complemented with Smash's nutty dance routines (perfected pissing about to 'Liquidator' in youth clubs) and equally demented yells of '*Hey, you!* Don't watch that, watch *this*. This is the heavy, heavy monster sound, one step beyond …'

Madness immediately attracted a skinhead audience, and encountered some heavy, heavy times to match. Suggsy had been an early second-generation skin (see Chapter 3, 'In the Beginning: Skinheads'). He'd also been a roadie for Skrewdriver back when they had no discernible political agenda. But his lasting friendship with Ian Stuart was to come back and bite him. In 1986, after Suggs had got involved with the Labour-supporting Red Wedge, The *Sun* published a picture of the two of them under the front-page headline SUGGSY'S NAZI PAL. Suggsy was devastated.

Both he and Smyth had knocked about with Right-wing gangs when they were too young to know any better, but from their late teens they were both genuinely pro-Labour.

After Madness started to break big, Suggsy also tried to play down his past as a juvenile Chelsea Football Club bootboy, claiming that 'when Sham came along I grew me hair', although *Sounds* uncovered pictures of him up to his shaven head in among a Sham stage invasion.

The band first encountered problems as the North London

Invaders when they played the Acklam Hall in west London, and, as many later bands would do, made the mistake of taking their mates. The Ladbroke Grove Skins reacted badly to the sudden appearance of a bunch of north London skins on their patch, and turned up to the gig 40-handed.

Suggsy recalls, 'Someone burst into our dressing room with an iron bar.'

Chas Smash, who was a fan, not a band member, at the time, adds, 'I was on speed and we had a fight in the toilets.'

Chris Foreman: 'We were pushing our vans to get them started and get away and one of the vans backfired. They thought we had a gun. Someone shouted "Oi! They've got a shooter!" Funny now, but at the time ...'

Chas: 'The band drove off and the police escorted the rest of us through the LGSs, who wanted to do us.'

Suggsy: 'Going to someone else's area with a load of your mates was taken as a threat. People would prepare for you to come and give you a welcoming committee.'

Trouble dogged the early Madness gigs, too. Suggsy describes them as 'rough times, we had to break up fights in the audience and jump offstage. There were stage invasions, stages collapsing, local rivalries – you had the Bridlington mods versus the Bridlington skins. Every fucking gig was just chaos.'

Apart from Hatfield, the worst night came when Madness played the Electric Ballroom with local R&B band Red Beans & Rice supporting. Red Beans had two black members, and when they went on stage a racist element in the crowd started to *sieg-heil* them. Suggsy and Chas Smash, who had been watching from the wings, jumped into the sea of skinheads and confronted them. Suggs reportedly put a couple of them in hospital with a microphone stand.

The first Madness single – their only 2-Tone release – was 'The Prince', a tribute to Buster, which reached a humble Number 16 in October 1979, securing the band a deal with Stiff. Thereafter, it was

Top Ten all the way and gig trouble became a thing of the past, although there were a few unpleasant reminders.

Suggsy recalls, 'We played Hammersmith Odeon once and it got a bit heavy. All the windows were going in and all these faces were coming in. The ugliest faces you've ever seen shouting, "Come on, you're our fucking band, let us in you cunts!" Talk about Frankenstein's monster gone wrong ...'

Next up for 2-Tone honours were the Selecter. Like the Specials, they hailed from Coventry, proving the city had more to offer than Chrysler and memories of Lady Godiva's mammaries. The original Selecter recording, on the B-side of the Specials' debut single, had all been the work of guitarist Neol Davies. By 1979 they'd become a fully fledged gigging entity. Neol recruited the all-black reggae outfit Hard Top 22 and wooed 'em away from the rootsy Rasta sound that was their forte. More ska-orientated and less rock-orientated than the Specials, the Selecter really came into their own live, where the band worked themselves into a frenzy, strongly resembling a hornets' nest 10 seconds after it'd been struck with a house brick, while pumping out their big, bouncy, overpowering rhythms.

The main visual draw was singer Pauline Black, who played the vivacious rude girl, bobbing and bopping all over the stage, never leaving the audience a minute to themselves. But the highlight of their early sets was a mock dust-up during 'Too Much Pressure' between her co-vocalist Gapper Hendrickson, the Marley lookalike bassist Charley Anderson, and hyper-active pianist Desmond Brown. Meantime, Neol (described by Pauline as 'Fonzi without the muscles') was content to impersonate a paralysed version of Walt Jabsco. 'On My Radio', a dynamic take of fickle passion and fossilised programming, was their first hit and 2-Tone's third.

Once the 2-Tone bandwagon was on the roll, the cynics were ready to gun down late additions as cash-in conmen, although it's amazing how many top quality bands were washed into the charts on the 2-Tone tidal wave.

Fourth recruits to the label were the Beat from Brum, who were immediately written off by some critics (Pete Silverton in *Sounds* called them 'fumbling' and 'nonsensical'), but in reality their sound was as different from the 'Big Three Bands' as they had been from each other. For starters, the Beat heat wasn't ska-based at all: it was more like a collision between the Ruts and Big Youth, more strictly roots than mohair suits. 'Black Punk' toaster Ranking Roger popularised Dillinger's style over supple punky reggae rhythms that spelled radical pop, sparkling teeth and hit tune after hit tune, starting with their one 2-Tone venture, the trampling of Smokey Robinson's poignant 'Tears of a Clown' (released November 1979, Top Ten January 1980).

The Beat's Brum chums UB40 were frequently mentioned in the same breath as 2-Tone early on, too, although in reality their laid-back and laconic brand of reggae was closer in spirit to contemporary black British outfits like Capital Letters than our feisty ska stars. Ironically, it was only after they'd established their own brand of mellow rhythms and whining vocals as a hit sound that the band raided their teenage memories to record an album of skinhead-style reggae called *Labour of Love*, which spawned three Top Ten hits in 1983.

North London band Bad Manners should have been the next 2-Tone signing – Dammers seeing and rating them at the same time as he first caught the Madness bug. But the band declined his offer of 2-Tone studio space for fear of attracting cheap cash-in jibes. In truth, the biggest attempted cash-in came from south-coast mod band the Lambrettas, who had a minor hit in March 1980 with a crass ska'ed-up version of the old Leiber–Stoller standard 'Poison Ivy'. Elton John's Rocket Records released the single originally on a 2-Tone parody label called 2-Stroke, with exactly the same design as a 2-Tone single but with 'Stroke' instead of 'Tone' and a parka-wearing mod instead of Walt Jabsco. 2-Tone didn't want to get heavy but they were considerably pissed off. They allowed Rocket to get away with the first 20,000 singles on the understanding that if they tried to press up any more than that in the same parody format they'd slap an injunction on 'em for 'passing off' quicker than you could say, 'Al Capone's guns don't argue'.

Seminal rude reggae rapscallion Judge Dread, a.k.a. ex-wrestler Alex Hughes, had also attempted to come back on the 2-Tone tide, releasing a single called 'Lover's Rock' in a 2-Tone black-and-white check cover the previous December, although he was forgiven because of his perverted place of honour in the skinhead reggae legacy and his inspirational influence on the aforementioned Bad Manners, who turned out to be the brightest of the whole bold new bunch and certainly the best laugh live.

Formed by the ginormous Doug Trendle from handpicked nutters among his north London schoolmates, the Manners originally congregated under the sticky-fingered moniker of Stoop Solo & the Sheet Starchers. (What? Not Onan and the Barbarians?) Doug's crooning career had begun years before that on Arsenal's north bank, where his penchant for football chants saw him nicked outrageously for alleged 'obscene singing' – the judge asked for a recital and even he had to grin when 'Who the fuck is Stanley Bowles?' wafted back across the courtroom. Eventually eight-handed, the Manners decided on their finest and most evocative handle at the start of 1978 and plugged away on the north London pub/khazi circuit, all the while evolving their own unique blend of ska and R&B – they called it Ska&B – coupled with a colossal carnival brass sound. Doug's comically crazed cavortings demanded a more fitting moniker, and so he became Buster Bloodvessel. Live, only the rabid rabbiting of rent-a-loon harpman Winston Bazoomies threatened to upstage him.

Bad Manners covered choice 1969 era reggae classics like El Pussycat, Double Barrell, Elizabethan Reggae and, of course, Fatty Fatty, along with a beefy, ska'd-for-life reworking of the *Magnificent Seven* theme. Their original songs scaled Olympian heights of partying pop, too, especially the intoxicating 'Special Brew' and the octosyllabic onslaught of 'Ne-Ne Na-Na Na-Na Nu-Nu' – their mighty Mork from Ork mutation debut single released by Magnet records in March 1980.

The last and least successful of the original 2-Tone wave was all-bird band the Bodysnatchers, whose chief attribute was their cocky cockney vocalist Rhoda Dakar, a Brixton-born-and-bred mixed-race beauty who could cut down hecklers like Bernard Manning in a bad mood and who later joined the Specials. The Bodysnatchers' best-known number was Rhoda's 'The Boiler' – a harrowing tale of a rape attack that stood out among the shambolic good cheer of their live set like a VAT man at a firm's office party.

The song ended up becoming the first single by the Specials not to make the Top Thirty when they released it after Rhoda joined the band in 1981. The radio just refused to airplay it. As a rule, the Bodysnatchers' own songs were more in the mood of original sixties reggae rather than the beefier vein of the Specials and the Selecter's ska sounds. Their other standout original song was the assertive 'Ruder Than You'. Live, though, the highlights of their set were all covers – '007', 'Monkey Spanner', 'Double Barrel' and 'Let's Do Rock Steady', which was released by 2-Tone as their first single in spring 1980, peaking at Number 22.

The abundance of cover versions in the 2-Tone bands' repertoire, coupled to the Specials' habit of peppering their own tunes with 'musical quotations', provoked a heated critical backlash from roots reggae authority Eric Fuller (in *Sounds*), who argued that the 2-Tone bands were building careers on Jamaican songs that would bring precious little financial reward to 'the obscure coloureds who did it all better first'. Prince Buster's 'One Step Beyond', for example, provided Madness with their first Top Ten hit, but Buster's cut from the song's publishers Melodisc was in danger of not getting through because the Brit bizman behind Melodisc had already retired! Similar problems seemed to dog the chances of Dandy Livingstone seeing many ackers from his 'Rudy a Message To You' – the Specials' second hit. In truth, however, this wasn't the fault of the 2-Tone bands, but 99.9 per cent to do with the shambolic nature of the Jamaican music biz, itself so rife with rip-offs and double dealings that *five separate publishing companies* tried to claim the royalties for that latter hit. So eager was the purist Fuller to use the situation to score propaganda points against the 2-Tone bands that he went on to accuse Dammers of simply speeding up Lloyd Charmer's song 'Birth Control', and 'marginally altering a few words' to produce the Specials' chart-topping smash 'Too Much Too Young'. In fact that song had been in the Specials' set as an original before Neville Staples suggested adding 'musical quotes' from 'Birth Control' (itself virtually a wordless dub track, disproving Eric's amusing but overhasty sniping).

Of course he was dead right to be suspicious. Black musicians had been had over by white business sharks since the 1920s. But nothing could have been further from Jerry Dammers's fertile mind. 'What amazed me,' Lynval Golding told me later, 'was that Jerry had to be one of the fairest blokes on earth. He's got no interest in money, none at all. When we put in the musical quotations from the ska originals he tried to make sure the money got through to the right person, 'cos in Jamaica everyone ripped off everyone, but Jerry would keep on trying to find the real writer. As long as he's got his music, food and a place to live, Jerry's happy. He could have paid Rico a session fee, but Jerry made sure he got the same as all of us. Rico will tell you about Prince Buster and the way he used to rip off all his musicians. The reason Rico stuck with us for so long was that we treated him fairly.'

Money and privilege were prime targets for Jerry's poison arrows. As his lyrics on 'Too Much Too Young' made clear, he didn't crave wealth or fame. His was a rather puritanical, lower-middle-class strand of socialism. Most of the 2-Tone bands, despite an early emphasis on fun, not protest, had Left-wing leanings. Their antiracism was inherent in the whole 2-Tone ideal of course. They didn't need to wear badges: their whole way of life was against racism and the creeping poison of racial hatred. Neol Davies made the point that class was the real divide, anyway.

On balance, 2-Tone was far more working class than punk had been. The musicians were largely working and lower-middle class.

Only a handful (Dammers, Panter, Pauline Black) had been students. Their following was even more down to earth – prole and lumpen-prole by a huge majority. Rude boys and rude girls were directly inspired into being by the bands they followed. In London, the rudies were drawn originally from the ranks of the capital's mod and skinhead scenes. There was a distinct rude look, identical for both sexes. Levi's Sta-Prest strides, or 2-Tone mohair ones. Braces, button-down shirts, loafers, white or red socks. Harrington jackets, pork-pie hats or trilbies.

Boys' hair was shorter, cropped of course, but closer to the mod's French crew cut than the skin's number one. But, as the music became more mainstream and the fans got younger, so the look became more sexually distinct – boys going for black two-piece suits, girls opting for dresses with black and white geometric patterns, black shoes, white tights and large earrings. The rude teen look went deeper and lasted longer in the Midlands than it did in London, where it swiftly submerged into skinhead, with 2-Tone having the effect of reviving the skin style that had started to decline after Sham. 2-Tone and rude style also had the distinction of being the first youth cult to attract significant numbers of black and mixed-race youth since skinhead a decade before, and many more of them, too. The reason it burnt out so quickly is that it was a relatively passive cult depending on the established bands for its momentum. Unlike punks and mods, the rudies weren't noticeably prone to form their own bands or write fanzines – they weren't doers. They lasted while 2-Tone lasted as a movement, which wasn't long. It went up like a rocket and then fragmented into a hundred pieces.

'2-Tone fell apart because Jerry really controlled it all,' Suggsy told me in 1984. 'It was one person's ideas controlling 32 people and when you think about it why should all those bands have carried on succumbing to his dream? I think the whole idea of 2-Tone was much stronger than the actual music. It became a musical fad, which is why I think it got eaten up and burnt out so fast. The ideas meant much more ...' While it was united, 2-Tone spelled marvellous times live, and undoubtedly the best came with the Taking It to the People 2-Tone tour in November 1979, which saw the near-perfect package of the Specials, Madness and the Selecter selling out Top Ranks, Tiffany's and polys with the same ease as their skanking singles were sailing up the charts. Mostly it was laugh-a-second stuff. I caught the show at Tiffany's in Edinburgh and can still grin at the memory of all three bands finishing the night off with a mass recital of the ol' skinhead moonstomp (Madness guitarist Chrissy Boy tried to entice yours truly up for vocals but, mercifully for the audience, I declined). Off stage, it was a giggle too, with Madness roadies Chalky and Tots perfecting quite a double act, including the old 'you push 'im, I'll kneel behind 'im' routine.

The only sour note of the tour came at the Hatfield Poly show. Had there been any justification for the Hatfield ANL's vicious attack on the audience? In truth, there was a BM element in the early Madness crowd, left over from Sham, and, though it never died away, it was swamped when, by as early as the following February, Madness's own headlining tour attracted so many young kids that *Sounds* was talking about them as 'the new Bay City Rollers'.

Older Right-wing-inclined skins, aided and abetted by the sickly sensationalist media, did make their mark on the younger kids in areas where they were strong, however. I remember my 13-year-old sister-in-law coming back from her Eltham youth club in the summer of 1980 saying, 'Skinheads are back – *sieg heil*!'

She had no idea what it meant. Nor did the kids who'd *sieg-heil* a band like the Selecter to show their enjoyment!

Pauline Black could never get her head round it. 'Why racists would listen to ska or reggae is a mystery in itself,' she said. 'And it's all the more bizarre that they should attend a Selecter gig where, of the seven band members, only Neol Davis was white.'

But the point was that, by playing to them, Selecter and the other bands helped to change opinions and stem a rising tide of racism.

2-Tone didn't spawn a Hitler Youth following. On the contrary, it boosted the ranks of anti-racists and non-racist skinheads, reaching out to black, mixed-race and Asian kids the way no UK youth cult had done before.

The extreme Right were deeply worried about 2-Tone's influence. The attempted stabbing of Buster Bloodvessel at the Ballroom did much to strengthen a growing groundswell of cynicism among the more sussed skins and terrace regulars who already referred to the BM as 'the German Movement'. The jailing of the notorious BM thug Matty Morgan in spring 1980 for assaulting the police (one officer was black, natch) did little to boost BM morale.

In February 1980 the second 2-Tone tour repeated the sell-out success of the first, this one featuring the Selecter as the headline act, the Bodysnatchers as the show openers, and, as main support, the promising pop act Holly & the Italians – a last-minute replacement for the Beat. Trouble was, the exciting Eyeties weren't ska and the whole tour was disgraced by audience birdbrains abusing them for that heinous nonconformity. Fighting frequently broke out during their set, so the Italians retreated, to be replaced by the Swinging Cats who later signed with 2-Tone.

Jerry Dammers found this narrow-mindedness abhorrent. He had no intention of sitting pretty in a musical cul-de-sac. Instead he guided the Specials along more experimental tracks, perfecting a mix of styles, including Muzak, trad MOR and even Latin American rhythms to produce the 'lounge music' of the Specials' second LP *More Specials*, which spawned the haunting hit singles 'Stereotype' and the addictive 'Do Nothing'. Internal dissent about direction coupled to the strain of making the 2-Tone movie *Dance Crazy* led to the Specials line-up splitting in 1981, but not until after the atmospheric chart-topping 'Ghost Town' had provided the perfect soundtrack for that summer's riots.

Out of the split, Hall, Staples and Golding emerged as the Fun Boy Three, scoring a string of deadpan hits and launching Bananarama on the road to stardom in their own right, before splitting themselves in 1983, leaving Hall to form the underachieving Colourfield.

For his part, Dammers recruited a new line-up, including vocalist Rhoda Dakar and, much later, temperamental new boy Stan Campbell, called the band the Special AKA again and spent over two years and half a million pounds making a follow-up LP. Called *In the Studio*, this passionate pop cocktail, drawing on a mixture of reggae, funk, jazz, afro, gospel and Latin rhythms, suffused with haunting melodies, was a vibrant testimony to Dammers's abilities, even though it was top-heavy with already released singles such as the ethereal, anti-Zionist song 'War Crimes' and the well-meaning but wrong-headed 'Racist Friend'. Best moment on it, and indeed the single of 1983, was the clenched-fist protest of 'Nelson Mandela' – Jerry's last-ever Top Ten hit.

Commercially, Madness fared much better, releasing the healthiest, and most diverse string of hit singles since the Beatles. They even broke into the US market, scoring a Top Ten hit in 1983 with 'Our House', something the Specials and the Selecter had both failed to do, despite their club success in the USA's 'armpit' cities of LA and New York – although the watered-down white reggae of the Police went platinum there. The only threat to their robust run came at Christmas 1983, when Mike Barson, the uncrowned band leader and keyboardist co-writer of all their best tunes, quit. Madness quit Stiff the following summer and had hits for a few more years on their own Zarjazz label. Suggsy also lent his production talents to Liverpool terrace popsters the Farm (see Chapter 13, 'Style Wars on the Terraces').

Poor old Selecter never seemed able to harness their live energy into a lasting studio career. Their first three singles, 'On My Radio', 'Missing Words' and 'Three Minute Hero', were fair to sensational, but thereafter their releases seemed to lack the sparkle that had made their live shows so special. They just sounded too earnest. Increasingly pissed off, the band split from 2-Tone and decided to change direction. The likable Desmond Brown quit while he was ahead, while Charley Anderson was mysteriously sacked (going on to form not very special band the People). They were replaced by a couple of white guys from the Pharaohs. The new band slowed down the former frantic Selecter pace, softened up, aimed to be more soulful – and still flopped. They split altogether in 1981, with Pauline Black attempting a solo recording career before coming into her own on the TV, where she graduated from presenting kids' show *Hold Tight* to serious/dull Channel 4 chat show *Black on Black*. She later became an actress.

Meanwhile, the mighty meaty Bad Manners had a string of sporadic hits on Magnet until 1983. Finally realising that the label was holding them back, they quit in 1984 but never bounced back into the charts.

For their part, the Bodysnatchers never really cut it on vinyl, evolving into the Belle Stars in 1981, who went Top Three two years later with 'Sign of the Times' and then faded away; while the Beat notched up a string of seven hits before Ranking Roger and Dave Wakeling quit in 1983 to form General Public, who never got higher than Number 60 in the charts.

Back in 1980, Dammers steered the 2-Tone label away from straight ska and consequently away from hits. The biggest tragedy was the failure of Rico's 'Sea Cruise' to chart – his *Jungle Music* LP was rightly heralded as a possible new direction for reggae but sagged disappointingly on the sales front as well. Flops from the Swinging Cats, the Apollinaires and the Higsons were both more predictable and more deserved. However laudable Jerry Dammers's attempts to widen the range and appeal of the 2-Tone label, it clearly wasn't what the people wanted. As the bands went their separate ways and no new 2-Tone talent came to fill the clubs and pubs they'd left behind, so the magic and the sense of unity fell away and with them the rude-boy cult. At street-level the skins found solace in the new Oi! movement, while the best 2-Tone bands deservedly went on to become part of the pop establishment. For myself, however, the image stamped on my brain from this era isn't one of any of the bands on *Top of the Pops*, but rather one from after the Selecter had finished their 'James Bond' encore at their Birmingham Top Rank gig. As the band trotted off stage, there was a stage invasion and a white rudy grabbed the mike and started chanting 'Rude boys'. Spontaneously, he reached out to a black rudy. They put their arms round each other and gave the crowd thumbs-up signs. That simple image probably says more about the 2-Tone dream than any words ever written.

POSTSCRIPT: I went to the USA with both the Specials and the Selecter at the beginning of the 1980s. Neither I nor the bands had any idea how influential those few club dates would be. Over the following decade, a third wave of ska, fuelled by 2-Tone, exploded in the US with bands such as the Mighty Mighty Bosstones (formed in 1983) and the Toasters (formed 1981) from the East Coast, and the Uptones (formed in 1981) in California at the helm. The Uptones influenced Operation Ivy, who became Rancid, and an entire Orange County ska scene that produced such exciting combos as the Aquabats. The Bosstones helped popularise the new ska-punk sound that merged the two musical forms, playing ska at a punk pace. Ska-core later blended ska with hardcore punk. But bands like the Toasters went for a more 2-Tone influenced trad ska style. Singer Robert 'Bucket' Hingley launched the hugely important Moon Ska Records label, whose latest incarnation, Moon Ska World, continues to release great ska acts such as the Dub City Rockers, the Big and the brilliant but batty Rhoda Dakar.

As I write this in 2009, the Specials are back together (without Jerry) playing to packed houses. And Suggsy's a regular TV presenter. Madness, who split in 1986 and re-formed six years later, have won new critical acclaim for their latest album *The Liberty of Norton Folgate*. Lee Thompson jokes, 'It's harder to get out of this band than the fucking Foreign Legion.'

## CHAPTER EIGHT

# WHITE RIOT?
# THE TRUE STORY OF OI!

'OI! EXPRESSES AN "US-AGAINST-THE-WORLD" ATTITUDE;
IT'S THE CONTINUATION OF THE TRADITION WHICH HAS ITS
ROOTS IN THE TEDDY BOYS OF THE 1950s.'
Simon Frith, sociologist, 1981

'OI! IS WORKING-CLASS AND IF YOU'RE NOT
WORKING-CLASS YOU'LL GET A KICK IN THE BOLLOCKS.'
Jeff 'Stinky' Turner

July 3, 1981. A pub gig in Southall, Greater London, ended in what the *NME* described as a 'race riot'. Cars and police vehicles were overturned and set ablaze, and the pub was gutted by petrol bombs. Forty officers were injured. Why?

It is commonly believed that neo-Nazi skinheads ran amok at the climax of an Oi! concert at the Hamborough Tavern; and that, furthermore, the gig had been put on to deliberately provoke the local Asian community into an uprising. One recent report in the London *Evening Standard* even managed to link the dreadful events of the day with the death of Blair Peach, who had actually been killed in street fighting between the police and anti-Nazi demonstrators in April 1979 – more than two years previously. A TV news report a few weeks after the gig claimed that 'hundreds of skinheads, many of them known National Front supporters' had been 'bussed in from the East End' for 'a full-scale race battle'. None of this was true. Yet that idea is now set like concrete in the public imagination.

In Britain, the image of Oi! music, bands and fans has been shaped by this absurd rewriting of What Actually Happened, even though there was never a significant or even noticeable National Front presence at London Oi! gigs. No Oi! band had ever expressed racist sympathies or recorded racist songs – in fact the opposite was true. And the skinheads, punks and other Oi! fans at Southall that night were witnesses to rather than participants in the trouble.

Nevertheless, back then Oi! managed to outrage all shades of polite middle-class opinion, right, left and centre. To this day the hippy Left perceive Oi! as a kind of cultural cancer. To the Establishment, Oi! was an upstart from a tower-block slum who wouldn't keep in line. He was raucous and obnoxious, a human hand grenade with a menacing disregard for authority. At best, Oi! bands and their fans were viewed as gurning barbarians gleefully pissing in the coffee-house latte. At worst, they were seen as modern-day Brownshirts responsible for the riots in Southall, Toxteth and the rest. Either way, Oi! was too hot to handle.

To the fast-talking wide boys who adopted its name, however, Oi! was something else entirely. Stripped down to basics, it was about being young, working-class and not taking shit from anybody. It was anti-police, anti-authority but pro-Britain, too. A lot of the Oi! kids liked a fight, and, yeah – this is no whitewash – there was a far-Right element among them; but Oi! was born in 1980 when the far Right were polling 15–20 per cent of the vote in inner-city wards. It would have been a miracle if there hadn't been a few NF sympathisers in the audiences. But what matters is: (1) Oi! never suffered from Nazi violence the way Sham 69 and 2-Tone had, and the aggro that blemished those early Oi! gigs was strictly football-related; and (2)

Oi!'s legacy is a worldwide street-punk movement that is vocally pro-working-class and against unemployment, state bureaucracy, racism and repression.

Discovered in the summer of 1981 (well into its second wind) by mass media rocked to their foundations by weeks of riots and youthful insurrection, Oi! found itself on the sharp end of the sort of tabloid crucifixion usually reserved for the more macabre mass murderers. Corrupting its meaning, the same media immediately tried to bury it. Inevitably their version of events was as watertight as a kitchen colander in a tropical monsoon. They said Oi! was for skinheads (but it was always more than that), that all skins were Nazis (only a minority ever were) and that therefore Oi! was the Strasser brothers in steel-capped boots (but the bands were either socialists or cynics).

Oi! became the most exciting, despised and misunderstood youth movement of all time. To really understand it, you had to be there.

Oi!'s roots were in punk, just as punk's roots were in the New York Dolls, but they weren't the same animal. For starters Oi! was the reality of punk and Sham mythology. Punk exploded between 1976 and 1979 because stadium rock had been disappearing up its own jacksie for years. The album charts were full of po-faced synthesiser twiddlers and pretentious singers belting out meaningless pseudo-poetic lyrics.

Punk seemed different. It was raw, brutal and utterly down to earth. Punk sold itself as the voice of the tower blocks. It wasn't. Most of the forerunners were middle-class art students. The great Joe Strummer, whose dad was a diplomat, flirted with stale old Stalinism and sang about white riots while living in a white mansion. Malcolm McLaren and Vivienne Westwood tried to intellectualise punk by dressing it up in half-inched situationist ideas, all the better to flog their overpriced produce to mug punters.

Sham 69, from Surrey, were the first band to capture the growing mood of disillusionment. Street punks were disgusted both by the proliferation of phoneys and posers and the King's Road conmen with their rip-off boutiques. But how much did Sham's Jimmy Pursey really know about borstals, football and dole queues, and how much was he feeding off the people around him? The Last Resort's Millwall Roi may have overstated the case but he summed up a common attitude when he wrote, 'I wish it was the weekend every day/ But Jimmy Pursey didn't get his way/ He liked to drink but he didn't like to fight/ He didn't get his fucking homework right.'

Cockney cowboys? As Julie Burchill observed, 'It must have been a bloody strong wind the day the sound of Bow Bells reached Hersham.'

The Oi! polloi didn't need punk's proletarian wrapping paper – invented backgrounds and adopted attitudes, accents and aggression – because they really were the cul-de-sac, council-estate kids the first punk bands had largely only pretended to be. The forerunners of Oi! were bands like Cock Sparrer, Menace, Slaughter & the Dogs and the UK Subs, although none of these bands were as successful as Sham, whose raucous brand of football chant punk dented the Top Ten three times.

Before he lost it, Jimmy Pursey gave the kiss of life to the two bands who defined the parameters and direction of original Oi!: the Angelic Upstarts and the Cockney Rejects.

Singer Tommy 'Mensi' Mensforth and guitarist Ray Cowie, known as Mond, formed the Upstarts in the summer of '77 after getting blown away by the Clash's White Riot tour. Childhood mates, they had grown up together on the Brockley Whinns council estate in South Shields and later attended Stanhope Road Secondary Modern school (Mensi got expelled from the local grammar school at 13 for delinquency).

Mensi worked as an apprentice miner after leaving school. Forming the band at 19 was his escape route from the pits. Mond worked as a shipyard electrician right up until their first hit. The Upstarts' original drummer and bassist quit after violent crowd reactions to their first gig in nearby Jarrow, to be replaced by bakery worker Stix and bricklayer Steve Forsten respectively. The band were also soon to recruit the services of Keith Bell, a self-confessed former gangster and one-time North Eastern Counties light-middleweight boxing champ, who as manager, bouncer and bodyguard was able to maintain order at early gigs on the basis of his reputation alone.

The Upstarts soon attracted the attention of Northumbria Police, who haunted the band's early career like a malignant poltergeist. Police interest stemmed from the Upstarts' championing of the cause of Birtley amateur boxer Liddle Towers, who died from injuries received after a night in the police cells. The inquest called it 'justifiable homicide'. The Upstarts called it murder, and 'The Murder of Liddle Towers' (b/w 'Police Oppression') was their debut single on their own Dead Records. Later re-pressed by Rough Trade, the song's brutal passion was well received even by music press pseuds, although not by the Old Bill, who infiltrated gigs in plain clothes. Charges of incitement to violence were considered. Only the Upstarts' mounting press coverage dissuaded them. For their part the band were uncompromising. They appeared on the front cover of the Socialist Workers' Party's youth magazine *Rebel* soon after and accused their area police of being largely National Front sympathisers.

Official police action may have been dropped but unofficial harassment continued unabated. Mensi claimed he was constantly followed and frequently stopped, searched and abused by individual officers. The band blamed unofficial police pressure for getting them banned from virtually every gig in the Northeast of England – via the promise of raids, prosecution for petty rule breaking, opposing licence renewals and so on. The Upstarts got the last laugh, though, when in April 1979 they conned a prison chaplain into inviting them to play a gig at Northumbria's Acklington Prison (where, ironically, Keith Bell had finished his last sentence). A hundred and fifty cons turned up to see a Union Flag embellished with the words UPSTARTS ARMY, a clenched-fist, the motto SMASH LAW AND ORDER and a pig in a helmet entitled 'PC Fuck Pig'. The band hadn't managed to smuggle in a 'real' pig's head (they usually smashed one up on stage), but the cons revelled merrily in the wham-bam-wallop of rebel anthems like 'Police Oppression', 'We

Are the People' (about police corruption) and a specially amended version of 'Borstal Breakout' retitled 'Acklington Breakout'.

The *Daily Mirror* splashed with PUNKS ROCK A JAILHOUSE (wrongly identifying me as the band's spokesman). The prison governor and local Tories did their nuts, with the Tynemouth MP, the appropriately named Neville Trotter, condemning the gig as 'an incredibly stupid thing to allow'. Only *Socialist Worker* printed a true record of the gig, quoting Mensi telling prisoners they'd be better off in the nick if Thatcher got elected that summer, and urging punks to vote Labour as 'Thatcher's government will destroy the trade union movement'. (In reality, Mensi's brand of sub-Scargill patriotic socialism was far removed from the SWP's revised Trotsky-lite posturing.)

The band's salty populism and savage post-Sham punk attracted a massive following of working-class kids in the Northeast, the self-styled Upstarts Army, while the power of their debut single persuaded Jimmy Pursey to form his JP label with Polydor. The Upstarts were the label's first signing and also their first sacking after a Polydor security guard took exception to their behaviour (word has it that the incident involved an aborted foetus, but I could never get to the bottom of it). He took on Mensi in a one-against-one fist fight and went down like the *Belgrano*. Polydor dropped the band. They never bothered to ask for Mensi's side of the story. Soon after, the Upstarts signed with Warner Brothers. Their second single, the Pursey-produced 'I'm An Upstart', was released in April 1979, charted, and was chased hard by the 'Teenage Warning' single and album.

The Cockney Rejects were also the real deal, this time the sons of dockers from London's East End, but their music wasn't political. Thirty years of lame Labour local government had stripped them of any worldview except cynicism. Their songs were about East End life, boozers, battles, police harassment and football.

I met them first in May 1979. Two cocky urchins adorned in West Ham badges bowled into my boozer spieling back slang and thrust their tatty demo tapes into my hand. Like them, it was rough, ready and

*Above*: When you're young … Mods and Skins soak up the sun on Southend beach, August Bank Holiday 1979.

*Below left*: These boots are made for … mindless violence. Teenage skinheads find a rocker in April 1980.

*Below right*: Sharp-dressed Teds lurk on a South London street corner – young peacocks forging their own style in the midst of post-War austerity.

*Above*: Local police lecture away-day Charlton Athletic skinhead fans, including Chris Weeks, at Southend Station en route to a match in 1970.

© *Getty Images*

*Below*: 1980: young skins hang out in Goulston Street, East London.

© *Getty Images*

*Above left*: Cocky Angelic Upstarts fans herald the dawn of 'New Punk'.
© *Getty Images*

*Above right*: Nicked! A London cop restrains a teenage punk in Chelsea, 1977.
© *Getty Images*

*Below*: Too much pleasure: The Bodysnatchers join The Selecter on the second 2-Tone tour.
© *Getty Images*

*Inset*: Too Much Pressure – Desmond Brown of The Selecter pounds away on his organ as Pauline Black sings.
© *Getty Images*

*Above*: Sham 69's Jimmy Pursey joins The Clash for a rousing chorus of 'White Riot' at Music Machine in 1978. © *Getty Images*

*Below*: The Sex Pistols, (left to right): Glen Matlock, Johnny Rotten, Steve Jones, Paul Cook. They look such nice boys too. © *Getty Images*

*Inset*: The funeral of Clement Blair Peach, killed in 1979 during violent clashes with the SPG at an Anti-Nazi protest in Southall, Middlesex.

© *Getty Images*

*Above*: The classic boot boy look. Cardiff v Manchester United, 1978.

© *Mirrorpix*

*Below*: Casuals discuss which of them should write the first tell-all book about terrace violence in 1989.

© *Mirrorpix*

*Above*: The Rolling Stones take a break to assess the trouble caused by Hell's Angels in the crowd at their free gig at Altamont, California.

© *Getty Images*

*Below*: The Hell's Angels were the most extreme element of America's outlaw biker tradition. Pictured here are members of the Berdoo and Fresno chapters in California.

© *Getty Images*

*Above*: Black Sabbath, pioneers of blue-collar metal: Geezer Butler, Tony Iommi, Bill Ward and Ozzy Osbourne.                    *© Getty Images*

*Below*: Iron Maiden, the leading lights of the New Wave of British Heavy Metal, with vocalist Paul 'The Beast' Di'Anno before the baldness took its toll.                                                              *© Getty Images*

*Inset*: The classic Motorhead line-up: Phil 'Filthy Animal' Taylor; Fast Eddie Clark and Lemmy (aka Ian Kilmister).            *© Getty Images*

*Above left*: Spandau Ballet, the pin-up boys of the New Romantics. No, don't mock.

© *Getty Images*

*Above right*: Marilyn Manson, 'not a true goth', displays early signs of swine flu.

© *Getty Images*

*Below*: The new face of urban gangs is usually masked.

© *Getty Images*

suffused with more spirit than Mystic Challenge. I put them in touch with Pursey, who produced their first demo tape. These songs re-emerged as the Small Wonder debut EP *Flares & Slippers*, which included the essential guttersnipe anthem 'Police Car' ('I like punk and I like Sham – I got nicked over West Ham …'). It sold surprisingly well and earned them the *NME* epithet of the 'brainstorming vanguard of the East End punk renewal', (although the student-orientated rag was later to virtually ignore Oi! until its arrival in the headlines forced its hand).

The kids were the Geggus brothers, Mickey and Jeff, the latter soon known to the world as Stinky Turner. Both had been good boxers – neither of them had ever been put down in the ring, and Jeff had boxed for the England youth team. They had little trouble transferring their belt onto vinyl. The Rejects' story began in the summer of 1977, when 17-year-old Mickey was first inspired to pick up a plectrum by the Pistols' 'God Save the Queen'. Incubating in back-garden performances in their native Canning Town as the Shitters, the Rejects emerged as a real group only after council painter Mickey recruited 21-year-old Vince Riordan as bassist in 1979. Previously a Sham roadie, Vince (whose uncle was Jack 'The Hat' McVitie) had marked time with loser band the Dead Flowers before he heard the Cockney call. Drummers were to come and go with the regularity of a high-fibre diet until Stix transferred from the Upstarts in 1980.

Live, the band hit like a mob of rampaging rhinos, with Mickey's sledgehammer guitar the cornerstone of their tough, tuneful onslaught. Schoolboy Stinky was a sight for sore eyes, too, screwing up his visage into veritable orgies of ugliness, and straining his tonsils to holler vocals best likened to a right evil racket. I was the Rejects' first manager – although those stories are best left for another book – and I stayed with them until Pursey and I had negotiated an EMI deal for them. After that, I bowed out to let a man I assumed was a pro take over. He was Pursey's manager, Tony Gordon, who went on to handle Boy George (in the management sense). So little was money my motivation that my price for signing the band over was a £100 meal at the Park Lane Hilton – not a patch on Manze's (I went with Hoxton Tom and our wives; Tony begged us to get him a receipt). In retrospect, Gordon was bad for the band. They really needed a Peter Grant figure, someone tougher and smarter than they were, to keep their energies channelled in a more, um, artistic direction.

Under Tony Gordon, the Rejects' career soared briefly then crashed and burned. After getting evicted from Polydor's studios for running up a damages bill of £1,000, the band got stuck into serious recordings with Pursey at the production controls. Their second EMI single, 'Bad Man', was superb, like PiL on steroids, but it made only the fag end of the charts. Their next release, a piss-take of Sham called 'The Greatest Cockney Rip-Off', did better, denting the Top Thirty. Their debut album, *Greatest Hits Vol. 1*, did the same, notching up more than 60,000 sales. It has gone on to sell more than 600,000 copies worldwide.

Unlike the Upstarts', the Rejects' first following wasn't largely skinhead; in fact at first skins didn't like them. Stinky's school pals the Rubber Glove firm aside, the Rejects crew came from football and consisted largely of West Ham chaps attracted by Vince's involvement and disillusioned Sham and Menace fans. Infamous faces included Gary Dickle, Johnny Butler, Carlton Leach – whose story inspired the movie *Rise of the Footsoldier*, Andy 'Skully' Russell, Andy Swallow, Hoxton Tom, Binnsy, H, Cass Pennant and Kevin Wells. Even as early as November 1979, their Hammers support was so strong that mass terrace chants of 'Cockney Rejects – oh, oh' were clearly audible on televised soccer matches – to the tune of Gary Glitter's 'Hello Hello I'm Back Again'.

Many of the East End Glory Boys swelled their ranks a little later, realising for the first time that here was a band exactly the same as they were.

The first standalone Oi! scene developed around the Cockney Rejects and their regular gig venue, the Bridgehouse in Canning Town, east London. It became the focus for an entire subculture. In 1980, this was the Life! None of these faces were 'Nazis'. Most of them weren't political at all, beyond the sense of voting Labour (if they bothered to vote at all) out of a sense of tradition. A tiny percentage were interested in the extremes of either Right or Left. As a breed they were natural conservatives. They believed in standing on their own two feet. They were patriotic, and proud of their class and their immediate culture. They looked good and dressed sharp. It was important not to look like a scruff or a student. Their heroes were boxers and footballers, not union leaders. Unlicensed boxing was a big draw, as were the dogs and stag comedians like Jimmy Jones and Jimmy Fagg. They liked to fight around football matches – the West Ham ICF (Inter City Firm) were fully represented at most local Rejects gigs. The young men oozed machismo, and some of the women were just as tough. But they weren't mugs. These were bright kids and a surprisingly large number of them have gone on to carve out successful businesses in fields as diverse as the music industry, pornography and clothing manufacture.

They're the ones who didn't end up dead or in jail, of course.

They related to the Cockney Rejects because at the time at least the Rejects mirrored their audience. Rarely in rock's history have a band and their followers been so identical.

The Rejects and the Upstarts had plenty in common – shared management, shared experiences of the Old Bill, shared class backgrounds – and were soon identified (by me) in the music press as the start of something different, a new, more class-conscious punk variant, which was known at first as 'Real Punk' or 'New Punk' and which had little in common with 1979's self-styled punk rockers in their second-hand images and wally bondage pants. It was a pairing they obviously approved of with both bands frequently jamming together at each other's gigs. Unlike Sham, the Rejects had little Nazi trouble. They wrote off the threat from the British Movement (we called them the German Movement) in their first *Sounds* interview. 'We can handle them,' said Stinky. 'If anyone comes to the gigs and wants to have a row, we'll have to row. Pursey couldn't do that. We're not gonna take no bollocks.'

Strong words that they had to back up the first time they played outside of the East End, supporting the Upstarts at the Electric Ballroom in Camden. When a large mob of BM skins started harassing punks in the audience, the Rejects and their 12-handed entourage (including two of the fledgling 4-Skins) took 'em on and battered them. Mickey Geggus commented, 'Our gigs are for enjoyment. No one's gonna disrupt them or pick on our fans. Troublemakers will be thrown out – by us if necessary.'

They had a second major run-in with the far Right at Barking station the following February, and once again the master race contingent got battered. Most of the Rejects' London gigs were trouble-free, especially the ones at the Bridge House, which was to London Oi! what the Roxy had been to punk. Managed by Terry Murphy and his tough boxer sons, the Bridge never saw a serious punch-up or any *sieg-heiling*. No one dared step out of line against the Murphys. Son Glen, the former barman, went on to play George Green on TV's *London's Burning*.

The Angelic Upstarts also fought – and won – a couple of sharp battles against the far Right. They played numerous Rock Against Racism gigs, too, including one at Leeds, where the band sported SWP 'Disband the SPG' badges. Like that of the Rejects, their real ag came from other areas – principally their manager, Keith Bell. Sacked by the band when he started to knock them about, Bell and his henchmen set about trying to intimidate Upstart fans, even assaulting people buying their records, before threatening Mensi's mother, smashing her house windows and making threatening and abusive phone calls to her. Reprisal incidents included Mensi and one time Upstarts drummer Decca Wade smashing one of the Bell firm's car windows and a midnight visit to Bell's own home by Decca's dad, club comedian Derek Wade and Mensi's brother-in-law Billy Wardropper, who blasted one of Bell's henchmen in the leg with a sawn-off shotgun.

Hitting back, Bell threatened to kill Wade Sr. Three of his cronies set fire to a stable belonging to Mensi's sister, causing almost £5,000 worth of damage. In ensuing court cases both Bell and Billy

Wardropper were jailed while Decca's dad copped a year's suspended sentence. Presiding Judge Hall told the Upstarts team, 'I accept that all of you suffered a severe amount of provocation, which was none of your seeking. But at the same time I have a duty to condemn the use of firearms, particularly a sawn-off shotgun.' The Upstarts recorded their opinion in 'Shotgun Solution': 'Shotgun blasts ring in my ears/ Shoot some scum who live by fear/ A lot of good men will do some time/ For a fucking cunt without a spine.'

With the Rejects, football was the trouble. And it was understandable because they'd been fanatically pro-West Ham aggro from the word go. Even at their debut Bridge House gig they decked the stage out with a huge red banner displaying the Union Flag, the West Ham crossed hammers and the motif 'WEST SIDE' (which was that part of the West Ham ground then most favoured by the Irons' most violent fans). Their second hit was a version of the West Ham anthem 'Bubbles', which charted in the run-up to West Ham's Cup final victory in the early summer of 1980. On the B-side was the ICF-pleasing 'West Side Boys', which included inflammatory lines like, 'We meet in the Boleyn every Saturday/ Talk about the teams that we're gonna do today/ Steel-capped Doctor Martens and iron bars/ Smash the coaches and do 'em in the cars.'

It was a red rag to testosterone-charged bulls all over the country. At north London's Electric Ballroom, 200 of West Ham's finest mob-charged fewer than 50 Arsenal and smacked them clean out of the venue. But ultra-violence at a Birmingham gig really spelt their undoing. The audience at the Cedar Club were swelled by a mob of Birmingham City skinheads, who terrace-chanted throughout the support set from the Kidz Next Door (featuring Grant Fleming, now a Left-wing film maker, and Pursey's kid brother Robbie). By the time the Rejects came on stage there were more than 200 City and Aston Villa skins at the front hurling abuse.

During the second number they started chucking plastic glasses. Then a real glass smashed on stage. Stinky Turner responded by saying, 'If anyone wants to chuck glasses they can come outside and I'll knock seven shades of shit out of ya.' That was it, glasses and ashtrays came from all directions. One hit Vince and, as a Brum skinhead started shouting 'Come on', Mickey dived into the crowd and put him on his back. Although outnumbered more than ten to one, the Rejects and their entourage drove the Brummie mob right across the hall, and finally out of it altogether. Under a hail of missiles, Mickey Geggus sustained a head injury that needed nine stitches and left him with what looked like a Fred Perry design above his right eye. Grant Fleming, a veteran of such notorious riots as Sham at Hendon and Madness at Hatfield, described the night's violence as the worst he'd ever seen. (For the full story see the next chapter 'The Battle of Birmingham'.)

Taken to the local hospital for treatment, Geggus had to bunk out of a 20-foot-high window when 'tooled-up' mates of the injured Brum City fans came looking for him. Back at the gig, the Londoners emerged triumphant from the fighting only to discover all their gear had been ripped off – total value, two grand. The next morning, the cockney contingent split into two vans – one that went on to the next gig at Huddersfield, the other containing Mickey and Grant that went cruising round the city looking for any likely punters who might know the whereabouts of their stolen gear. Incidents that morning in Wolverhampton Road, Albury, involving Geggus, three locals and an iron bar resulted in Mickey being charged with malicious wounding. Eight months later, both he and Grant had the luck of the devil to walk away with suspended sentences.

Maybe as insurance, in the summer of 1980, the Rejects played two Bridge House benefit gigs for the Prisoners' Rights Organisation, PROP, arranged by me and Hoxton Tom with the help of Terry Murphy. Tom's aunt was involved with London PROP because his uncle, Steven Smeeth, had been jailed for his part in George Davis's doomed comeback caper. The gigs were two of the best I'd ever seen the band play.

Brum had meant the end of the Rejects as a touring band, however. They had to pull a Liverpool gig when literally hundreds of tooled-up Scouse match boys came looking for confrontation. Road manager

Kevin Wells was threatened at knifepoint. At first Mickey seemed to revel in it all, acting as if he was living out some Cagney movie. The band's second LP called, surprisingly enough, *Greatest Hits Vol 2*, reflected his apparent death wish with sleeve notes boasting, 'From Scotland down to Cornwall, we dun the lot, we took 'em all.' On the song 'Urban Guerrilla' he spoke these words: 'Some folk call it anarchy, but I just call it fun. / Don't give a fuck about the law, I wanna kill someone.' Me? I think he meant it.

But, in the long build-up to the trial, a change came over Mickey. He swapped his little blue pills for ganja and started to mellow. Correspondingly, the Rejects' music began to move away from hooligan racket towards more mainstream rock: 1981's *The Power & The Glory* sounded like *The Professionals*; 1982's *The Wild Ones*, produced by Pete Way, was more like *UFO*; and, from a punk point of view, if 1984's *Quiet Storm* had been any more laid back it could have been bottled and sold as Valium. *The Wild Ones* remains a great rock album, with standout tracks such as 'City of Lights'; but the old fans were actively hostile to their new sounds, while abysmal marketing meant potential new fans never got to hear them. Stalemate.

The Angelic Upstarts lost their momentum in 1980 as well, getting dropped by Warner's in the summer. And although they were snapped up by EMI, going on to release their finest studio album, *Two Million Voices* in April 1981, they barely played live and fans were getting frustrated.

During 1980, hooligan audiences, especially in southeast London, found new live laughs in the shape of Peckham-based piss-artist pranksters Splodgenessabounds, whose brand of coarse comedy and punk energy scored three Top Thirty singles that year. Their debut single, 'Two Pints of Lager', was a Top Ten smash. Tongue in cheek, I dubbed them 'punk pathétique' along with equally crazy bands like Brighton's Peter & the Test-Tube Babies and Geordie jesters the Toy Dolls.

Singer Max Splodge insisted, 'The pathétique bands are the other side of Oi! We're working-class too, only, whereas some bands sing about prison and the dole, we sing about pilchards and bums. The audience is the same.' Pathétique peaked in the autumn of 1980 with the Pathétique Convention at the Electric Ballroom. West Ham's bootboy poet Barney Rubble was Man of the Match.

Elsewhere a second generation of hardcore Oi! bands had been spawned directly by the Upstarts and the Rejects. The Upstarts inspired Criminal Class from Coventry, and Infa-Riot from Plymouth via north London. The Cockney Rejects inspired the ferocious 4-Skins, and Sunderland's Red Alert. Edinburgh noise terrorists the Exploited also cited the Rejects as their major influence. In London, a whole host of groups sprang up around the Rejects, too, including Barney & the Rubbles and Stinky's Postmen combo. A movement was evolving at the grass roots.

I called it Oi!

Oi! was and remains a cockney street shout guaranteed to turn heads. Stinky Turner used to holler it at the start of each Rejects number, replacing the first punks' habitual 'One, two, three, four'. Before him, 'Oi! Oi!' had been Ian Dury's catchphrase, although he'd probably lifted it from cockney comic Jimmy Wheeler, whose catchphrase had been 'Oi, oi! That's yer lot.' Entertainers Flanagan and Allen first used 'Oi!' as a catchword in their 1930s variety act.

As I was compiling *Oi! – The Album* for EMI (released in November 1980), more like-minded combos sent demo tapes from all over the country. There was Blitz from New Mills, outside Manchester, the Strike from Lanarkshire and Demob from Gloucester. But the first real challengers for the Rejects' crown were the 4-Skins. They made their debut supporting the Damned at the Bridge House in 1979 with Mickey Geggus on drums. The 4-Skins developed through various line-ups playing low-key London pub gigs sporadically before arriving at their definite line-up towards the end of 1980: Gary Hodges, vocals; Hoxton Tom, bass; Rockabilly Steven Pear, guitar; and John Jacobs, drums. There was a real charisma about the band, and their raw brand of barbed-wire roar was blessed with a driving dynamism. Their standout song was 'Chaos', a horror-movie fantasy of urban chaos and skinhead takeover. But most of their three-minute blasts of fury concerned unemployment and police harassment ('ACAB', 'Wonderful World'), the horrors of war ('I Don't Wanna Die'), thinking for yourself ('Clockwork Skinhead') self-pride ('Sorry') and class ('One Law for Them').

Both the 4-Skins and Infa-Riot were emphatic about the need to learn from the Rejects' mistakes and get away from football trouble. The 4-Skins favoured no one team (Hodges was West Ham; Hoxton, Spurs; Steve, Arsenal and Jacobs, Millwall) and no one political preference (Hoxton was a liberal; Steve, left Labour; Jacobs, apolitical; and Hodges, a reformed Right-winger very pro-anti-unemployment campaigns). Infa-Riot were the same, professing no football affiliations. Mensi wrote their first *Sounds* review and he and Jock McDonald got them their first London gigs. Musically, they were a lot like a lither, wilder Upstarts. Like most Upstarts-influenced groups, Infa-Riot played gigs for Rock Against Racism (an apparently noble campaign that was actually a front for my old party, the extreme Left SWP). Criminal Class played RAR gigs too, and a benefit for the politically dubious, Republican/Irish nationalist front Troops Out of Ireland movement.

The 4-Skins refused to play RAR gigs, not wanting to be poster boys for Trotskyism.

The Oi! bands converged to publicly thrash out their stance at the Oi! debate held at *Sounds* in January 1981. Everyone agreed on the need for raw rock'n'roll, and the sense of benefit gigs, but there was a heated difference of opinion on politics. Stinky Turner was violently against politics and politicians, claiming simply that 'Oi! is working-class and if you're not working-class you'll get a kick in the bollocks.' Mensi argued that Labour still represented proletarian interests and claimed that 'the Tories still represent the biggest threat to our kind of people'. It was the same divide as had always separated the Rejects and the Upstarts. They managed to agree about reclaiming Britain's Union Flag from the fascists for the people, but that was it.

Although a few black and immigrant kids were into Oi!, it was mostly a white working-class phenomenon. The West Indian kids into Oi! were cockney blacks like the now infamous Cass Pennant, who'd rejected the pull of Rastafarianism and reggae. No Oi! band professed racist or Nazi leanings (in fact Demob had two mixed-race boxers in the band) and the teething trouble that dogged early gigs was all to do with the football legacy bequeathed by the Rejects. As *Punk Lives* magazine commentated later, 'Anyone who went to Oi! gigs could tell you you didn't get sieg-heiling at them ... ironically Madness and Bad Manners had the most trouble with Nazi skins at the time. All Oi! went on about was class.'

For the first half-year of the Oi! movement in London there were only two incidents of gig violence, both around Infa-Riot and neither of them worth writing home about. The band headlined the first 'New Punk Convention' at the tail end of 1980 with the Upstarts and Criminal Class. It ended in a brawl as Poplar Boy West Ham fans slugged it out with a smaller Arsenal crew led by the then infamous Dave Smith, an ex-boxer with a lethal jab, who followed the Upstarts.

In March 1981, Infa-Riot played the Acklam Hall in west London with Millwall-supporting skinhead band the Last Resort. Tooled-up local Queens Park Rangers fans, skins and football geezers, besieged the venue looking for West Ham. At one stage they tried to smash their way in through the roof. Ironically, most Hammers Oi! fans were safely in Upton Park at the time, watching their boys battle a Russian team.

The model of the sort of gig the bands wanted came in February 1981 with the second New Punk Convention, this time held at the Bridge House with the 4-Skins headlining (and introduced by the king of rude reggae himself, Judge Dread). The pub venue was packed far over capacity with a motley crew of skins, working-class punks and soccer rowdies drawn from the ranks of West Ham, Spurs, Millwall, QPR, Arsenal and Charlton. There wasn't one ruck all night.

This gig set a precedent for peaceful co-existence that lasted even when Oi! shifted venues to Hackney's Deuragon Arms. It was living proof that Pursey's old dream of the Kids United could happen. But united for what? It was around this time that I and the leading bands entered into a conspiracy to pervert the course of youth-cult history. We held a conference to plan the way the Oi! movement could develop in a positive, united manner. The idea was not only to arrange gigs and set up an Oi! record label, but also to plug away at the central theme of the folly of street kids fighting each other over football teams. We wanted to give Oi! a purpose by playing benefit gigs for working-class causes.

At the time I was living on the Ferrier estate in Kidbrook, southeast London, as was Franky 'Boy' Flame. And bands frequently made the pilgrimage there to stay in our deluxe council maisonette while they were playing London or just to shoot the breeze in the Wat Tyler pub. Some petty jealousies and band rivalry existed, but the Oi! scene was far more united than any other youth cult in British history. We tried to build on that.

The first Oi! conference was a small affair attended by reps from the Rejects, the 4-Skins, Splodge, Infa-Riot, the Business and the Last Resort, the last two being the latest recruits to the burgeoning movement. The Business were then known as 'pop-oi' because of their tuneful anthems. They came from Lewisham, south London. They were fronted by Mickey Fitz (Michael Fitzsimmons), who, like guitarist Steve Kent, had attended Colfe's Grammar School in Lee (as I had done) and had developed a terrace following that peacefully included West Ham, Chelsea and Millwall. Kent was a truly talented musician. The Business were managed by West Ham terrace veteran Laurie Pryor, who was also known as Ronnie Rouman.

The Last Resort were a skinhead band from south London via Herne Bay, Kent, based on the Last Resort shop in Petticoat Lane, east London and financed by the shop's owner Michael French. They too saw Oi! as being bigger that skins. 'Oi! is uniting punks, skins and everyone,' growler Millwall Roi told *Sounds* in their first interview. 'Now we've just gotta get away from football.'

Lee Wilson of Infa-Riot agreed. 'Oi! is the voice of street kids everywhere,' he said. 'That's why we're gonna grow, that's why we're gonna win.' And Oi! was growing all the time. By spring, as I was compiling the second Oi! compilation, *Strength Thru Oi!*, for Decca (released May 1981) more than 50 bands had aligned with the movement, including the Oi!/ska squad the Buzz Kids, whose singer Garry Johnson's lyric writing far outshone his vocal ability. He'd already had some lyrics published in a poetry collection by Babylon Books called *Boys of the Empire*. I encouraged him to ditch the band and branch out as Oi!'s first entirely serious poet. Johnson's humour and his bitterly anti-Establishment verses added yet more credence to Oi!, as did the plethora of good fanzines that had sprung up around it – the best being *Rising Free*, *Ready to Ruck* (which became *New Mania*) and *Phase One*. In June a second Oi! conference was held in the Conway Hall at Red Lion Square, attended by 57 interested parties including reps from bands all over the country. There was much concern voiced about the movement's violent image, which was felt to be unjust. The sublime Beki Bondage from the Oi!-bolstered punk band Vice Squad complained that the aggressive skin on the front of *Strength Thru Oi!* made the movement look too skinhead-orientated. Everyone agreed. And once again conference voted unanimously to back pro-working-class campaigns. Ron Rouman was delegated to write to the Right to Work Campaign that week to set up gigs. The main themes of the day were the need to unite working-class kids, and stick together. *Punk Lives* called it 'a glimpse of the future Oi! could have had'.

When the 4-Skins, the Last Resort and the Business played a gig at the Hamborough Tavern in Southall six days later, the riot that surrounded it and the acres of hysterical newsprint that ensued drowned out that possibility, and any chance of Oi! getting a fair hearing, for good.

When the shit hit the headlines during 1981's summer of discontent, I sincerely believed that the truth would out. That the smears against the Oi! bands would be laughed at in the way that the similar ridiculous slurs against the Sex Pistols and the Clash had been.

The whole idea that the bands had gone into Middlesex to provoke a race riot was absurd. We'd been talking strike benefits, not NF marches. No Oi! band had sported swastikas, as the Sex Pistols had done. No Oi! band had sung lyrics like 'too many Jews for my liking', as Siouxsie Banshee did. No Oi! band had lifted their name from the SS, as Joy Division had done ... What contributed to Oi!'s undoing, however, was the movement's utter hostility to the middle classes in general and the trendy Left in particular (see the Garry Johnson/Business anthem 'Suburban Rebels'). So, as well as incurring the wrath of the Right-wing establishment, Oi! also alienated the Left wing of the middle-class media, whose backing had seen the punk bands through their own particular backlash and who were later to defend rap and hip-hop (which were far more violent than Oi! had ever been, and anti-Semitic to boot). Besides me, there was no one else in the media to defend the bands. Very few rock journalists had ventured into the East End to see the gigs. (Indeed, the idea that the *NME* was ever *the* punk paper is a complete myth. That paper rubbished 'Anarchy in the UK' and their first review of the Clash suggested they 'should be returned to the garage, preferably with the motor running'.) Parsons and Burchill loved Joe Strummer and co. for their politics alone.

The Oi! bands and their fans were guilty of that most terrible of crimes – being white and working-class with chips on their shoulders. Ironically, Alan Rusbridger, now the editor of the *Guardian*, was the only journalist to give Oi! a fair hearing.

The superficial evidence against the Oi! bands seemed strong – the Southall riot and the *Strength Thru Oi!* album. The Oi! gig at Southall's Hamborough Tavern had been arranged by west London 4-Skins fans fed up with having to travel to the East End to see the shows. The press painted sinister pictures of East End skinheads being 'bussed' into a predominantly Asian area.

FACT: There were just two coaches hired by the Last Resort, who hired coaches to transport their away firm of fans whenever the south-London-based band played anywhere outside of their local area. TV and radio reports gave the impression of skinheads battling Asian youths and the police.

FACT: The Oi! fans were all inside the Tavern enjoying the gig when the first Asian petrol bomb sailed through the window. The cops were protecting the Oi! kids. The press said the peaceful Asian community had risen spontaneously to repulse Right-wing invaders who had terrorised the town.

FACT: There'd been just one incident involving young skinheads from the Coldharbour estate in Mottingham, Kent, in a chip shop earlier in the evening. 'They probably asked the geezer how many rupees a packet of chips cost,' Max Splodge later shrugged.

The sheer quantity of petrol bombs used by the Asians indicated they'd been stockpiling them for some days before. The young Asians were definitely on the offensive. Young white Oi! fans were assaulted by Asian youths on buses going *to* the gig, and a minibus containing Business fans from Lewisham and radical poet Garry Johnson was attacked by Asians wielding swords without any provocation (see Johnson's book *The Story of Oi!* for full details). In fact, the apparently placid Asian community was to riot again within the week with no 'outsiders' to pin the blame on.

The idea that the bands had gone to Southall to deliberately provoke a race riot just to be able to cash in on the ensuing publicity is just daft. It goes completely against everything they'd been trying to achieve for the previous eight months. The 4-Skins' manager Garry Hitchcock said, 'If we'd really wanted to go to Southall and smash it up, we'd have come with geezers – and left all the birds and the kids behind.'

'People ask why the Oi! bands played Southall,' commented Hoxton Tom, 'but you've gotta remember, in them days any gig was welcome. No one thought for a minute that there'd be trouble there. The Business had played Brixton before. The Last Resort had played Peckham, we'd played Hackney often, and they're all areas with large black populations, and yet those gigs were always trouble free. Oi! had to break out of the East End to have any chance of growing.'

To the mass media, the events of 4 July were manna from heaven: Yobs. Immigrants. Anarchy. The Thin Blue Line … But the Oi! crowd were reluctant participants. As soon as it was obvious real havoc was brewing, the Oi! bands attempted to negotiate with the Southall Youth Movement through the police. They didn't want to talk. 'We didn't want trouble,' said Tom, 'but that's all they had on their minds'. Under attack, the Oi! polloi had no other option but to fight a defensive rear-guard action and retreat. The Hamborough Tavern was razed to the ground. And the press distortion began. According to some reports Right-wing hate leaflets had been found in vans the following morning – the vans that had been torched. Were the leaflets printed on asbestos? Hacks even descended on the Bridge House and tried to bribe kids into *sieg-heil*ing for their cameras, offering £5 a salute. One was kicked out of the pub by Si Spanner, who was Jewish. But who cared about the truth? Storm-trooping skins made shock-horror headlines.

The fighting at Southall could have been worse. Scores more Oi! fans were turned back by the police before they'd even got to the gig, including an Indian workmate of Hoxton Tom's (the press never mentioned the few black, Asian and Greek kids inside the Tavern). Ironically, reports of a race riot on the radio induced mobs of west London bikers to rush to the scene eager to stand alongside their old enemies, the skins, against the Asians. The cops turned them back too.

I take full responsibility for *Strength Thru Oi!*. I gave the album its title. But it was never knowingly a pun on the Nazi slogan 'Strength Through Joy'. Let's be honest, who knew? How many people my age were up on the minutiae of Third Reich sloganeering? I'd been an active anti-fascist for years and had never heard the expression. The Skids had released an EP called *Strength Through Joy* earlier that year, and that's what I based the pun on (asked later, Skids singer Richard Jobson – who became a dapper TV movie reviewer – said he'd taken it from Dirk Bogarde's autobiography). It was either that or *The Oi! of Sex*, which I dismissed as too frivolous. *Doh!*

Selective quotes from my sleeve notes were used by the *Daily Mail* to fit their theory of Oi!'s 'Brownshirt' philosophy. Naturally, this meant they had to omit the favourable mentions of black sportsmen, including Jesse Owens, the American athlete who'd triumphed so dramatically at the 1936 Berlin Olympics. The fact that there wasn't a single racist lyric on the album didn't seem to matter. 'Blood on the Streets' by RAR stalwarts Criminal Class actually made the point that black and white youth faced the same state oppression. Not that this stopped one TV news reporter ludicrously quoting the lyric of the song to 'prove' that the Oi! bands were 'pro-violence, anti-black, anti-police'.

The biggest argument Oi!'s detractors had was the picture of the aggressive skin on the front cover. This turned out to be bin-man Nicoli Crane (a gay Nazi who later died of AIDS). Clear evidence of a Right-wing plot, you might feel. But the truth is far more mundane: the original model for the album had been West Ham personality and then bodybuilder Carlton Leach. Carlton had turned up for one photo session at the Bridge House that didn't work. He never turned up for the second one. Decca came up with their own cover illustration, a naff aerial shot of a cropped head with the album title emblazoned across it. It wasn't strong enough. Under looming deadline pressure I suggested using a shot from a skinhead Christmas card that I had pinned on my office wall. The image was strong but unclear, with all of the colours bleached out of it. I thought it was a still from US movie *The Wanderers*. In fact the shot had been taken by English skinhead photographer Martin Dean. It wasn't until the very last minute, when Decca had mocked up the sleeve, that the photo was sufficiently clear to reveal Nazi tattoos on the arms. We had the option of either airbrushing the tattoos out or putting the LP back a month while we put a new sleeve together. Said Splodge manager Dave Long, 'Blame it on youthful impetuousness but the wrong decision was made. It was a mistake, but it was an honest mistake. There's nothing else on that LP or in Oi! that could possibly be construed as dodgy.'

Another crucial point the critics skipped over was that it wasn't only me who hadn't realised the picture was of an obscure half-Italian dustman with a penchant for cock. The far right hadn't either. That album had been out for two months before the *Daily Mail* 'exposed' it (and me!) and yet not once had it been referred to in Right-wing publications. It was a bitter irony. Me, at that point in my life a dedicated socialist (used to having 'Bushell is a red' chanted at me relatively good-naturedly at gigs), accused of masterminding a Right-wing movement by a newspaper that had once supported Mosley's Blackshirts, Mussolini's invasion of Abyssinia, and appeasement with Hitler right up to the outbreak of World War Two!

The *Mail*'s ferocious attack on Oi! – which four years later was completely disowned by Simon Kinnersley, the journalist who wrote it – was obviously related to the fact that *Sounds* was owned by their rivals, the Express Newspapers.

Southall proved the catalyst for a spate of anti-government riots and there was no doubt where the Oi! bands stood on that issue, with the 4-Skins, Blitz and the Violators celebrating the popular uprisings with songs like 'One Law for Them', 'Nation on Fire' and 'Summer of '81'. In *Sounds* and in his book *The Story of Oi!*, Garry Johnson called on black and white youth to unite to fight the Tories. *Sounds* and I started libel proceedings against the *Mail*, while the Oi! bands now shaped up to deal with a problem that had never seemed an issue before – Nazism.

Naturally the far Right loved it. Young National Front (YNF) organiser Joseph Pearce (brother of Soft Cell's Stevo) popped up in the press out of nowhere claiming that the Oi! bands were the musical wing of the National Front. Joe Pearce had never even been to an Oi! gig.

Out of journalistic interest, I surveyed skinheads in the Last Resort shop on the Sunday after Southall. Most of them cited some immigrant ancestry from Irish to Pakistani through to Russian Jew. Last Resort fan Khalid Karim from Leytonstone, who was half-Pakistani, swore he had never been hassled at any Last Resort gig. 'Gappy' Eddie from Poplar claimed to personally know at least 30 'nonwhite' skins, including West Indian skins from Hackney, Brixton, Ladbroke Grove and Walthamstow, a half-Pakistani suede-head from Dalston and another half-Pakistani skin called Rob from Wimbledon, who I remember was always at Oi! gigs taking pictures. Sixteen-year-old Nicky Holder from Lewisham named other nonwhite skins – Gary Singh from Belvedere, West Indian Colin McClean from Lewisham, Arab skin Mushti from New Cross, and a huge black Orpington skin called Sanya. Jewish skinhead Tony Stern from Epping claimed to know 'loads of Jewish skins and no one gets any trouble. Where are all the "Nazi" skins now? That's what I wanna know.' Danielle Lux, from an orthodox Jewish family, was always down at the Hackney gigs. She went on to become a successful TV executive.

When *Socialist Worker* ran a report based on the *Mail* article, it was inundated with letters from socialist skins and punks complaining how out of touch it was. Sheffield skins wrote to *Sounds* to say that, the month before, 500 black and white skinheads had marched together in protest against unemployment and police harassment bearing placards proclaiming 'JOBS NOT JAILS'. SWP skin poet Seething Wells was outraged by the all-skins-are-Nazis line, pointing to the literally thousands of Northern skins and rudies who had swelled June's anti-Nazi Leeds Carnival. He might have mentioned Liverpool's 'Skin Fein' Republican skins too.

It was harder to get the truth into the nationals. A freelance journalist called John Glatt came and spoke to skinheads at length and filed a sympathetic report to the *News of the World*. His copy was slashed and distorted to make a cheap sensationalist slob story.

Even if Oi! had just been a skinhead phenomenon, it was dishonest and dangerously lazy journalism to suggest that anything more than a small minority of skinheads at this time were Nazi sympathisers.

The Oi! bands realised that simple facts weren't enough to win the propaganda battle. They had to prove their protestations of innocence. Gary Hodges went on TV to say that the 4-Skins would play an antiracist gig as long as it was organised by an independent body, although the band split before it occurred under the tremendous pressure and after just one more gig – advertised as country band the Skans! – at a Mottingham pub. The Business declined to play Rock Against Racism gigs for the old 'RAR as Trot front' reasons, but instead put together their own unwieldy-named 'Oi Against Racism and Political Extremism But Still Against the System' tour with Infa-Riot, Blitz and the Partisans. Infa-Riot played a Sheffield RAR gig and Blitz played at the Blackburn leg of the Right to Work march.

After Southall, a few of us met up with Red Action, a working-class street-fighting splinter group from the SWP, to clear the air about Oi!. Their leading member, Mick O'Farrell, knew me from the Right to Work marches and even contributed a judge-bashing poem to the fourth Oi! album sleeve called 'Chairman of the Bench'. It was a short-lived union, however. Although they called themselves socialists, Red Action were led by Irish nationalists and we disagreed passionately about Ulster and the Falklands. But that didn't stop Red Action from putting on Oi! gigs and writing about the bands and the music positively in their papers. As O'Farrell said at the time, 'Oi! is working-class, and anything that is part of and comes from the working class has got to be good.'

In late August 1981, I compiled the third Oi! album, *Carry On Oi!*, released by Secret Records in October of that year. Eager to stand by the bands, I re-formed my own seventies punk group the Gonads to contribute 'Tucker's Ruckers Ain't No Suckers' – a spoof of football hooligan songs – to the compilation. On first release it sold 35,000 copies. *Melody Maker*'s review stressed that Oi!'s intentions 'weren't to divide but to unite the working classes'. The same month the Exploited smashed into the Top Forty with 'Dead Cities' (shame about that *Top of the Pops* appearance), while the Business released their superb debut single coupling their live anthem *Harry May* with 'National Insurance Blacklist' – an attack on the unofficial employers' blacklist operated against militant trade unionists in the building trade: 'Job chances seem very thin/ It's a losing battle we must all win/ The CBI are winning, keeping down the pay/ Mysterious people calling early in the day/ The

"X" has appeared, another lost life/ No tears are shed for the children and wife/ The dailies ignore it, or treat it with tact/ Still when have they been known to report fact?/ In our country so fair and free, / So say the holders of the economy, / There is a monster said not to exist:/ They call it the employers blacklist ...' Their next single, 'Smash the Discos', got to Number 3 in the Indie Chart.

Paradoxically, the period from September 1981 to the end of 1982 saw the strongest ever Oi! releases, thanks to Secret, and the excellent Malvern label No Future's series of 22 singles from the likes of Blitz, the Partisans, Red Alert, Peter & the Test-Tube Babies, and Derbyshire *Clockwork Orange* band the Violators. *Punk Lives* magazine calculated that Oi! sold more than 2 million records in the first four years (by 2001, total worldwide sales by Oi! groups and groups influenced by Oi! stood at well over 11 million).

Recognising its significance, Left-wing playwright Trevor Griffiths wrote a play called *Oi for England*, which was broadcast by ITV in April 1982 as well as being taken around England on a theatrical tour. The play was more than a little far-fetched. It featured four unemployed skins in an Oi! band approached to play a Nazi gig, and revolved around their arguments about it and the riot outside. What Griffiths seemed to be saying, however, was that, in any group of skins, you'd have one susceptible to the lure of race and nation, one drawn to class struggle, and two who couldn't give a toss about politics.

Unfortunately, Oi!'s vinyl health during 1982 wasn't reflected on the streets. The 4-Skins split, and then re-formed with drummer Jacobs on guitar, new boy Pete Abbott on drums, Hoxton Tom still on bass and roadie Panther (Tony Cummins) singing. After Hodges's leonine growl, Panther's vocals were closer to Bagpuss with man flu. Later, Millwall Roi sang with them. But by then Tom was the only surviving original, and sales had slumped almost out of sight. They split 'for good' in 1984.

The Rejects were dropped by EMI in 1981, disowned Oi! for HM, and didn't play again for over a decade. The Upstarts soldiered on, playing the US punk circuit in 1982, but musically they went down the khazi. Under pressure from EMI, the Upstarts released a poor synth-pop-saturated LP called *Still from the Heart*, which was perceived widely as a sell-out and flopped miserably. (Infa-Riot tried a similarly doomed direction change, releasing an LP of unbelievably ordinary rock in 1983 before finally breaking up the following year.) The Upstarts were the subject of a Channel 4 documentary in 1984, but their chart success was long behind them.

The Last Resort never ever got to the singles stage. They weren't allowed a life independent of Mickey French's boutique. What he wanted was a house band, a singing advert for his T-shirts. Before Southall he opposed moves to send the bands on a US tour – he wanted the scene to stay at the small-club level. The cynics claimed he didn't want commercial competition for 'his' skinhead clothes market.

Sadly, the Resort suffered when their London fans smashed up a pub in King's Lynn called the Stanley Arms. Virtually the same crowd were also involved in a televised ruck with local skins at Benny's Club in Harlow – featured in BBC2's *Arena* series. Both incidents happened in January 1982, at a time when everyone else was trying to prove that Oi! meant more than rucking. The Last Resort split with French later in 1982 to re-emerge as the Warriors, but back then they were never sufficiently motivated to build on their potential. (Supporting the Resort at Benny's, were skinhead band Combat 84, whose singer, Chubby Chris Henderson, was a public-school-educated Right-winger. The other band members did not share his views and broke up after he made a racist comment on *Arena*. Henderson became actively involved with CFC hooligan mob the Chelsea Headhunters; Combat 84 briefly re-formed 18 years later without him.)

The Exploited, meantime, had shed their skin look, adopting a mutant Mohawk image and becoming the darlings of the Apocalypse Now punk revival. Singer Wattie went on to close down two-thirds of Western Europe to other punk bands by smashing up dressing rooms. Losing gifted guitarist Big John (to Nirvana!) along the way, the band play on to this day.

Back in 1982, Blitz and the Business had clearly emerged as the new vanguard Oi! desperately needed. Blitz specialised in belligerent boots-'n'-braces brickwall Oi! – pure youth anthems like 'Fight to Live', 'Razors in the Night' and the haunting 'Warriors'. Their debut LP, *Voice of a Generation*, went Top Thirty and was the Oi! LP of 1982, but they were never that hot live. A disastrous gig at the Hammersmith Clarendon at the end of 1982 was the beginning of the end. In 1983 Blitz split in two, their former engineer Tim Harris taking over from the popular Mackie as bassist (Mackie later formed the short-lived Rose of Victory with Blitz guitarist Nidge Miller) and pushing the band into trendier synthesiser sounds with scant public appeal. They didn't last into 1984.

The Business split and got punkier. Guitarist Steve Whale (ex-Gonads) contributed greatly to their harder sound. They were haunted by politics – internal and external. To back up their 'Blacklist' song, Business manager Ron Rouman and the Oi! organising committee (an ad hoc body set up after Southall) met with blacklisted building worker Brian Higgins and other trade union militants to organise a big pro-union benefit gig. But the band bottled out and sacked Rouman, replacing him with bikers' pin-up Vermilion Sands. Deprived of Rouman's drive and terrace connections, the band fell temporarily apart. The Business re-formed in 1984 and were smart enough to realise you had to tour to survive (ironically, they signed to Rouman and Mark Brennan's Link Records). They have been playing ever since to growing audiences, especially in the USA, where they inspired another Oi! wave and the new street-punk bands.

Back home, though, Oi! as we first knew it had died by the end of 1982. It never had room to grow, and its vanguard fell apart ignominiously. To paraphrase Mao, it was like a stream: when it's moving it stays healthy, but when it gets blocked up and stagnant all the shit rises to the top. The Oi! stream was definitely blocked up. And the relatively poor quality of the new combos showcased on the fourth Oi! LP, *Oi! Oi! That's Yer Lot* (produced by Mickey Geggus and released by Secret in

October 1982), confirmed it. The new bands were too unoriginal, too weak or, in the case of Terry Hayes and Skully's East End Badoes, too limited in their appeal to a square mile of Poplar to mean much.

When promising Oi!-influenced bands did break through in 1983, they all fell at early fences. Croydon's Case were cracking – they specialised in a ballsy brand of high-octane pop fresher than Max Miller chewing Polos in a mountain stream, and were fronted by the exceptionally expressive Matthew Newman. Case attracted acclaim from most quarters (including the *Daily Mirror* and Radio One) but fell apart when Matthew swapped the stage for domestic bliss with Splodge co-vocalist Christine Miller. Similarly, Taboo rose from the ashes of the Violators and specialised in non-wimpy pop. But the band split when wonderful, vivacious vocalist Helen decided to get pregnant and leave.

Finally there were the Blood, one of the best Oi! bands ever to come out of Blighty. Emerging from the wild excesses of Charlton's Coming Blood, the Blood's debut LP, *False Gestures for a Devious Public*, was an invigorating blend of Stranglers, Motörhead and Alice Cooper influences, which hit the UK Top Thirty and was voted one of the year's best by the *Sounds* staff. On stage they were awesome and OTT in equal measure. They filled blow-up dolls full of butchers' offal and cut them up with chainsaws. And their lyrics were a cut above the usual, with lines like: 'The Pope said to the atheist, "In God's name I do swear, you're searching blindly in the dark for something that ain't there."/ The atheist said to the Pope, "There ain't no getting round it, you too were searching in the dark for nothing ... but you found it."' But the band were lazy bastards who never wanted to tour, and the days when you could scam your way to chart success were long gone.

Cock Sparrer re-formed in 1082 and the following year released the LP they always should have made, *Shock Troops* (Carrere), but they never had chart success in the UK again. Modesty forbids any mention of the Gonads, considered by many to be the finest Oi! band of them all (see the album *Glorious Bastards* for the proof in handy CD form).

At the fag end of 1983, Syndicate Records launched a new series of

Oi! albums that lacked both the bite and the sales of the originals – *Son of Oi!* was nudging up to the 10,000 mark when Syndicate went bust in December 1984, that bankruptcy itself a reflection of Britain's shrinking Oi! market. The two best new bands were Burial and Prole (the latter a studio creation put together by me and Steve Kent). Scarborough's Burial cited Oi! and 2-Tone as forebears and mixed the sounds of ska and rowdy bootboy punk in their set. The only Oi! band to have any success were the Toy Dolls, who scored a Top Ten novelty hit with their version of 'Nellie the Elephant' at Christmas 1984.

As British punk degenerated after its 1981 boom, the skinhead scene became a political battleground and turned sour. The cream of the 1981 generation went casual. A few even turned rockabilly. Meanwhile, Nazi kids who'd never been part of Oi! started turning up at the gigs, obviously attracted by the media's 'reporting'. When they found that the truth was different, they turned nasty: Garry Johnson was beaten up by Nazi skins in Peckham; I was attacked by a mob of 15 Nazis (not skins) at an Upstarts gig at London's 100 Club. There were three of us, we had no chance. Si Spanner was stabbed by the Nazi who'd tried to stab Buster Bloodvessel at the Electric Ballroom. Attila the Stockbroker, the Left-wing Oi! poet/wally, was whacked on stage in north London. Infa-Riot were attacked at the 100 Club by Nazis. You get the picture.

In east London, it was a different story. The British Movement were taken out of the frame by the Inter City Firm. In early 1982, Skully and other Oi! regulars had organised a march protesting about the jailing of their fellow ICF member Cass Pennant. The BM threatened individuals, putting pressure on them to cancel this 'march for a nigger'. The following Monday the ICF had been planning to take on Tottenham fans (as West Ham were playing Spurs that night). Instead, they confronted and smashed the east London neo-Nazis who were drinking in the Boleyn Arms. They were never a significant presence on the West Ham terraces again, but they remained a problem elsewhere.

When they couldn't find Oi! bands to toe the master-race line, the neo-Nazis created their own global underground of nationalist skinhead bands around the Blood & Honour banner (see Chapter 15, 'The Battle of Waterloo').

Skrewdriver, the veteran punk band first featured on Janet Street-Porter's punk TV documentary in 1976, came back as skinheads and were the cornerstone of the new hate-punk sound. Opposing them were a raft of equally extreme Trotskyist bands and performers, such as the Redskins, the Newtown Neurotics, Attila and Seething Wells. The Upstarts moved steadily to the Left throughout the 1980s, with Mensi becoming directly involved with Anti-Fascist Action, led by Trotskyites and Irish nationalists. Although his heart was in the right place, Mensi's ideological journey reached a revolting nadir with the recording of 'Brighton Bomb' – a song justifying the 1984 attack on the governing Conservative Party. The IRA planted a 100lb bomb in the Brighton Grand hotel set to explode during the Tory conference. It killed five and seriously injured 34, including two Cabinet members.

Quietly, and apart from all the polemics, a small, smartly dressed alternative skinhead scene developed underground. *Hard as Nails* fanzine reflected this growing trend. It was run by two young kids from Canvey, Essex, both Labour Party members. But they insisted the 'zine was about style, not politics. They had some crossover with the scooterist scene, which flourishes to this day, with thousands subscribing to George Marshall's marvellous *Pulped* mag and enjoying a drip feed of classic Oi! CDs from Mark Brennan's label Captain Oi!, the world's leading punk reissue label.

The British Oi! scene didn't really perk up until Link Records came along in 1986, creating a truly independent platform to showcase new bands like Section 5 and Vicious Rumours. But Link alone couldn't reverse the decline. In Britain Oi! fizzled out and turned into a vacuum for many a barren year. But the fuse we lit went on to detonate explosive scenes around the globe. Oi! had taken off in most European countries by the mid-eighties, producing exciting distinctive bands such as Oxymoron in Germany and Discipline in Belgium. There is even an underground Oi! scene in mainland China. In Berlin, MAD Marc and Ute did what English Oi! should have done: he built an alternative promotion group along with his own fanzine and record store. It has now been running for more than a quarter of a century and has been hugely influential in keeping the real spirit of Oi! – working-class hooligan youth, black and white – alive.

MAD Tour Booking were a major force in bringing British Oi! back to life. As Marc says, 'Like the English bands, we lived our lives and fought our fights, only we stayed forever in the front line. We cared and still care for the revolution of what punk and Oi! was all about.' Great Oi! bands still flourish in Germany, Scandinavia, France, Poland, Belgium, Greece, Spain and Italy. Germany's Stomper 98 are particularly impressive. But it was bands in the USA who really made the music their own. Oi! was always viewed for what it was in the States: a distinctive brand of working-class punk. Hardcore bands like Negative Approach used to cover Oi! songs in their sets. Sick of It All covered Sham 69's 'Borstal Breakout'. Hardcore heavy hitters Agnostic Front invited the Business to play there.

The first actual US Oi! bands were formed in 1981. Frontrunners included DC's Iron Cross, the Effigies from Chicago, New York's Warzone, the hardcore punk skin band founded by US Navy vet Raybeez, and the Press, the socialist Oi! band from New York, whose anthem 'Revolution Now' was directly inspired by the Gonads.

The Templars – formed by black and white skinheads – emerged in 1991; Oxblood a year later.

In 1987, New Yorker Marcus Pacheco founded the group Skinheads Against Racial Prejudice (SHARP) – see Chapter 16, 'Blowing in the Wind' – to demonstrate that skin culture had nothing to do with racism or political extremism. André Schlesinger of the Press and Jason O'Toole of hardcore band Life's Blood were among the movement's earliest supporters. (At the time, an all-black skinhead gang called the Doctor Marten Skins were active in NYC; they wore authentic gear and were into Oi. Later the DMS would become just another street gang, losing the skin look and recruiting members who weren't black.) Two years later, Roddy Moreno of Welsh Oi! band the Oppressed was inspired to set up a British chapter. Germany and France followed, although in Europe SHARP is less organised than in the States, and more about individual expression.

In the States, Oi! took off in earnest from the mid-1990s on, with inspired outfits such as Boston's own Dropkick Murphys, plus the Bruisers from New Hampshire, the Anti-Heros from Atlanta, the Kicker Boys and the Vandals. The clear catalyst was the Business, whose album *The Truth* was to become the cornerstone of the new street-punk scene. Guitarist Steve Whale took all the best bits of early Oi! – the street-socialist principles, terrace camaraderie, mob choruses – and deliberately fashioned them into something new and exciting.

The impact of *The Truth* can readily be heard in albums by Agnostic Front, the Murphys, the Anti-Heros, the Briggs, the Street Dogs, the Bouncing Souls and scores more. Street-punk acts are now one of the biggest branches of punk rock worldwide, with global sales well in excess of 10 million (although hardcore Oi! fans view many of these bands as too poppy and prefer the more brickwall sound of blue-collar US bands like Patriot, Hammer & the Nails, the Workin' Stiffs, Fully Loaded, Oxblood, and Tommy & the Terrors).

One of the best Oi!-influenced bands was Operation Ivy, whose ska-punk numbers were punctuated with oi-oi terrace chants (this became a ska-punk tradition). Operation Ivy became Rancid, one of the hottest punk bands around. Rancid's Oi! anthem 'Avenues & Alleyways' appears with their permission on the album *The Kings of Street Punk*, released by G&R records – the label formed by Mickey Geggus and Andy 'Skully' Russell. And Lars Frederiksen from Rancid has produced the debut album from ex-Business star Steve Whale's brilliant new punk band the Masons, with guest vocalists including Stinky Turner, Charlie Harper and Steve Ignorant. Other major US punk bands, including No Doubt and NOFX, played Oi! songs; NOFX were unashamedly inspired by Blitz and the Partisans. The Briggs cite the

Cockney Rejects as a major influence; the Dropkick Murphys have performed with Liberty Hayes – daughter of Terry Hayes, of the East End Badoes – and so it goes on.

In 2000, I Scream Records released the first of two compilation albums called *The Worldwide Tribute to the Real Oi*. This featured major US bands like Agnostic Front, the Dropkick Murphys and Sick of It All performing classic Oi! songs. The second volume included the Bouncing Souls and Roger Miret & the Disasters. Incidentally, the world's largest organised tour against racism happened in the USA, featuring bands like Less Than Jake and the Toasters, and was sponsored by the Moon Ska label, which is now run in Europe by rotund Oi! stalwart Lol Pryor. Drawn out of retirement by overseas interest, most of the original British Oi! bands are still playing and small trouble-free scenes still exist around the UK, with many small bands playing regularly, including the Badoes, Control, the Warriors and Superyob. Exciting younger UK bands tend to cite Oi! as just one influence, along with other strands of punk, new mod and ska.

In April 2001, the US rock mag *Spin* put together their Top 50 most influential punk albums ever. *Oi! – The Album*, the record I had compiled for EMI 21 years previously, was in there with these words: 'The white riot becomes a soccer riot: Oi! was punk dumbed down to a hilariously catchy chant and a knee in the bollocks.' Not perfect but at least there wasn't a sniff of any Nazi nonsense – unlike in Britain, where apparently professional journalists like John Sweeney of the *Observer* feel free to trot out the same old rhetoric without reporting all the relevant facts and the whole truth. Posers who work for *Kerrang!* and *Metal Hammer* still refuse to write about the Business, even though they gleefully write about bands who *cite* south London's finest as their inspiration. And in 2001 UK CD manufacturer Disctronics declined to re-press well-known 'Nazi' CDs like *Oi Oi Music* by the Oppressed (the world's leading anti-fascist Oi! band!) and *100% British Ska*. Yeah, we still wind up the mugs.

The latest miscreant is Robert Elms. His book, *The Way We Wore*, starts with a lovingly accurate depiction of skinhead fashion in the sixties but goes on to dismiss Oi! out of hand. Yet it's clear from the text that Elms has no personal knowledge of the Oi! scene, had never been to any gigs and has only a tenuous idea of when Oi! happened and which bands were involved in it. It's an odd book. Elms, an LSE graduate, lost his father at a young age and clearly looked up to his tougher brother Reggie and his skinhead pals with something approaching misty-eyed hero worship. He's hot for hooliganism ('working-class teenage boys liked to dress up; working-class teenage boys liked to fight'), and praises its 'violent brilliance'. Yet strangely, although gang warfare and terrace culture are fine in 1969, kids just like his brother's gang ten years later are completely written off. Elms admits (crassly) that he was attracted to punk by the awful rip-off fashions created by Vivienne Westwood; and by the politics of the Clash (nothing wrong with that). The music never really came into it. To him, Oi! was an ugly 'monosyllabic' thing (unlike those colourfully polysyllabic cults such as mod, punk, goth, Ted etc.). He manages to link the Southall gig with the death of Blair Peach, who was killed by the Metropolitan Police's later-disbanded Special Patrol Group (SPG) more than two years before, simply because they happened in the same town. He writes that the 'predominantly Asian area … was set alight during a riot at an Oi gig in a pub', disingenuously failing to mention who was throwing the petrol bombs and who was doing the rioting.

Inevitably, by the early eighties, Robert was closely associated with the New Romantics (i.e. the camp-clown end of British youth cults; see Chapter 12, 'Journeys to Glory') and was busy writing pretentious poetry for Spandau Ballet. In fact, Elms gave them their name – taken from Spandau prison, which housed one Rudolph Hess. That kind of Nazi flirtation is so bold and decadent, doncha know? Spandau wrote some quality soul-edged pop songs, of course, and I have to admit to a tinge of envy regarding Elms's love life (he dated Sade); but his views on Oi! are laughably poor journalism. Besides, it's hard to be lectured by someone who finds Blue Rondo A La Turk more exciting than Cock

Sparrer, and Steve Strange more noteworthy than Hoxton Tom. Make your own mind up which has more lasting worth.

The veteran punk writer Tony Parsons was more astute when he noted, 'Oi! is punk without the theatrical overtones, punk without 'O' levels, punk that has never been to art school. This is the genuine voice of council estates. Real working-class music. Unlike every musician since Elvis, Oi! bands don't play with the mythology of danger. They were and are the real thing. It isn't pretty.'

The chances of Oi! ever becoming respectable are slim. But I do know this: the movement that *NME* once said I had 'invented' is still going strong three decades on. In the last year I've been filmed by Bravo and by Asian Oi! fans, talking about the Oi! movement. And I've just been approached to take part in a 30th-anniversary retrospective for the *Guardian*. Pretty much any Oi! band that ever existed has now re-formed. And the message is still the same as it always was. Oi!'s self-definition of 'having a laugh and having a say' got it right on the button. The laughs were ten a penny for Jack the Lads knocking back pints and pills and pulling at the pubs, rampaging at the football grounds and revelling in rebel rock'n'roll at the gigs. Oi! reflected that, but it also cried out against the injustices weighed up against the young working class. In that sense Oi! was a real voice from the backstreets, a megaphone for dead-end yobs. At its best, it went beyond protest, and dreamed of a better life: social change; the kids united.

## OI! IN ITS OWN WORDS

'This generation won't keep quiet / Work, work, work – or RIOT!' – the Business, 'Work or Riot', 1981

'All you kids, black and white / Together we are dynamite' – Angelic Upstarts, 'Kids on the Street', 1981.

'Wankers hand out leaflets / They never ever let it be  / I don't care what they say / But they better not come near me ...' – Cockney Rejects, 'Fighting in the Streets', 1979

'They always put the blame on us / And they tell the public lies / But that don't mean that we have lost / 'Cos our spirit never dies.' – East End Badoes, 'The Way It's Gotta Be', 1982

'What we want's the right to work / Give us jobs, not jails / Don't throw us on the scrapheap because your system fails.' – the Gonads, 'Jobs Not Jails', 1981

'45 Revolutions on my stereo, not one revolution on the streets' – Blitz, '45 Revolutions', 1981

'The voice of Oi! is unity / No "them and us", just you and me / Think how strong we could be / United against society' – Garry Johnson, 'United', 1981

## CHAPTER NINE

# THE BATTLE OF BIRMINGHAM

The real problem with Oi! was football-related, and the very worst example of it was the Battle of Birmingham, when the Cockney Rejects attempted to play a gig at the Cedar Club. That night was the worst violence ever witnessed at a UK rock concert. Brutal and relentless, it made Sham 69 at the Finsbury Park Rainbow look like a day trip to Alton Towers. The night ended with scores of casualties, including Mickey Geggus. In Jeff Turner's words, 'There were people being cut, bottled and glassed, the PA was utterly destroyed, there was claret [blood] everywhere. Men and women were in tears. It was the rock'n'roll equivalent of [the Battle of] Rorke's Drift, only, instead of a hundred and forty redcoats with guns facing four thousand Zulus, we were twenty-odd cockneys battling more than two hundred Midlands skinheads in vicious hand-to-hand fighting.'

It was the opening night of their tour, and two vanloads of the 'Firm' mates had come up for the crack, among them Johnny Butler, Dickle, H, Swallow, Danny Harrison, Danny Meakin, John O'Connor, Bruce, who was one of the Ancient Brit crew, and Brett Tidman, all 'in the mood for a party' to take them out of the equation. Jeff describes the day.

'We did the sound check in the afternoon, which was fine, and got back to the gig just after seven. Kevin Rowland, from Dexys Midnight Runners, owned the club and he was there on the night. It was an odd place, very poorly designed. The stage was right at the back but there was no backstage area. There were stairs in the middle of the venue, which went up to the changing room, so you had to walk through the crowd to reach the stage.

'We were due on at 9pm. As soon as we got there you could sense there was a hostile atmosphere. It was packed to capacity, with five hundred or so crammed in. A lot of the crowd was skinheads but there were a lot of straight football hooligans there too; they were a mixture of Villa and Birmingham City, which in itself was strange, because normally they'd hate each other's guts. It was like West Ham and Millwall coming together to face a common foe, which was unimaginable to us. At that time it would never have happened: the hatred between south and east London was too great.

'We had to walk through the body of the crowd to play the gig. As soon as they saw us, they started gobbing at us and not in a punky way. It was pure loathing. "Fuck off!" they were going. "Fuck off, you cockney cunts!" The atmosphere was poisonous, the worst atmosphere I'd ever experienced. The entourage came with us as usual and stood at the back of the stage behind us. There was a pair of steps that went down to two exit doors at the back. The only other way to leave that club was through the crowd.

'We started playing. Some of the crowd was clearly into it, but a big belligerent section weren't. They were just verballing us from the off. They didn't wanna know. There were a lot at the front going, "Come on, you wankers; come on, you cunts." I couldn't really focus on performing because I could tell it was going to go off. One particular bonehead sticks in the memory. He was down the front wearing a Fred Perry shirt and he had an Aston Villa tattoo on his arm. All he kept doing was screwing us and saying, "Come on, come on," offering us out with his hands. I looked at Mick. We both really wanted to get down there and give it to them, but we were trying to keep calm.

'We were in the middle of "Where the Hell is Babylon", probably the fourth number, when the first pint glass came flying over. And I did the worst thing possible.

'I stopped the set and said, "Whoever chucked that glass, fight your way to the front of the stage and we'll go outside, one to one. We'll see who's fucking big then." I should never have said it. It was the worse thing I could've done, because then they all started milling up and the air was full of things being slung at us: fag packets, coins, beer, nothing too heavy but there were a few more glasses in the bombardment too.

'I remember seeing Mick in his yellow vest – we used to call him the Canary – exchanging a few words with these boneheads down the front.

'We finished the song, and Vince started tuning his bass. I turned round to see how he was getting on, and the next minute I heard a commotion. I looked and Mick wasn't standing next to me any more. He was in the audience on his own just having it with this mob. So that was it. We all jumped down and it was proper going off. We were battling these skinheads. Vince swung his boot as he leapt in from the stage and kicked some gobby geezer right in the mouth. Knocked him spark out.

'There were only twenty odd of us, and initially there were about eighty of these Brummies who wanted to know, but we pushed them right back to the bar. We were beating 'em, no problem, and that was when I saw a geezer take a glass and stick in right in Danny Harrison's face. There was blood everywhere. Over to my right, Johnny Butler was cut as well. Some of the opposition had tools, but, where we had been pushing them all back to the bar, the others were getting their hands on glasses and bottles. Armed, they started to turn the tide of battle. We were having to move back towards the stage now, stepping over their casualties on the floor, who we'd already battered the fuck out of.

'I looked back and H was standing up on the stage. Some huge bonehead came from the side and smashed him right in the mouth. He was lucky he never broke his jaw. But H didn't even go over; he just turned round and upped him.

'We reached the stage and starting pulling over all the PA equipment to throw at them. There was nowhere else to retreat to. We had to make a stand here. We could have gone through the exit but that would have meant defeat and we couldn't contemplate that; we couldn't give in. We were on that stage trying to hit them with everything we can lay on hands on: the bass drum, the stool, the mike stand, the lot. The shower of bottles started up again. I looked up and saw what looked like a UFO spinning over. It appeared to be moving in slow motion. It was a big glass ashtray, and it bounced off Mickey's forehead. The claret poured out of his head like a waterfall. But that only made me madder, and I punched my way back into the mêlée.

'At this stage the bouncers finally decided to make a show. They pushed their way up to the stage and started shoving us through one of the exit doors into a small area. The street was the other side of the next set of doors. The bouncers locked us in with one of their blokes in there with us to keep us in check. We looked around and realised that Mick, Andy Swallow and three others were still out there. I told the bouncer to open the door. He didn't move. I lost me rag: "Open that fucking door now," I shouted. "We've got five men out there." He was a big geezer, but not that old, probably twenty-six, twenty-seven, but he was shitting himself. Vince said, "If you don't fucking open that door now, we're gonna do you." The geezer started crying. He said, "I can't take no more of this." He went to pieces. We pushed him to one side and kicked the door out. There were bits of iron in the room from disassembled clothes rails; not heavy but if you whacked someone round the head with one they'd know all about it. We grabbed what we could carry and went back into the fray. Our five were still on their feet holding the fort. They'd dragged a couple of big tables on stage to use as a shield. There were people unconscious all over the floor. There was broken glass everywhere; the PA was all smashed to fuck. The row had been going on for about twenty minutes. We had to finish it off. This was do-or-die time. We burst back into action giving it everything that we'd got. We were smashing them, cutting them, hitting them. We drove them back through the club, past the bar and clean out of the venue.

'As they were retreating they were all shitting themselves, which just shows what wankers they were. We'd fought our toughest battle, we'd fought as a firm against the odds, and we'd won. They had all showed so much heart and bottle to stand their ground like that. If it had happened in wartime and we'd been wearing uniforms we'd have got the VC for it.

'At the moment of victory, about thirty Old Bill arrived, which was just as well because that created a sense of calm. I looked at my brother's face and it was ruined. He had claret everywhere, a gaping head wound. Danny Harrison was bleeding, Johnny Butler was cut badly. The place looked like a battlefield: there were geezers being stretchered out. Poor Robbie Pursey was as white as a sheet. He was the same age as me, but I was used to it. All the Kidz Next Door came from cosy little places around Hersham. They'd had nice upbringings. They must have thought, What the fuck were we doing here?

'As soon as the cops got there they wanted to nick Mick. For some reason they always seemed to go for him. I was livid. I said, "Here's twenty of us and all that fucking scum start on us and you wanna arrest one of ours? What were we supposed to do?" The Old Bill were speechless. Give Kevin Rowland his due: he never complained, he backed us up. He said, "You had to do what you had to do." He was apologising to us. The poor sod was shell-shocked. His bouncers were useless. The only show they made was when they cordoned us off on the stage and pushed us through the exit door. But they didn't do a thing about the row.

'Looking back now, there's no doubt that Birmingham was the beginning of the end for us. It was a horrible night. Bouncers crying, birds crying, geezers I looked up to had been cut to bits, but they wouldn't go to hospital because they wanted to go round the town looking for the other side. I was sixteen. I don't know if the experience toughened me up or fucked me. I really don't. Once the adrenalin had worn off you realised it was just terrible. A lot of people probably never got over it. I don't think Mick ever did. Within four years he'd lost all his hair. I mean, baldness runs in the family, but not *that* early. It was traumatic. This wasn't like the kind of "riots" at venues the music press wrote about. This was a fight for survival. It was vicious and nasty and our songs were the main cause of it. We saw mates getting glassed. These were geezers who always stood together and never gave in, geezers you thought were invincible, yet they were vulnerable too. They could be stabbed and cut like anybody else.

'We were lucky no one died.'

# SOUTHALL, AND THE DEATH OF BLAIR PEACH

On 25 April 2009, journalist Alison Roberts wrote a piece in the London *Evening Standard* that again wrongly linked the death of Blair Peach in Southall with skinheads. In fact, no skinheads were involved in the riot of 23 April 1979. The fighting occurred entirely between the police and the far Left, who were protesting against the far-Right National Front, who were holding a lawful public election meeting at Southall Town Hall in support of John Fairhurst, their general election candidate for the area.

I have no truck with the NF or their racial theories, but I do cling to the old-fashioned notion that journalism should involve the facts. And the facts here were that this was not 'a rally' of skinheads or 'an act of deliberate provocation', as reported, but a meeting on council property, which the fascist party, though loathsome to most people, were legally entitled to hold. Most of those present inside the hall were middle-aged members of the Front's long-established Ealing branch. Of cropped heads, Ben Sherman shirts and Doc Martens there were none.

The NF had stood in local and parliamentary elections for Southall before without violent incident, and Mr Fairhurst, an ex-serviceman born and bred in the Middlesex town, had been fully entitled to stand in the election. Their meeting was due to start at 7.30 that night. The SWP and other far-Left activists, along with Asian militants, started kicking off at about 1pm without a single fascist in sight.

There were no 'clashes between white skinheads and "pretty angry Asians youths" ', as the *Standard* reported. The fighting during which New Zealander Peach unfortunately died happened entirely between anti-fascists and the cops – specifically the SPG. The 33-year-old special-needs teacher, who worked in Tower Hamlets, east London, suffered fatal head injuries after being struck with a truncheon. More than 40 people were hurt in the riot, 21 of·them police officers. Three hundred were arrested – none of them members or supporters of the National Front. The only violence involving the NF took place at Southall railway station at about 7pm, when a gang of Asian youths ambushed a retired ex-serviceman in his 70s, Richard de Jongh Wagenaar, and kicked him unconscious on to the railway track. He was later awarded a four-figure sum by the Criminal Injuries Compensation Board.

Martin Webster, the NF's national activities organiser, chaired their Town Hall meeting. Members of the public who attended included eight members of the Southall Indian Workers' Association committee. After the speeches, Webster invited them to ask questions but instead they marched out of the hall in silent protest, as was their right.

White Marxists, most of them middle-class professionals, and younger Asians had a different approach. The far Left then, as now, viewed the very existence of a far-Right party as a provocation and took the view that they should be brutally smashed every time they raised their heads above the parapets. You may or may not agree with that. I was certainly an active participant in many violent anti-fascist activities in the 1970s and our attitude was it was our right to attack them and stop them organising by any means necessary. We instigated mob violence regularly and gleefully – and the press reports equally gleefully blamed the NF.

In her piece, Roberts quoted only Jo Lang, whom she identified as a 'Hackney teacher'. Jo was actually an SWP member; her view was entirely partial.

In May 1980, the jury at the inquest into Blair Peach's death returned a verdict of death by misadventure. Paul Holborow of the Anti-Nazi League said the verdict proved 'the police killed Blair Peach'. News reports at the time did not state that Holborow was also a central committee member of the SWP. No police officers were ever charged with the attack. Mr Peach's girlfriend, teacher Celia Stubbs, said they 'got away scot-free'. However, nine years later, the Met reached an out-of-court settlement with Peach's brother after the family gained access to part of the internal police report, which named six officers.

## CHAPTER TEN

# REALITY ASYLUM: ANARCHO-PUNK

'WE SEEK A FUTURE THAT IS OUR OWN, AWAY FROM THE OPPRESSION,
HISTORY AND TRADITION. WE SEEK SOME REALITY THAT IS OURS,
YET ALL AROUND ARE THE LITTLE PEOPLE.'
Crass, The Feeding of the 5000

October 1979 witnessed the most brutal riot ever seen at a London punk gig. The concert was headlined by Crass, the anarchist or hippy-punk band. Forty or so Skinheads, members and supporters of the neo-Nazi British Movement (BM), had turned up for the show at the Conway Hall, a benefit gig for a group of arrested activists known as Persons Unknown. Anarchist Martin Lux, a veteran anti-fascist street fighter, recalls, 'A dozen of them were large brutes, ugly-looking bastards, real hard nuts, with another dozen or so inner core; the remainder were runty followers, but dangerous if mob-handed or tooled-up.' As per usual, the Nazis amused themselves by taking the piss out of the largely terrified and intimidated punk audience. Unfortunately for them, however, their arrival had been spotted by members of the Socialist Workers' Party who happened to have been meeting close by. Frantic phone calls followed, and a team of the most violent Left-wing headcases in London was swiftly mobilised.

Before Crass went on stage, the half-dozen hard-core anarchist street fighters present had been swollen by a dozen tooled-up SWP hooligans who stormed the gig.

They were largely from north London, mostly Man United Cockney Reds, with a few Celtic and Arsenal. Armed with coshes, spanners, iron bars, chains, bottles and hammers, they attacked the BM contingent with extreme prejudice. 'It was merciless and very bloody,' says Karen H (who has asked for her identity to be withheld). 'I had seen trouble at gigs before, but nothing like this. It actually made me feel physically sick.'

Martin Lux, who in common with many of the SWP activists was of Irish Catholic descent, remembers it as 'a bloodbath … the BM were battered and beaten all over the venue'.

Another eyewitness reports, 'It proper went off. It wasn't just a five-minute thing: the BM fought back viciously. There were injuries on both sides.' Eve Libertine just recalls 'swathes of people covered in blood'.

Crass went ballistic. They distrusted the far Left as much as they disliked the far Right; they preferred to have a dialogue with 'the boneheads', and win them over one on one. After the Conway Hall carnage, Crass furiously denounced the Trots as 'red fascists'. Later they wrote them off as 'Left-wing macho street fighters willing to kick arse' and revealed their own 'bigotry and blindness' in the process.

Many of the anarcho-punks who followed them found the band's attitude infuriating, however. They saw Crass's apparent defence of the BM as proof of the band's detachment from the depressing reality of their lives.

Much of Crass's audience was made up of out-of-town runaways and squatters; Nazi skins had been attacking them for months, particularly around the King's Cross squat estates. There are many horrific anecdotal reports of rapes and beatings, and of terrified punks being doused in petrol. Now the attacks intensified.

From that night on, Crass started to experience regular trouble at their gigs. 'Retribution took place,' says singer Steve Ignorant. 'People were getting chased down train lines outside the Moonlight club; they were ambushed on the way to the gigs.'

These brutal tactics were to spawn a new, tougher breed of anarcho-punks. Some of them were later drawn to Class War – a violent, revolutionary anarchist organisation formed in 1983 by Ian Bone and Martin Wright. Meanwhile, those SWP hooligans went on to form Red Action, and later Anti-Fascist Action, after being expelled from the Party two years later (see Chapter 16, 'Blowing in the Wind').

In fairness to Crass, their patient conversations with self-styled far-Right skins did occasionally pay off.

'A few of them were proper ideological Nazis,' says left-wing poet Garry Johnson. 'But most of them were confused teenagers looking for an identity and Crass did get through to a few of them. They made them think. The irony is, if the BM ever had come to power, kids like them would have ended up in jail – if they were lucky.'

The Conway Hall riot was a mighty long way from the hippy roots of the anarcho-punk scene. The key figure in this movement was Jeremy John Ratter, a posh-boy art student turned *avant-garde* performance artist, who in 1967 set up a pacifist commune/squat in Ongar, Essex, called Dial House (a Grade 2 listed, 16th-century cottage). Middlesex-born Ratter, soon to be better known as Penny Rimbaud, was heavily involved in the free festival movement of the early seventies at Windsor and Stonehenge. Rimbaud took his name from the gay French poet Arthur Rimbaud ('alf-a-penny, geddit?) and was a hippy through and through. So it came as some surprise when in 1977, at the age (he said) of 34, he formed the punk band Crass with Steve Williams, a young working-class Bowie fan. Williams was born in Stoke on Trent, but grew up with his grandparents in Dagenham, Essex, after his parents divorced. The Crass connection came about because Steve's elder brother Dave, a Zen Buddhist, had been involved with Rimbaud in the performance-art event EXIT. Steve had wanted to be a priest, but seeing the early punk bands and listening to Penny's poetry reading won him over. He was reborn as Steve Ignorant.

Rimbaud had taken the Sex Pistols 'Anarchy in the UK' as a genuine statement of political intent. But punk anarchy was never that. The Pistols had used the word to signify a vague nihilistic rebellion, self as social incendiary device. For the Damned, anarchy was one long custard-pie fight. For Wattie Buchan of the Exploited it was apocalyptic chaos. But Crass saw themselves firmly as political activists in the tradition of the Angry Brigade. An early Crass poster claimed, 'GERMANY GOT BAADER-MEINHOFF, ENGLAND GOT PUNK. BUT THEY CAN'T KILL IT.' It was typical Rimbaud cobblers. Baader-Meinhof were also known as the Red Army Faction and were a German terrorist group. They described themselves as Communists, grew out of student protests of the sixties and were responsible for 37 murders. Yet Rimbaud's lyrics advocated pacifism, woolly-minded feminism and rural self-sufficiency – surely some contradiction here?

Crass represented an attempt to hijack punk by the kind of hippies the first punks detested. Or they were a righteous alternative to the way punk's first standard-bearers were selling out across the board. You decide.

Either way, what made them significant is that they believed in something, and they took punk's DIY ethic to the logical extreme by releasing their music on their own label, booking their own gigs and bringing out their own publication, *International Anthem* ('a nihilist newspaper for the living').

At first it was going to be just the two of them, Rimbaud and Ignorant, performing as the Stormtroopers, but Crass blossomed into a seven-piece: Ignorant (vox), Rimbaud (drums), Joy De Vivre (vocals, guitar, keyboard), Phil Clancey, a.k.a. Phil Free (guitar, vocals), Eve Libertine (vocals), Andy Palmer (guitar), Pete Wright (bass, vocals).

Their name came from a line in Bowie's 'Ziggy Stardust': 'The kids were just crass' (not sure who had the 'God-given ass' – possibly Eve). The band's first gig was at a squatters' free festival and their first release was on Small Wonder, the small east London label that also brought the Cockney Rejects mewling and puking into the music business. *The Feeding of the Five Thousand* was a 17-track EP, including the song 'Punk is Dead': 'Punk was just a way of bemoaning the fact / A whole generation was afraid to act.' The first song, 'Reality Asylum', was a virulent attack on Christianity. Pressing-plant workers in Ireland were so offended by it that they refused to press it up, so it was replaced by two minutes of silence called 'The Sound of Free Speech' (easily the best track on the EP).

The music was minimalist, devoid of melody; the lyrics were uncompromising but largely impenetrable.

Intrigued by an early tape of the record, I gave Crass their first ever review. The piece I wrote in *Sounds* was gently mocking: 'Such is the strength of their beliefs that they hide away in a cottage commune where they pick potatoes ...' I also mentioned their mostly middle-class backgrounds and Rimbaud's age, before summing it up as 'thirty minutes of invigorating energy'. I liked their rage and stencil lettering, if not particularly their sound, their image, or their macrobiotic communal living. They wore black and appeared to flirt with fascism (their look was half-inched from Woody Woodmansey's U-Boat, formed by Woody after he had left Bowie's Spiders From Mars band). Their symbol – a deleted cross in a circle – looked uncomfortably like a swastika.

But the lyrics of songs like the anthem 'Do They Owe Us a Living?' (*no!*) placed them firmly at the dropout end of old-fashioned 'underground' politics.

When the record was released, my review was harsher. 'They claim to be anarchists and hide behind CND badges,' I wrote. 'How relevant. They write lyrics a lot like/this and sometimes LIKE/THIS and being middle class they think class doesn't matter.' The lyrics were 'Teach Yourself Anarchy', punctuated with plenty of fucks for street cred (Crass's rage often bordered on childish petulance). The piece concluded that the band were 'full of shit, spirited shit maybe'. In

*NME*, Tony Parsons concurred, calling Crass 'facile and offensive'. They later hit back with the splendid song 'Hurry Up Garry (The Parson Farted)'.

Neither bad reviews nor the later violent backlash from neo-Nazis could derail the Crass train.

As the punk scene split and spiralled off in wildly different directions, Crass were surprised to find that they were developing a street army of followers – many of them were dropouts and, as we've seen, out-of-town runaways living in squats; displaced radicals, hungry for an ideology to suit their lifestyle. Crass with their hatred of Little People and normality gave them that. They also glorified their giro-cheque ethic – living on state benefits was redefined as subversion in 'Do They Owe Us a Living?' – and created an omnipresent look.

Crass bequeathed to their followers the standard anarcho-punk uniform of black, black and more black. (If they're all rebels, why do they look identical? asked cynics.) It was scruff-bag chic, often with related hygiene issues, a million miles from the cleanliness and aspiration of mod or the smartness of real skinheads.

'They were the not-so-great unwashed,' laughs mod turned scooterist Barrie Taylor. 'Horrible, scruffy bastards; worse than the rockers because they made such a racket and got on your tits with their preaching. Fuckin' Crass. All Crass meant was the hippies were wearing black now.'

For Rimbaud, wearing nihilistic puritan black was a protest against the 'peacock preoccupations' of the fashion industry. The anarcho-punk look was easy to copy, cheap and readily replenished in charity shops and army-surplus stores. And it helped on demos – making it harder for the cops to identify individuals. Leather went out the window – no animals would be harmed or farmed in the making of this uniform. Brand-name jeans were out too. It was all durable cotton and moleskin jackets.

Male and female dressed identically. Anarcho-punk was as non-sexist as it was sexless – which is why part of the audience would be wooed away by the likes of Adam & the Ants and Bauhaus. And, as a depressing contrast to punk's love affair with sulphate, Tuinal was to be the squatter-punk's drug of choice – a powerful barbiturate depressant that promotes dependency and comes with a high risk of OD'ing. The ultimate escape from reality.

As well as attacking their critics, Rimbaud laid into rival strands of punk, disingenuously dismissing Oi! as 'the greatest working-class rip-off'. If any of the Oi! bands had been bothered, they might have asked the question, Are Crass real anarchists? Many genuine anarcho-syndicalists disliked the band's rekindled hippy ethos, and their retreat into personal politics.

Above all, they took the fun out of punk.

Yet Crass rapidly attracted and inspired other groups into their orbit, releasing records by the Poison Girls, Flux of Pink Indians, Omega Tribe, Rudimentary Peni, Anthrax, Annie Anxiety, the Cravats, the wonderful teenage runaway Honey Bane, Icelandic band Kulk, and Conflict, who represented the working-class wing of the movement, living on the Coldharbour Estate in Eltham, south London, and advocating direct action for the Animal Liberation Front etc. Crass released Conflict's debut EP, *A House That Man Built*, in 1982. They were angrier and far more confrontational than their mentors but just as tuneless.

Crass seemed to realise the limitations of their musical straitjacket. By their third album, 1981's *Penis Envy*, they consciously softened their sound. They even found a sense of humour and began to pull off clever stunts, the best being the flexi-disc they conned *Loving* magazine into giving away: 120,000 copies of a track from the album – 'Our Wedding' by Joy De Vivre – were distributed free with this soppy romantic mag aimed at teenage girls; the band's anti-marriage feminist claptrap reached a much wider audience than 'Reality Asylum' ever would. The giveaway offer came from an outfit called Creative Recording and Sound Services – CRASS.

Twenty-thousand copies of another flexi-disc, the antiwar 'Sheep Farming in the Falklands', were slipped inside the sleeves of other records by sympathetic bods at the Rough Trade Records distribution warehouse.

Crass pulled off a more sophisticated hoax after the war, when the band used samples of Margaret Thatcher's and Ronald Reagan's voices to fake a conversation that suggested Europe would be nuked in any conflict between the USA and the Soviets. This 'Thatcher-gate' tape was leaked anonymously to the press. The CIA suspected the KGB, but the *Observer* revealed the true perpetrators.

After Maggie was re-elected in 1983, Crass brought out the single 'Whodunnit?' on 'shit-coloured vinyl' with the lyric, 'Birds put the turd in custard, who put the shit in Number Ten?'

Crass broke up in 1984, although Rimbaud and some of the others continued as the Crass Collective. They were an important band in that they revived the fortunes of CND in the eighties, and their legacy lives on in the shape of crusties, Stop the City demos, Poll Tax rioters, hunt saboteurs, New Age travellers and deep-green and anti-globalisation protestors.

The po-faced new puritans who recently invaded Heathrow telling working-class travellers their holidays were 'immoral' almost certainly owe their doom-mongering existence and apocalyptic vision to Crass and the movement they spawned.

It is a movement that has underlined the failure of modern protest to reflect or connect with mainstream opinion. The wilful separateness of 1980s-style radical politics has succeeded only in alienating the very masses – Rimbaud's hated 'little people' – upon whom social change is dependent.

All Crass really offered was an asylum from reality.

# CHAPTER ELEVEN

# WELCOME TO HELL: HELL'S ANGELS AND HEADBANGERS

'DESPITE EVERYTHING THE PSYCHIATRISTS AND FREUDIAN CASUISTS HAVE
TO SAY ABOUT THEM, THE HELL'S ANGELS ARE TOUGH, MEAN AND
POTENTIALLY AS DANGEROUS AS A PACK OF WILD BOAR.'
Hunter S Thompson

27 April 2002. A simmering turf war between two rival motorcycle gangs, the Hell's Angels and the Mongols, erupted into violence early on a Saturday morning at Harrah's hotel and casino, Las Vegas. Highways in and out of the desert town were closed for several hours as police called in from all over the state struggled to contain the fighting.

Around 30 Angels had ridden to Harrah's in search of Mongols, with whom they had been feuding for 18 months. An initial face-off between rival gang members turned into a brawl involving around 70 people as gamblers in the casino took cover beneath slot machines and gaming tables. Aniko Kegyulics, 25, who was at the casino bar, said 'We saw a bunch of people fighting and then suddenly we heard gunshots. Bang! Bang! Bang! Everybody hit the floor.'

A police spokesman said videotapes from the security cameras showed 'a lot of shooting and a lot of stabbing. It's horrific.' Thirteen people were treated in hospital for gunshot and stab wounds. Three bodies, believed to be bikers involved in starting the trouble, were found. Another biker, 28-year-old Christian Tate, was found dead beside his motorbike less than an hour later on the highway near Ludlow. Police say he was shot on his bike and that his death was 'likely connected in some way'.

The following year, armed cops raided dozens of Hell's Angels clubhouses in the climax of a two-year undercover operation that implicated them in prostitution, drug dealing and drug manufacture, gambling, arson, extortion, contract killings and murder. The operation, the largest coordinated action against the Angels for almost two decades, resulted in the confiscation of 127 firearms, 1,000 rounds of ammunition, military explosives, methamphetamine and four stolen vehicles. Fifty-five gang members and their associates were arrested and many faced federal murder charges – primarily over the Vegas shootout (which had been billed as a bikers' 'peace conference' during the annual Laughlin River Run convention).

The Hell's Angels were never a youth cult. When the American popular press caught onto them in 1964, all post-1945 generations were represented in their ranks. The Angels were the most extreme element of America's outlaw biker tradition, which really took off after the end of World War Two, swelled by disillusioned/discontented demobbed veterans. A riot in Hollister, California, on Independence Day 1947 was an early warning of the madness to come. Four thousand cyclists converged on the town, gatecrashing a speedway event. Drunkenness and brawls abounded. When seven bikers were arrested, a mob of riders descended on the town jail and freed them. The police were powerless to prevent them.

The Hell's Angels were just one of hundreds of outlaw biker gangs that had been formed mainly by angry and frustrated young men back from the war. Outlaw bikers rapidly became America's national bogeymen. They proudly sported a '1%er' badge to signify their allegiance to the alleged 1 per cent of US bike riders the American Motorcycle Association understandably spurned. Brando's *The Wild One* established the biker worldwide as a potent symbol of rebellion and nonconformity.

The Hell's Angels Motorcycle Club was first founded in San Bernardino, California, in 1948, and steadily built up a reputation for violence, rape and criminal activities (principally dealing in narcotics). Members were distinguished by their 'colours' – a patch embroidered on the back of their cut-off denim jackets showing a leering winged death's head wearing a motorcycle helmet, with 'HELL'S ANGELS' written above, and 'MC' and the area of origin below. Scruffiness was a virtue. Angels had long, unkempt hair, were unshaven or bearded, and wore 'lived-in' T-shirts, jeans held up with a length of bike chain, which doubled as a weapon, and heavy boots. The basic uniform was augmented by Nazi patches and badges (the better to outrage respectable society), and a '13' patch denoting the 13th letter on the alphabet, M, standing for marijuana. Their traditional mode of transport was a heavy US-built bike, principally the Harley-Davidson. They were the souped-up sons of the old Wild West outlaws who were so obviously their spiritual forefathers.

For years they lived out their lives of brutality and coarse sexual practices (for example, an Angel could earn his 'red wings' by performing cunnilingus on a menstruating woman) unnoticed by straight society. But then media coverage of the Monterey rape trial in September 1964 jettisoned the biker gang into international notoriety.

Four Angels were charged with raping two underage girls. It didn't matter that the men were acquitted of charges, the news hounds had scented blood – not to mention guts, beer and semen – and they proceeded to spray their scandal-hungry readership with the whole sordid package. The effect was immediate. In California, the Angels' numbers rocketed, and all over the US 'chapters' of Angels were given the right to use the name.

West Coast liberals immediately identified with the Angels,

simplistically seeing them as being on their side because of the vitriol the press and the Establishment unleashed in their direction. It was the old 'my enemy's enemy must be my friend' syndrome. Alan Ginsberg and Ken Kesey eulogised them. Mick Farren wrote, 'The Hell's Angels Motorcycle Club is the American Dream. They are self-proclaimed Outlaws, their creed is one of freedom, of pride, of male domination. They drink, they brawl, they act like Lords of Creation. Current society is unable to tolerate the degree of individualism that it takes to become an Angel.'

But the middle-class wet dream of the street-brawling Angels as their revolutionary, noble-savage strike force was shattered for ever when, not long after the 'Summer of Love', the Angels sided with Reagan and Rockwell and smashed into a Berkeley peace march, their swastika medallions glistening in the sun.

Ralph 'Sonny' Barger, the head of the Oaklands chapter, even offered to lead a crack troop of hardened Angel guerrillas against the Vietcong (see Chapter 16, 'Blowing in the Wind').

In December 1968, two Angels flew into London, where they met up with the legendary east London rocker Buttons. Impressed, they persuaded Buttons to sample the Angel lifestyle. After spending half a year living like a new barbarian with the Californian gang, Buttons returned to Blighty with the official club charter for the Hell's Angels, England. When an unofficial chapter opened in Windsor in 1979, the Angels shot them.

It certainly wasn't the first, or the last, killing associated with the gang.

On 6 December 1969, the Rolling Stones gave a free concert at the Altamont Speedway track in California. The bill included Santana, Jefferson Airplane, the Flying Burrito Brothers and Crosby, Stills & Nash. The Grateful Dead were scheduled to play but pulled out because of the atmosphere of violence at the event. The Altamont gig is remembered not for the line-up but for the murder of an 18-year-old black man called Meredith Hunter by Hell's Angels high on LSD. It is widely but wrongly believed that the Stones hired the Angels as security for the venue, paying them with $500 worth of beer. The venue's owner, Dick Carter, however, insists that he had hired sufficient security guys and that the Angels were just there for the gig. 'Most of the articles about Altamont are filled with bull,' he says. 'We had every off-duty police officer available and every security guard in Northern California there. About seventeen Angels came to the concert because they were in Oakland for a convention. Sam Cutler, then the Stones' manager, asked if the Angels would escort the Stones through the crowd on motorcycles and then sit around the stage during the show to protect the band. We had purchased $500 worth of beer for the bands, and Cutler told the Angels they could have some.'

Cutler himself said, 'The only agreement there ever was ... the Angels would make sure nobody fucked with the generators, but that was the extent of it. But there was no "They're going to be the police force" or anything like that. That's all bollocks.'

As the evening progressed the excited crowd pressed towards the stage and the Angels fought them back. Among them was Meredith Hunter and his white girlfriend. High on methamphetamine, Hunter started brandishing a handgun. The Angels said that he waved it at Mick Jagger and threatened to kill him – the documentary film *Gimme Shelter* clearly shows him wielding a pistol. One of the Hell's Angels stabbed him, and others kicked him to death.

Jagger later wept as he watched the murder replayed in slow motion. But Stones guitarist Keith Richards said, 'People were just asking for it ... all those nude, fat people. They had victims' faces.'

The case went to trial, where the judge ruled that Meredith Hunter's death had been justifiable homicide. But Jagger refused to use the Angels as security again. Years later, a BBC Radio 4 documentary reported that the Angels were so infuriated at what they saw as an outrageous snub that they cooked up a plot to murder Mick at home at his estate in the Hamptons in Long Island, New York.

They planned to enter the property by sea so that they could come up through the grounds avoiding his front-gate security. The assassination attempt was aborted only when their vessel capsized in rough seas. They were thrown overboard. All survived, but no further attempts were made on Jagger's life. The BBC reported that the plot had been discovered by the FBI, who later infiltrated the gang. Mick hadn't known a thing about it.

The following summer, the English chapter ran riot at the Bath Music Festival at Shepton Mallet. President Buttons said, 'The festival is not a place to recruit people. It's a place to annihilate them.'

In August 1971 three English Angels were jailed in Colchester, Essex, after 39 of them had terrorised the Weeley pop festival. Hundreds of pounds' worth of catering equipment was smashed with iron bars after a fight erupted between the bikers and stallholders. When vigilantes vandalised their motorbikes, the Angels were 'hell-bent on revenge'. The prosecution told of an orgy of 'robbery, violence, blackmail and terror'.

The following year, in Winchester, an Angel marched a 14-year-old Girl Guide off the street and raped her in a café in front of 'laughing, cheering' gang members during a national Hell's Angel convention. Ian 'Moose' Everest, 18, of Rochester, Kent, pleaded guilty to abduction and rape.

It quickly became obvious even to radicals with the rosiest-tinted bins that one thing the Angels weren't was revolutionary. But they did capture the public imagination. In Britain, a mass market in Angels-related fiction sprang up to rival the Richard Allen Skinhead series of books. The big sellers were by Peter Cave, Alex R Stuart, Mick Norman and Thorn Ryder. Norman's *Guardian Angels* put the outlaw bikers on a pedestal: 'These were not men of the nineteen-eighties,' he wrote, 'used to slick suits and the soft answer. There was a primitive violence and strength in the Angels.' Girls in Norman's world were 'for screwing and nothing else'. Rather riskily, he even hints of latent homosexuality in an Angel initiation ceremony. 'Gerry Vinson, who had been drinking heavily ready to play his part, stepped up first and took the honours as president. He unzipped his trousers and urinated over the prospect's back, shoulders and legs, reserving a little for the last to spray into Shelob's hair.' In *Angels on My Mind*, Norman's fourth and final Vinson story, the Angel is kidnapped by a crazed cop and disappointingly subjected to therapy by his shrink girlfriend.

When the bottom fell out of the market for Angel-related fiction, Peter Cave turned to soft porn and Stuart took bikers into the occult in *The Bike from Hell* and *The Devil's Rider*.

Globally, the Hell's Angels moved inexorably into organised crime to sustain their nonconformist lifestyle. Drugs, prostitution and protection rackets came first, followed later by killings.

During the 1990s, however, the Angels had tried to shed their criminal reputation, claiming they were now more concerned with charitable work than hellraising. In the USA, rallies were staged to raise money for children's hospitals. However, the rise of rival gangs – the Pagans and Outlaws on the East Coast, the Bandidos in Texas and Mongols in California – caused an intensifying of the turf wars over prostitution and drugs profits.

Many of the new gangs were primarily Hispanic and from inner-city areas. The Angels responded with a recruitment drive in which small gangs were persuaded to join them for a share of the spoils from their various rackets.

In July 2003, FBI agents in Arizona arrested 18 Angels and their associates on charges that included a murder-for-hire scheme and illegal weapons use. The follow-up raids occurred in Southern California, Arizona, Nevada, Washington and Alaska. They involved several hundred federal agents. In San Francisco, the gang's city headquarters on Tennessee Street was raided at 6am. Agents armed with assault rifles ringed the street while officers broke down the wall from an adjacent house to get into the building.

Donald Kincaid, of the Bureau of Alcohol, Tobacco, Firearms and Explosives, said the operation had exposed the continued criminal nature of elements within the motorcycle gang. 'If you have a toys-for-tots run on the same day you're cooking methamphetamine, which is your real persona?' he asked.

However, George Christie, a long-time Angels leader in Southern California, dismissed the raids as a stunt. 'How many of the guns were illegal?' he asked, adding, 'I didn't know it was against the law to have ammunition. How many people were actual members? We're a long way from this getting into a courtroom.'

The Hell's Angels' capacity for limitless brutality won them the respect of even the hardest of their opponents. The Angels, and other not-quite-as-notorious but still heavy rival gangs such as the Road Rats and the Outlaws, persist in Britain and Europe to this day.

In November 2008 seven Outlaws were convicted of the murder of a Hell's Angel – the first killing on British soil after four decades of bloody global rivalry between the world's largest and most fearsome biker gangs. Gerry Tobin, a Canadian living in London, was gunned down by members of the Outlaws gang as he left a biker festival in Warwickshire. Three of the guilty men followed Tobin for 30 miles as he left the Bulldog Bash in August. They waited until he was on the M40 before pulling up alongside his Harley and shooting him in the head.

The police believe Tobin was targeted not because of who he was but simply because he was a Hell's Angel. The Outlaws have never been happy that the Bulldog Bash, a Hell's Angels festival, is held in their heartland. Detectives are also convinced Tobin's murder was, and had to be, sanctioned by the Outlaws' bosses in America. Superintendent Ken Lawrence, from Warwickshire police, told reporters, 'I can't imagine a local chapter carrying out an act such as this without sanction or awareness from someone in a much higher position.'

The seven were senior members of the Outlaws' South Warwickshire chapter. While president Sean Creighton, 44, Simon Turner, 41, and Dane Garside, 42, were in the car, Malcolm Bull, 53, Dean Taylor, 47, Karl Garside, 45, and Ian Cameron, 46, lay in wait ahead ready to murder Tobin should the initial plan fail.

The hatred between the US-based gangs began in 1969 when a

member of the Outlaws raped the wife of a Hell's Angel. Her husband and other Hell's Angels later beat the rapist almost to death in New York. In turn, three Angels were kidnapped by the Outlaws and executed at point-blank range, before their bodies were weighted down with rocks and thrown in a Florida quarry.

Since then there have been tit-for-tat incidents all over the world, with increasing activity in Britain. In 1998, the Outlaws made a specific bomb threat to the Bulldog Bash. In 2001, a Canadian man survived despite being shot three times as he left the festival. In January 2008, the machete-wielding gangs clashed violently and openly at Birmingham Airport. Four Angels and four Outlaws were arrested and charged.

And in November that year, David Melles, 52, an Outlaw from Selsey, Gloucestershire, was jailed for 12 years for amassing an illegal armoury of guns and bullets. Police found them while investigating a proposed showdown between the two gangs in Cinderford, Gloucestershire.

In August 2009 police spent more than a £1 million and used the Terrorism Act 2000 to keep order at the Bulldog Bash after failing to get it banned. Warwickshire Assistant Chief Constable Bill Holland claimed that the four-day event, which attracts up to 15,000 bikers, is a cover for organised crime and poses a risk of a violent clash between the group and its arch-rivals, the Outlaws. But the Hell's Angels themselves claimed the event was innocent fun. One, called Woo, told *The Times*, 'I came to the Bulldog Bash in a Range Rover towing a caravan,' he said. 'The wife – well, she's a bit of a five-star luxury kind of girl. I even had to leave the Harley at home.' Woo, 50, is one of 200 Hell's Angels who policed the Bash. The local cops hired officers from five neighbouring constabularies to carry out stop-and-search procedures. The 'intelligence-led' operations involved sniffer dogs. But one biker, called Slim, told reporters, 'I've just got back after eight months in Afghanistan, trying to prevent terrorism. Using the Terrorism Act to stop me is disgraceful.' Slim, now working as a civil servant at the Ministry of Defence, added, 'It wasn't intelligence-led – it's because I am wearing motorcycle-club patches on my leathers.'

Peter Barnes, chairman of Warwickshire County Council, who opened the show amid a deafening roar of engines, accused Mr Holland of wasting taxpayers' money. 'The police have overreacted. The show brings great benefits to the area's local economy.'

The Bulldog Bash prides itself on being family-orientated and raising money for charity. Help for Heroes, which raises funds for members of the forces wounded in Iraq and Afghanistan, does particularly well. Liz Murray told *The Times*, 'Some bikers are ex-servicemen, others are simply patriotic. Last year we collected £11,000.'

The local Rotary Club stall has raised more than £100,000 for charity in its 18-year association with the event.

Woo, who first joined motorcycle clubs during Northern Ireland's Troubles because they were one of the few organisations where religion was irrelevant, defended the movements. 'We have corrupt police, but not all police are corrupt. We now know that some MPs are corrupt, but not all MPs. Every organisation is made up of good and bad eggs. The Hell's Angels is no different.'

One biker from the Predators club said, 'I pulled up my leathers and showed the officer my bulletproof vest. I'm a grandfather. You can never be too careful – it's a bit like wearing a helmet,' he said. 'But the most aggressive things are these bloody wasps.'

# HEADBANGERS!

As the 1970s arrived, the Grease – the rockers and their descendents – identified less with primal rock'n'roll and increasingly with the emerging hard-rock genre (itself ironically fathered by guitar gods like Eric Clapton, formerly of mod band the Yardbirds, and Jimi Hendrix, whose own roots were in black R&B).

The most significant band to emerge were Black Sabbath, the

pioneers of heavy metal. Sabbath were no-future, working-class hooligan youth in black leather, four dead-end kids raw on talent and high on hopes, armed with savage riffs — many of them were shamelessly pirated by later punk bands. Their music was inner-city white noise coupled to lyrics about madness and the futility of war. ('War Pigs' still has a resonance now, sneering at politicians who start conflicts and leave the poor to do their fighting for them.)

Singer and housebreaker Ozzy Osbourne had been a skinhead when he met bassist Terry 'Geezer' Butler. Guitarist Tony Iommi had lost the tips of two fingers of his right hand in an industrial accident at the sheet-metal plant where he worked. These were credentials that the Clash would have given their eye teeth for.

In their first band, Earth, they'd hit on the ruse later used by the Sex Pistols of turning up at venues uninvited and claiming to be the support. They broke into chocolate-bar vending machines and ate raw vegetables pilfered from allotments to keep them going. Ozzy went on stage wearing pyjamas years before the Boomtown Rats.

Butler's song 'Black Sabbath' gave the band a new name that suited the way they felt. 'Everyone else was into flower power,' Ozzy told me. 'It made me sick and it made me angry because it was so senseless. It was all right for rich hippies in California lying back and smoking pot. But what did we have to do with that, living in Aston, Birmingham, without two pennies to rub together. The music we developed was loud and furious because that was the way we felt.'

And the audience they attracted live were just like them: mostly blokes, long-haired but too hard to be hippies, chanting 'Sabbaff, Sabbaff' as if they'd all just arrived *en masse* from the Clock End to revel in those great slabs of sound as bleak as Wormwood Scrubs and Ozzy's lyrics about youth revolution that came dripping in frustration and sedition.

Heavy metal was prole rock, and Black Sabbath were the ultimate English exponents. As Andrew Weiner wrote in 1973, 'They relate to casual street-fighting and mind-numbing boredom and schools that are day internment camps, and, above all that, the prospect of dead-end factory jobs. They relate to the entire depressing English working-class experience.'

Punk, according to its own propagandists and salesmen, was angry rock music made by working-class kids trapped in dead-end factory jobs. By that definition, Black Sabbath were a lot more punk than most of the artists and art students who adopted the name in London and New York in the mid-seventies.

At the time, their followers were known contemptuously as hairies. They wore their hair long over greatcoats bought from army-surplus stores. Loon pants were popular; baths less so.

The bulk of the emerging heavy-metal audience were non-violent. Mostly they were working-class and lower-middle-class. Regular guys. The same kind of blokes – and the audiences were predominantly male – who would follow Iron Maiden in the later part of the decade.

In 1975, prior to punk's official arrival, Ian Kilmister, better known as Lemmy, was booted out of Hawkwind 'for doing the wrong drugs' – sulphate, the punk drug of choice. The bassist immediately formed his own band, which he wanted to call Bastard, but compromised on Motörhead (motorhead is street slang for amphetamine). Speed was his drug, speed was his sound; they were louder and faster than any 1970s punk band. Lemmy wanted Motörhead to be the 'dirtiest rock'n'roll band in the world', adding, 'If we moved in next door to you, your lawn would die.' Like Sabbath, Lemmy saw his high-energy racket as the antidote to drippy-hippy flower-power drivel. In rock-dream terms, Motörhead were cowboys riding iron horses into the wildest Wild West town: the ultimate rock ambassadors of biker subculture.

Although spurned by the music press, the band made a big impact on live audiences. Their debut album, called *Motörhead*, came out in 1977 and went Top Fifty. The seminal punk fanzine *Sniffing Glue* gave it a glowing review. Mark Perry called it the most relevant album ever released. Hit singles 'Overkill' and 'Bomber' weren't far behind. By the summer of 1980 they had their first Top Ten smash. Motörhead are often cited as a forerunner of the punk–metal crossover of the eighties, but, like Iron Maiden, they were actually a parallel development to punk. They were knocking out their brand of no-fuss, no-frills rock at the same time as the Ramones. It was harder, more brutal and less melodic, but it was just as raw and just as much an antidote to the stadium rock/virtuoso orthodoxy of the time. Lemmy's lyrics didn't dilly-dally in arty allusions or lost legends: he glorified speed, war and romanticised losers. But the band saw themselves as being closer in spirit to US bands like the MC5 than heavy metal as it was then understood, which Lemmy dismissed as 'slow and ponderous'.

Stiff released a Motörhead single in 1977 ('White Line Fever') and the band played gigs with the Damned. But at no time did Lemmy cut his hair or compromise the band's sound and vision. Motörhead did their own thing their own way. They were louder, harder and heavier than the rest. But, for all the venom of their onslaught, Motörhead wrote great songs, anthems like 'Ace of Spades', 'Iron Fist' and 'Bomber', and they picked up as many punk fans as they did metal ones. The real punk–metal crossover could be seen right there in Motörhead's audiences, and the bands who sited them as influences. Those East End gutter punks the Cockney Rejects were covering Motörhead in their live set from as early as 1979.

If Lemmy had a message it was oblivion: his words urged us to escape from reality through noise.

September 1979. More than 500 fans – double the number that fire regulations allow – are packed like pilchards into the Bandwagon Heavy Metal Soundhouse. It's a glorified sweatbox of a venue on the side of the Prince of Wales pub in Kingsbury, northwest London; and the audience are the antidote to fashion, awash with denims, black-leather jackets, T-shirts, boots and hideous flares. We've all come along to see an unsigned, unfashionable, long-haired rock group from the arse end of east London. No one goes home disappointed ...

Iron Maiden were a revelation. Raw, admittedly; but everything we now associate with the cockney kings of metal was already evident in the primeval mix: that savage stampede of sound, the twin guitars blazing like forest fires, bold tempo and key changes, the emphasis on performance and those rowdy melodies, so kick-arse boisterous they'd make a vanload of tanked-up Millwall fans sound like a church choir. They were awesome.

Iron Maiden were less than a month away from landing a record label.

In five more months – on 22 February 1980 – they would make their *Top of the Pops* debut. Before another year was out they'd be on their first headlining tour of the USA and I'd be tipping my titfer at Paul Di'Anno's groupies from afar.

This particular September they were already a phenomenon – rapidly expanding fish in the small pond that was the nascent New Wave of British Heavy Metal. This cumbersome name, conjured up by *Sounds* editor Alan Lewis to accompany a piece by Geoff Barton, was to stand the test better than most. Maiden were the vanguard, then Saxon, Def Leppard, Venom, Angel Witch, Blitzkrieg, Demon, Diamond Head, Raven, Sledgehammer, Tank, Samson, Savage, Satan, the Tygers of Pan Tang, Witchfynde, Bastille, Ethel the Frog, Toad the Wet Sprocket and more. But where had they come from? How was this happening? Heavy metal was dead and buried. The *NME* had held a wake and everything. Trouble is, no one seemed to have told the fans.

'I liked some punk,' says metal fan Darren Brown. 'I liked the Pistols and that. But I couldn't stand all the bollocks that went with it. All those silly-bollocks see-through strides and bondage pants. What a fucking rip-off! You'd read all the shit in the music press about punk coming from council estates and tower blocks and when you met them they were all students or dropouts from a rich background. Fakes in other words.

'Me and my mates were from a Hackney council estate. We grew up loving Aerosmith and Thin Lizzy and we weren't going to stop loving them because some tosser in the *NME* had decided they were out of style. We'd go and see bands like Maiden early doors because we loved their music and they were down to earth like we were. It was good honest rock for good honest people. It didn't pretend to be something it wasn't. That's why it caught on.'

Iron Maiden were the most important group in the whole NWOBHM phenomenon. To begin with, with the notable exception of *Sounds*, the music press treated Maiden with the same disdain as they did Motörhead. The band were seen as an aberration and as such they were to be ignored or written off as musical throwbacks. When neither tactic worked, the east London band were redefined as 'post-punk' metal. Wrong again. Consider the history. The first Iron Maiden line-up got together at Christmas 1975, more than 11 months before the Bill Grundy TV interview dragged the Sex Pistols and punk rock kicking and gobbing into the national consciousness. And the seeds of this apparent 'overnight success' had been planted as long before as 1972.

At 15, Steve 'Harry' Harris had packed in training for West Ham's youth team to pursue a dream of rock'n'roll infamy. 'I wanted to drink and I wanted to chat up women; the training got in the way,' he explained a few years later. And, of course, rock offered far more chance of scoring.

He bought himself a Copy Fender Telecaster for £40, taught himself to play and jammed with schoolmate guitarist Dave Smith. They were into bands like Wishbone Ash, Jethro Tull, Deep Purple and UFO; later Judas Priest and the Scorpions. With Paul Sears on drums and singer Bob Verschoyle, the two pals became Gypsy's Kiss, rhyming slang for— Aw, work it out yourself – it's no big riddle.

Harry left Leyton County High School in Leytonstone, east London, with four O-levels and landed a job as an apprentice draughtsman. When he was made redundant he swept streets and worked briefly as a dustman.

What he did as a day job didn't matter that much to him as long as the band could rehearse and play at night.

The Gypsies gigged sporadically, slashing their way through a set that consisted mostly of period-piece covers such as 'Paranoid', 'All Right Now', 'Smoke on the Water' and 'Blowing Free'. In between, they'd play their own early Harris-penned originals with names like 'Heat-Crazed Vole' and 'Endless Pit' (*not* rhyming slang!) – part of which was to become the Maiden anthem 'Innocent Exile'.

After six gigs, the Gypsies kissed off and Harry joined another east London outfit called Smiler, a no-brains rock-a-boogie blues band who gigged regularly. The experience was invaluable for Harry, but he felt restricted. Smiler did play a boogified version of 'Innocent Exile' but turned down what H calls his first 'proper song', 'Burning Ambition', on the grounds that 'it had too many key changes'. How sick must they feel now?

So Harry quit. 'I knew I had to form my own band,' he told me. 'I knew what I was aiming for. I wanted a hard-rock band who would take risks with tempo changes and experiment a bit.' That band was Iron Maiden, the name taken from an obsolete instrument of torture (and not from Maggie Thatcher, who some said shared that definition).

Fired by Harry's determination, Maiden defied music-biz trends, stuck to their guns and carved out something unique, long-lasting and magical.

Their first line-up was Harry (bass), Terry Rance (guitar), Paul Day (vox), Dave Sullivan (guitar) and, don't mock, Ron Rebel (drums).

Their first gig was at the Cart & Horses pub in Stratford, east London. 'A khazi,' Harry recalls with a grin. 'The place was so small we had to change in the bogs.' Their first set included such seminal Maiden standards as 'Prowler', 'Transylvania', 'Innocent Exile', 'Burning Ambition' and the messianic set-closer 'Iron Maiden' itself, which included the immortal line 'Iron Maiden's gonna get you, no matter how far ...'

At the time he wrote them, young Steve Harris had no idea how prophetic those words would prove to be.

Over the following years Iron Maiden gigged solidly round the east

London circuit, working such infamous rock pubs as the Bridgehouse, Canning Town and the Ruskin Arms in East Ham.

Their existence had no presence in the music press save for the gig guide adverts where they always billed themselves poetically. 'The only band worth seeing … bleed, shock and rock,' boasted one ad. 'We break, shake, shock and rock – we make the rest look average stock,' read another.

Ever the perfectionist, Harry tinkered with the line-up constantly until he got both the sound and the level of visual energy he desired. For a while the band were about as stable as an Italian coalition government.

Out went Paul Day, in came Smiler's old singer Dennis Wilcock, who later quit and was replaced by Jack the Lad Essex boy Paul Di'Anno – a real showboater who won over fans with his cheeky-chappie stage persona. Nimble-fingered Maiden favourite Dave Murray was an early recruit as lead guitarist, until after six months he rowed with Wilcock and went off to join Urchin with his pal Adrian Smith. Ron Rebel was replaced by Barry 'Thunderstick' Purkis, who in turn handed on his stool to Doug Sampson (also ex-Smiler). Harry experimented with an organist, Tony Moore, for one gig only. When Moore didn't work out Dave Murray's replacement Terry Wapram (ex-Hooker) quit, so Harry talked Murray back into the frenetic fold. There were other line-up changes along the route, including guitarists Tony Parsons (not the *NME* writer) and Paul Nelson, but, as Harry insisted, 'We had to get it right.'

And what was right? As their own advert modestly put it, Iron Maiden became the 'best visual, high energy, loud but talented, good-looking, tasteful, heart-breaking, hard-hitting, bloodsucking, mind-blowing hard rock band in London.'

Paul Di'Anno has a more jaundiced take on it, saying, 'Steve was the one with the driving ambition. Iron Maiden was his baby and it definitely wasn't a democracy. But he was proved right. If you cut Steve in half – and the thought did occur to me a few times when I was in the band – he'd probably have "Iron Maiden" running through him like a stick of rock.'

Di'Anno's commitment was less impressive. By his own admission Paul had gone to the audition in the Green Man, Leytonstone, only because he wanted to pull the Swedish barmaid who worked there.

Along the way the band accumulated a following withcrowd-pleasing singalong anthems such as 'Charlotte the Harlot' and the other elements of Maiden imagery that remain part of their splendid, soaraway shtick to this day: horror visuals, historical epics and, of course, Eddie, their monstrous mascot, who started as just a mouth spewing blood.

In 1977, Maiden's big problem was getting gigs outside of east London. Nearly every other venue in the capital had gone over to punk. Various record companies, agents and wannabe managers tried to persuade the band to lop off their locks and sell out for short-lived fame and fortune of the filth-and-fury kind. One pushy wannabe manager even booked them into punk's most legendary club, the Roxy. But Harry resolutely refused to change and the Roxy gig was never played. 'They said heavy rock was as welcome as a dose of clap,' he recalls. 'But as soon as anyone told us we were good but we should go New Wave or commercial we'd just say OK and leave.'

As punk rapidly became big business, this determination not to sell out took real guts. Instead, Maiden slogged away on the East End circuit, branching out further east to places like the Plough & Harrow in Leytonstone and the Harrow in Ripple Road, Barking – even further afield from anywhere record company A&R men dared to venture. But the band's fans from Stratford and Canning Town followed them out. Suddenly, they had an away crowd: bikers, and factory workers, football fans – a solidly working-class bunch. There was no uniform, but the fans had a fairly standard look: black leather or denim jackets, hair worn shoulder length or longer, T-shirts, boots or trainers, belts (often studded) and straight jeans. Maiden dressed like their head-banging fans and vice versa. Not for them the appalling fashion *faux pas* associated with certain rock bands (coloured leathers, jockstraps worn over trousers, loin clothes ...).

It was only when Maiden travelled to Lancashire and Yorkshire later on that they encountered the famous Northern 'trouser problem': young teenage metal fans sporting flairs wide enough to house the entire Nolan Family clan. Tragic.

Devil-may-care vocalist Di'Anno cemented the band's already strong relationship with the audience. Di'Anno, with his short hair, pork-pie hat, bellowed lyrics and barrow-boy persona, was far more blue-collar than sour-faced 'punk' scribes such as Ian Penman and Paul Morley. 'When we get time off we go and see West Ham and I act the hooligan,' he said. He compared Maiden to Australia's blue-collar hard-rock heroes AC/DC: 'regular guys' in a 'no-nonsense group … like us, they're down to earth.'

The Ruskin Arms became Iron Maiden's base – they could play it four nights a week and still pack it out every gig. But Harry knew they had to go beyond local-hero status and so, on New Year's Eve 1978, the band began recording their first demo tape at the Spacewood Studios in Cambridge.

In two days, at a cost of £200, they laid down four tracks, all Steve Harris compositions: 'Iron Maiden', 'Invasion', 'Prowler' and 'Strange World' (and all, incidentally, written on a bass and in pieces – one of the keys to their distinct sound). Because they were penniless, the band relied on Di'Anno's charms to sweet-talk a local nurse into putting them up for the nights. Paul paid a terrible price in the shape of a nasty little rash. 'And her a nurse,' he later moaned. 'No wonder the NHS is falling apart.' His sacrifice was worthwhile. These songs were the band's passport out of the pisspot pubs of east London. The demo led them to the three not-so-wise men who would play crucial parts in their destiny: Neil Kay, Rod Smallwood and Geoff Barton.

Kay, the resident rock DJ at the Soundhouse in Kingsbury, was a peculiar-looking cove, much akin to a sawn-off Catweazle; but he believed in metal with a fanaticism worthy of the Japanese imperial army. The Soundhouse wasn't a disco, it was a crusade – and he used it to promote new rock bands. Requests from Kay's regulars were compiled into a Top Twenty chart that ran in the rock weekly *Sounds*. Maiden's frequent appearance at Number 1 caught the interest of staff writer Geoff Barton and when Kay took his rock crusade on the road, it was the visionary editor Al Lewis who lumbered the phenomenon with the accurate if unwieldy name of the New Wave of British Heavy Metal or NWOBHM for short.

The bands on the bill were Samson, Angel Witch and Iron Maiden. Later names such as Saxon, Def Leppard and Sledgehammer were tossed into the mix. There was no doubt in Barton's mind that Maiden were the big hitters – as EMI's later abortion of a compilation album, *Metal for Mothers*, was to prove. This era also gave the world mad Maiden fan Rob Loonhouse and the new circle of hell that is air-guitar playing.

Rod 'Small-wallet' Smallwood enters the picture around this time – a non-graduate of Trinity College, Cambridge, who once promoted May balls with his student pal Andy Taylor. Yorkshireman Smallwood booked Maiden two showcase gigs out of the East End. 'I was very impressed,' he told me. 'I'd never seen a band who looked the audience straight in the eye and enjoyed themselves like they did – and do.' Rod became a key player in the Maiden story. Not only did he become the unofficial sixth member of the band, keeping them clean and scandal free (a big job in Di'Anno's case), but also with Andy Taylor he put the whole operation on a business footing, sowing the seeds for their long-time financial growth and stability.

Smallwood put together Maiden's first UK tour dates. He also blagged them their first Marquee headliner (19 October 1979) – the West End venue had turned them down umpteen times before – in order to lure lazy industry talent scouts out to see them. By December they had signed with EMI.

Two months later they made their first appearance on *Top of the Pops* and caused off-camera grief by refusing to mime. Paul Di'Anno was the first person to sing live on the BBC1 show for almost a decade.

But he was to last only two albums with the band before his love of what was euphemistically called the rock'n'roll life-style (i.e. drink, drugs – mainly coke and speed – and dubious women) got too much for the rest to take. They got their kicks from booze, soccer and Jimmy Jones comedy tapes.

I won't mention the Reeperbahn if they don't.

With the Soundhouse tracks released independently as a limited 5,000 pressing for fans, Maiden set about recording their first studio album with producer Will Malone, who had cut his teeth on *Tubular Bells*.

Martin Birch, who'd worked with Deep Purple, produced the second. By this stage Clive Burr was on drums and funny cockney guitarist Dennis Stratton had been and gone – replaced by Adrian Smith, Dave Murray's childhood pal from Hackney. They'd already toured Europe supporting Kiss. To promote *Killers*, Maiden embarked on their first world tour, making initial inroads into the USA (on later US tours they imported British beans and Ruddles beer to sustain them). The final sound-defining line-up change was Di'Anno's replacement, former Samson singer Bruce Dickinson, in many ways an even bigger rebel than he was. Even Paul acknowledges Bruce was 'the best singer the band has ever had'. Di'Anno was rougher, rawer, more 1979 British rock. Bruce, the 'human air-raid siren', was more suited to the international arena and Maiden's future as a world-class rock act.

The proof in plastic came with the Martin Birch-produced *The Number of the Beast*, the band's classic third album. From this point on the Maiden story is pretty well established. Michael 'Nicko' McBrain joined as drummer for the Piece of Mind tour and has stayed ever since. He had double appeal for the rest of the lads. Not only had they seen him play with French band Trust on their Killers tour, but he'd also once played with their favourite funny man Jimmy Jones (who had sacked him for being 'too loud').

Maiden's shows have got bigger, but their feet stayed resolutely on the ground. Every time I catch up with Harry he wants to talk about football, music and movies. He still loves the Hammers with a passion. And he still makes sure the fans get value for money. Pleasingly, years of international acclaim haven't changed him or the band one jot.

Behind Maiden the band to make the biggest impact in Britain were Saxon, the big teasers from Barnsley. These tea-drinking sons of Yorkshire miners were signed up as early as 1979 and for the first couple of years gave Maiden a run for their money in terms of album and singles sales. Their first two albums went gold and they clocked up four Top Twenty hits in 1980 and 1981: 'Wheels of Steel', '747 (Strangers in the Night)', 'And the Bands Played On' and 'Never Surrender'. Other new-metal bands were spawned in their wake, many of them incubating punklike on small independent labels such as Neat, Ebony, Heavy Metal and Bludgeon Riffola.

Neat gave the world satanic so-and-sos Venom, who were to be significant for their influence on the growing thrash-metal scene, where punk and metal met head-on in a crude car crash of aggression and tuneless racket. The trio – Cronos on bass and vocals, Mantas on guitar and Abbadon on drums – were the pioneers of black metal. Live, they sounded like sticking your head into a giant cement mixer. As someone once wrote, 'Home taping is killing music. And so are Venom.' The band from Newcastle upon Tyne were the most successful of the ludicrously named North East New Wave of British Heavy Metal (NENWOBHM). Venom debuted in 1981 with the single 'In League with Satan', which was followed by the 1982 album *Welcome to Hell*. Their second album, *Black Metal*, was the one cited as kick-starting thrash (some scholars cite the Gonads song 'TNT' as the first punk-metal musical hybrid; modesty forbids any comment from me).

In terms of global success, none of the NWOBHM bands came close to Def Leppard. It helped that they were younger and prettier than the rest, but what cracked it for them was their songs and the expert production and co-writing skills of AC/DC's producer Robert John 'Mutt' Lange.

For all their glamour, Leppard were as down to earth as their home town of Sheffield. Bassist Rick Savage, guitarist Pete Willis and drummer Tony Kenning formed a band called Atomic Mass while they were still at school. An equally young glam-rock fan called Joe Elliott auditioned to become second guitarist and ended up as singer. It was Joe who thought of the name change. The lads were working as van drivers and at a local factory when they were joined by another guitarist Steamin' Steve Clark, a lathe operator. Kenning quit and was replaced temporarily by Frank Noon. Full-time drummer Rick Allen, then just 15, joined the band in November 1978.

That year, they recorded a three-track EP called *Def Leppard* and released it on their own Bludgeon Riffola label. John Peel picked up on one track, 'Getcha Rocks Off', and gave it a good airing; that and rock-press interest were enough to get the majors sniffing around. When they signed with Phonogram in 1979, Leppard were all still teenagers. Their debut album, *On Through the Night*, came out in March 1980 and, although the single 'Hello America' charted, it seemed to piss off British audiences, who suspected the lads of being keener on breaking the States than enjoying UK success. The dimwit backlash saw Leppard pelted at the Reading Festival that August. It was Britain's loss. The band teamed up with genius producer Mutt Lange for their next album, *High 'n' Dry*. MTV played 'Bringin' on the Heartbreak'. In the summer of 1982, Pete Willis (a.k.a. 'the alcoholic midget') was replaced by the more photogenic Londoner Phil 'Phyllis' Collen, a former electrician from glam band Girl. Things were building up nicely but no one was prepared for the success of their third album. The Mutt Lange-produced *Pyromania* was a smash, selling six million copies in 1983 and spawning a trio of US hits: 'Photograph', 'Rock of Ages' and 'Foolin''. 'Photograph' overtook Michael Jackson's 'Beat It' as the most requested video on MTV.

The working-class lads from Sheffield had made it big time. I joined them on the Massachusetts leg of the tour and it was like Beatlemania, with teenage girls screaming their name and making offers that could have seen us all in jail. They were playing the Earls Court-size Cape Cod Coliseum. And the venues kept getting bigger. They ended in September playing to 55,000 in the Jack Murphy Stadium at San Diego, California. The tour was a complete sell-out, with tickets going faster in most areas for Leppard than for the

Rolling Stones. T-shirt sales were breaking all house records, including Styx and the Stones.

It was hard to credit that just four short years before Leppard were playing Woodborough Dale Miners' Welfare Club!

Leppard outsold and outstripped Iron Maiden in the USA, becoming as hysterically popular over there as Duran Duran were in Blighty. When one commentator jokingly likened them to a cross between AC/DC and the Bay City Rollers, he inadvertently hit on a perfect analogy, one that conveys both the excellence of their music and the extravagance of the audience acclaim. Yet at home *Pyromania* peaked at Number 18 in the charts; bizarre, because it was the hard-rock album of the year, establishing the band as the true inheritors of primetime UFO's mesmerising blend of muscle and melody. They had power, raunchy atmospherics, tasteful tunes and colossal chants; and the whole cataclysmic caboodle was suffused with the energy, excitement and exuberance of a lifer let loose in a Soho brothel.

Despite snooty attitudes back home, in the States they performed in Union Flag stage strips. The red, white and blue lovingly adorns their merchandising, too, resulting, comically, in hundreds of Yank fans sporting Union Flag shorts and shirts. At the time, I wrote, 'George Washington, where are you now?'

In Detroit their first show sold out in three hours of the box office opening – i.e. as fast as is humanly possible. The gig was postponed because of Joe's throat problems. Of the 28,000 Detroit tickets sold, only 50 were returned! A local radio station opened its lines to get-well messages from fans. These included one sweet-talking young lady who said, 'Hi, Joe, I wanna fuck the hell out of you,' and another who called leaving the missive 'I'm gonna chain myself to the door and I ain't gonna leave till Joe Elliot fucks me.' Rock'n'roll, doncha just love it!

Talking to Joe after the Cape Cod show, I was surprised to find how open-minded he was about music. Like most people his age, he'd grown up on glam and had more than a passing interest in punk. He adored UFO, AC/DC *et al.* – that was given – but Joe had also gone to see Chelsea and Slaughter live, had queued up to get Siouxsie's autograph, he loved *Never Mind the Bollocks*, adored the Skids, he'd lapped up the first Clash album …

'But I don't like the Clash any more,' he told me. 'They're not working-class, they're middle-class – they're making money but they're embarrassed about it. We've had nothing for four years. I guarantee when I make money, I'll let everyone know … you'd be surprised how many records we've had to sell to pay our debts back. This album did cost a lot but we'd rather do something that's quality than ship out cheap rubbish, y'know. We're not one of these take-the-money-and-run bands who are ripping yer public off.'

Real working-class punks never had a problem with rock bands. Pistols Cook and Jones were huge Thin Lizzy fans, and happily played with Phil Lynott as the Greedy Bastards in 1978. The Stranglers loved the Doors. The Damned were closet Hawkwind fans. Cockney Rejects adored Aerosmith and UFO, not to mention Queen. The affection went both ways. As early as 1977, Rob Halford of Judas Priest said, 'Punk to me is rock … I saw the Pistols and I got something from the band … our music is like an advancement of their music.'

Most 1976 punks also owed a huge debt to glam rock. Marc Bolan of T.Rex was instrumental in breaking many of the first wave on his TV show.

Punk begat the poncier New Wave and the trend took over the entire music business. Suddenly anything 'rock' was deemed unutterably unfashionable. But, for those of us on the ground, there were disturbing side effects. The so-called 'proletarian' rock revolution had ushered in a new generation of middle-class tossers. Many of us punks felt we had more in common with good, honest blue-collar rockers like AC/DC (debut album, 1977) than we did with, say, the Gang of Four.

Metal's new wave was just as down to earth as punk had been, and just as uncompromising. Maiden signed to EMI at the same time as the

Rejects, who spearheaded another anti-fashion movement, the street-punk wave known as Oi!. Like Maiden, the Rejects were thoroughly working-class and were equally hated by the UK music-press snobs. They had the same 'fuck the world, we'll do it our way and our way rocks' attitudes.

Although starting as a brick-wall punk band, after four albums the Rejects released *The Wild Ones*, produced by UFO's Pete Way and a minor classic of backstreet hard rock that stands the test of time.

As we saw earlier, Singer Jeff 'Stinky' Turner summed up the Oi! attitude as 'working-class and if you're not working-class you'll get a kick in the bollocks.' Is it any wonder the Rejects felt they had more in common with ex-burglar Ozzy Osbourne than ex-teacher Sting?

When David Coverdale remarked, 'I only drink champagne,' Ozzy retorted, 'I only drink dog's piss.' But if that had been reported as a Stinky Turner quote no one would have doubted it.

In the end, attitude, class and music mattered a damn sight more than fashion and tribalism. In Britain it always does.


At the start of the 1970s, there were still greasy gangs of rockers; the eternal minority, like black leather evergreens they never went away. The rockers' look and attitude was adopted by many notorious American street gangs and crews such as the Savage Nomads, the Skulls and the Seven Immortals, in New York City as well as other large cities and rough neighbourhoods. And it was revived by many punk bands.

The early 1980s saw a rocker revival. The rocker Reunion Club, started by Len Paterson and a handful of original Chelsea Bridge Boys, held rocker reunion dances and organised nostalgic motorcycle runs to the south coast. As many as 12,000 revivalists turned up at Brighton Beach – enough grease to chill the heart of the hardest mod.

The style lives on to this day in rockabilly and psychobilly circles. The modern day rocker style has followers all over the world, notably in Japan, the US and Australia.

Rockabilly started to reinvent itself dramatically in the 1980s under the influence of exciting new US bands such as the Cramps and the Stray Cats, becoming punkier and more adventurous, and introducing elements of sexual fetishism.

Today there are vibrant scenes all over the US, particularly on the West Coast; in Europe and Japan too. Rockabilly cross-pollinated with hot rod vintage car enthusiasts and other retro lifestyle elements from home furnishings to tattoos. Like any other self-respecting cult, it is a complete way of life.

# CHAPTER TWELVE

# JOURNEYS TO GLORY: THE NEW ROMANTICS

'FROM HALF-SPOKEN SHADOWS EMERGES A CANVAS /
A KISS OF LIFE BREAKS TO REVEAL A MOMENT WHEN ALL MIRRORS ARE
REDUNDANT / LISTEN TO THE PORTRAIT OF PERFECTION ... LADIES AND
GENTLEMEN, THE SPANDAU BALLET.'
Robert Elms introducing Spandau Ballet on stage
'Pretentious? Moi?'
Mr Johnson (*Fawlty Towers*)

Early 1979, on any Tuesday night, there was only one place for London's latest teenage fashion peacocks to gather: Billy's in Meard Street, Soho, was where you had to be, where you had to go to be seen. In reality, it was a dump, a tiny basement under a brothel, but something was happening here, something significant, and, for many observers, quite horrible: it was the birth place of the New Romantics.

For a short time, the West End was witness to a shameless breed of preening dilettantes sporting silk gowns, rubber T-shirts, riding boots and fancy chiffon scarves – and the girls were just as bad. There were no real rules. The only point was to be different, to be noticed. You could sum up the message of this new scene with one simple phrase:

'Look at me!' That's why it started out like an am-dram re-creation of prewar Berlin decadence and ended up with posers flouncing about dressed like Marie Antoinette, Dick Turpin and Widow Twanky (with a silent 'T').

In the course of the New Romantics' rapid rise to mainstream cultural phenomenon, its adherents donned everything from spats and monocles to full pirate regalia via frockcoats, wing collars and plaid. This was a movement based on raiding the dressing-up box; Narcissus reborn on a student grant.

Makeup was applied with trowels. Blusher became king. Even hair became an art form (experimental of course), sculptured and shaped into gravity-defying fringes. 'Everything else was grey,' recalls Lisa Wright. 'The punks were so angry and so class-obsessed. Skinhead was Neanderthal. Mod was yesterday. 2-Tone when that happened was monochrome. What was wonderful about us was we had colour and imagination. It was getting back to punk before it became a uniform but adding the magic of glam. For a girl like me from a south London council estate it was an escape into a fantasy life, a revolt into style.'

Why be irate, when you could be pirate?

The men to blame were colourful characters: Steve Strange and Rusty Egan. Strange was born Steven John Harrington in Porthcawl, South Wales, in 1959. The fading seaside town, once considered the Blackpool of the Glamorgan coast, was far too parochial for such an exotic creature. Steve left home at 15 and ended up in the Smoke, where he befriended the Sex Pistols and ended up working for Malcolm McLaren. By 1978, as the first wave of punk was but a distant memory, Strange hit on the idea of something completely different.

Billy's was a gay club based in the Gargoyle Club, in Soho, later to become Gossips. Tuesday nights were dead there, so Vince, the owner, a big black diamond-loving Soho character, had nothing to lose when Steve approached him and offered to fill it with his friends. Strange ran the door while his style partner, Rusty Egan, deejayed, playing a mixture of Bowie, Kraftwerk, Roxy Music, Gary Numan and Georgio Moroder.

Rusty had been 19 when he began deejaying at the Speakeasy in 1977 – the same year as he had started drumming with one-hit wonders the Rich Kids, a short-lived, overhyped, power-pop outfit formed by ex-Pistols Glen Matlock, with Midge Ure on vocals and Steve New on guitar. In 1978, Egan, Ure and Strange formed the studio-only band Visage, who became significant two years later.

By 1979 Rusty was pioneering the new sounds of German electro-dance music and Japanese synth-pop (Yellow Magic Orchestra), providing an exciting new electro soundtrack that suited the elitist and poseur-friendly feel of the club. Many of the earliest clientele were ex-punks from the exhibitionist end of the scene. At most there were 70 of these overdressed regulars who, being mostly students, weren't spending enough dosh to keep the owner happy. (On other quiet nights, the rooftop part of Gargoyle's hosted soul discos and, more significantly, the fledgling Comedy Store, although the new acts were never quite as funny as the self-regarding fops of Tuesday nights at Billy's).

By the summer Vince had kicked them out and Strange and Egan had relocated to Blitz in Covent Garden, where the scene really took off. The cloakroom attendant was a young George O'Dowd; regular faces included Marilyn, Midge Ure, Adam Ant, Steve Dagger, all of Spandau Ballet, Chris Sullivan, Toyah, Jeremy Heeley, John Galliano, Sade, Kirk Brandon (Spear of Destiny/Theatre of Hate) and the then London School of Economics student Robert Elms, who was to play a crucial role in breaking news of this dress-up-and-dance movement to the nation.

It was a weird club, blitzed with images from World War Two. But Steve Strange was in his element as the greeter here, piously deciding who was suitably attired to get in and who wasn't. He let David Bowie in (of course) but famously turned away Mick Jagger for being insufficiently stylish.

The bulk of the ultra-chic clientele were art and fashion students, their numbers swelled by faces from the gay end of the fashion world, hairdressers, young artists and hip filmmakers. Ponces, largely. But in among them were a small mob of Spurs fans from Hackney, who were members of the hardcore Trotskyite faction Red Action, and some of the Angel Boys, an Islington gang whose members included a good-looking, grammar-school-educated kid called Gary Kemp.

Kemp had seemed destined for fame. He'd trained at the Anna Scher theatre school and had jumped on the power-pop bandwagon, forming a band called the Makers in 1978. They changed their name to Gentry that year and asked Steve Dagger (social secretary of the LSE students' union) to manage them. It was Dagger who suggested that guitarist Gary should recruit his brother Martin (also a stage-school kid) to play bass on the grounds that 'he's the best-looking guy we know'. Gary did, teaching him rudimentary bass-playing in a month. They were joined by singer Tony Hadley, drummer John Keeble and Steve Norman (sax, although he started as second guitarist). Gentry were nothing special. They played their first gig at Kingsway College, wore pastel suits and were very sixties. They were soul boys at heart, drinking at pubs like the Champion and the Edward at the Angel.

With Dagger, seen by many as the sixth band member, at the helm, it wasn't much of a logical leap to change their image to fit in with the newly emerging Blitz scene. And it was Dagger's LSE pal and the band's occasional roadie Robert Elms who suggested that they should change their name to Spandau Ballet – taking the phrase from graffiti he'd seen sprayed on the wall near Spandau prison (sole inmate, Rudolph Hess) during a student trip to Germany. Gary Kemp loved it. The new name was perfect. It was pretentious and utterly meaningless all at once.

Spandau Ballet became the first band associated with the new youth movement, defining the New Romantic genre. Their rise was extraordinary and so crooked that even McLaren would have taken his hat off to them. They played their debut gig at a warehouse party in Battersea (the tickets bore the slogan 'a crash course for the ravers' from David Bowie's song 'Drive-In Saturday'). At Dagger's instigation, the show was reviewed by Elms, who hand-delivered it to 'rock bible' the *NME*, which duly printed it. So the band's manager got their roadie to review their first ever gig in glowing terms and the *NME* published it! Chutzpah or what? Better than that, fawning professional trendy Janet Street-Porter read it and immediately wanted to film them for her TV series *20th Century Box*. Dagger swiftly put on a gig at the Scala cinema, Janet's cameras rolled and, *voilà!*, pop history was made. By November 1980 they were in the charts with their debut single 'To Cut a Long Story Short' (peaking at Number 5). In the video, the group from the highlands of Highbury wore kilts.

At first Spandau mixed funk and synth-pop, with suitably posy Constructivist imagery (Soviet chic, so very hip doncha know – just forget the millions murdered by Uncle Joe). Later, they became a mainstream pop act paying their respects to the great Marvin Gaye in their first chart topper, the soul-boy classic, 'True', which also slips in a sneaky reference to amphetamines (although this song also included some of the worst words in the history of pop, with an anguished Tony Hadley asking why he finds it so hard to write the next line; inspiring many a cynic to respond: Dunno, give up. Is it because Gary Kemp is a crap lyricist).

The rock press was mostly sniffy about the New Romantics. I was no exception. My take was that they'd taken something real and edgy and turned it into pantomime. But there's no denying that the look caught on big time.

It had its own house magazine in Nick Logan's *The Face*. It had clubs: after Blitz, other venues such as the St Moritz, Le Kilt, Club for Heroes and the Beat Route became fashionable. It had a look – the early handmade and second-hand fashions soon replaced by fashionable boutiques such as Modern Classics in Hoxton. Vivienne Westwood jumped on the bandwagon, too, with a set of strongly 'influenced' designs. She opened a shop absurdly called Nostalgia of Mud, run by Philip Salon and Simon Withers (the designer who had run up much of Spandau Ballet's early clobber).

'New Romantic became a genuine alternative subculture because it filled a gap,' opines Barrie 'the Mod' Taylor. 'These clubs kids had had enough of heavy politics and bland clothing. This was about glamour, about looking fantastic again, and, as an old mod, I could relate to that. But, like mod, what was individual style quickly became a marketable look and something laughable.

'Could you imagine a Shepherd's Bush face dressing as a fucking pirate? They had no quality control. They looked like a joke.'

Pillage idiots, even.

Lisa Wright disagrees: 'The music press hated the New Romantic scene because they couldn't control it, and because they were either hippies, politicos or Oi! Herberts – no disrespect. It wasn't about fighting or demonstrations or cock-rock guitar solos; no one wanted any of that hackneyed old rubbish. I was seventeen, I wanted to be cool, and to look fabulous; we dressed to impress. Inevitably, though, what started on the club scene was bastardised and exploited.'

The term 'New Romantic' was coined by Spandau's first album producer Richard James Burgess (writing in *The Face*, Elms had tried to lumber it with 'The Cult With No Name', which really tripped off the tongue). There was no doubt the movement put bums on seats. And in the charts, too. After Spandau, the floodgates opened and it seemed that everyone who had ever been associated with the Blitz Club was destined to have a pop career. Visage got to Number 8 with 'Fade to Grey'; Eltham's own George O'Dowd became Boy George and twinkled his way to Number 1 with Culture Club's 'Do You Really Want To Hurt Me?'; Adam Ant was transformed from punk has-been to a dandy highwayman hit machine; while Midge Ure's Ultravox waltzed off to the big time with 'Vienna' – hilariously kept off the top spot by Joe Dolce's 'Shaddap You Face'. Sultry Sade had to wait a few years for her chance to shine, but she's massive now. Of the original wannabes, only Chris Sullivan's Blue Rondo A La Turk/Berks flopped. Their debut single peaked at a less than impressive Number 40.

Other cities threw up scenes of their own, too, most notably Birmingham. Spandau Ballet played their first out-of-town gig at the Botanical Gardens there in 1980 and were amazed to discover a parallel style-and-dancing vibe going on. Duran Duran (first hit, 'Planet Earth', February 1981) were in the audience. John Taylor and Nick Rhodes had formed the band in 1978 with the idea of fusing punk energy with the style of Bowie and the dance sounds of Chic. They took their name from the sci-fi movie *Barbarella*, toured with Hazel O'Connor, were signed by EMI, hit their stride with their second album, *Rio*, and have never looked back. As well as good looks, mullets and *matelot* shirts, they had decent songs – twelve hits in their first three years – and were one of the pioneers of remixes. Internationally, they were bigger than Spandau.

Duran Duran made the cover of *Rolling Stone* in 1984, just as the New Romantic was officially washed up as a youth phenomenon in England, although the backlash had begun in the central London clubs as early as the summer of 1981, where the music was getting funkier and the style harder and altogether less of a pose.

Dressing up like a clown may have made sense as an antidote to 2-Tone puritans, skinhead sternness and punk purists, but, as riots swept the UK, such sartorial escapism suddenly seemed out of step and out of time.

# CHAPTER THIRTEEN

# STYLE WARS ON THE TERRACES: CASUAL

'WE ARE I, INTER-CITY / WE ARE C, COOL AND CASUAL / WE ARE F,
FIRM-HANDED / WE ARE FIIRRM / WE ARE I.C.I.C.F ...'
West Ham ICF chant to the tune of 'D.I.S.C.O.'

The mass media cottoned on to casual in 1984, a good three years after the style had come into its own. The newspapers were baffled by the combination of style and violence, but the parallels with previous street cults stood out like a shuttlecock shoved down the front of your Fila shorts. Casual involved a modish obsession with clothes, a modish attachment to the latest black sounds and a fanatical thirst for violence at football matches that mirrored skinhead at its most aggressive. Well-groomed hooligans, loving the hippest black urban music, giving it large – we'd seen it all before, but now it came in Sergio Tacchini tracksuits with a soundtrack from Morgan Khan's hotter-than-Hades Streetsounds label.

Casual was the coming together of two traditions. The soul boy and the terrace warrior were, for a brief while, dressing identically, both groups chasing the same pricey goal of streetwise sartorial elegance and maximum working-class flash. There were overlaps, of course.

They were the same sort of kids from the same pubs and council estates (sometimes the same kids altogether) but their traditions were quite different. And so, correspondingly, are the claims about where casual came from. The new look incubated on the terraces, but which ones? Every club with a well-dressed crew wants to take the credit. Much as I'd personally like to make a case for that good-natured band of Beau Brummells from the Valley, Floyd Road, as (more or less) an impartial observer, I can state without fear of serious contradiction that the rise of casual is a tale of two cities – Liverpool and London. And within London a tale of two clubs – West Ham and Arsenal. ('Outraged' of Stamford Bridge, feel free to send protest letters and incendiary devices c/o Piers Morgan, the Emirates Stadium.)

For a few glorious years, no self-respecting urban British youth would be seen dead out on the town if they weren't wearing upmarket European sports brands. But, before we dissect the evolution of the look, let's peer briefly into the origins of the football hooligan.

If you believe the hand-wringing newspaper reports, fighting on the terraces is a recent development, doubtless caused by a combination of liberal laws, Dr Spock's lax approach to childhood discipline and watching too much of *The Sweeney* on TV (continued the *Daily Mail*, *ad infinitum*). The puritan Phillip Stubbs was more on the ball, though, when he observed in 1583 that football 'may rather be called a bloody murdering practice than a sport or pastime'. More recently, Patrick Murphy at Leicester University has discovered more than 4,000 incidents of crowd violence at football matches that occurred in the 20 years before 1914, with more than a hundred examples of clubs being disciplined for the behaviour of their supporters.

That's not a misprint. Crowd disturbances and violent disorder were a regular matter of fact at football games before World War One.

Newspaper reports at the time illustrate clearly that one Victorian value strangely overlooked by Lady Thatcher was hooliganism.

The big difference between then and now was not the behaviour of the crowd but the manner of the reporting. For example, the Leicester

*Daily Mercury* of 3 April 1899 ran a match report that stated, 'The referee's decision had caused considerable dissatisfaction, especially that disallowing a goal to Loughborough in the first half, and at the close of the game he met a very unfavourable reception, a section of the crowd hustling him, and it was stated that he was struck.'

A referee mobbed, jostled, punched? That would be front-page news in today's tabloids. Then, it was a throwaway line.

It wasn't an isolated incident, either. Horror stories in the newspaper reports uncovered by Patrick Murphy included the case of a Northeast team mercilessly attacked by a gang of 'Brumwickian roughs' who showered them with 'sticks, stones and missiles' in 1895. While in Leicester in 1909, the enraged crowd broke down the barricades, poured whisky on them and set them ablaze. As the flames spread to the pay boxes, firemen who'd rushed into action were set upon by the mob.

Far from being a recent phenomenon, football violence has been part of English life for more than a century. All that has changed in modern times is the degree of organisation. The hooligans of the late seventies/early eighties operated more like small armies, with generals, captains and soldiers; they used forward planning and attack strategies. And it's certainly arguable that the very way that terrace trouble was written about in the national press has encouraged this development.

The *Daily Mail* was one of the first tabloids to publish a 'league table' of hooligans in the 1970s, unwittingly inspiring rival firms to compete for top place. Similarly, the BBC *Panorama*'s infamous seventies documentary on Millwall hooligans made Harry the Dog and 'F-Troop' heroes among their peers.

Newspapers caught on to the limitless potential of the football hooligan as potent new folk demons because fighting, especially at football matches, was such an integral part of being a skinhead first time round.

The first big fuss I remember was in 1971, when the Leeds United ground at Elland Road was closed down for three matches by the FA following a particularly enthusiastic pitch invasion by the home supporters in a match against West Bromwich Albion. The underground football fanzine *Foul* appeared briefly in the early seventies featuring such heroes as Rupture and the Oaktree Skins – Rupert Bear relaunched as a 'Nutwood United' bootboy. The mass media failed to see the joke, although unwittingly they were to provide endless hours of fun for real hooligans themselves. They had two main problems. First, the original skins and bootboys had made such a marked impression on their minds that throughout the eighties Fleet Street hacks would ring me up asking if I could direct them to 'skinhead bootboys' for 'Soccer Savages' type exposés – despite the fact that no top-ranking football firm had been skinhead-orientated for years.

Secondly, even when the papers did manage to find a kid who looked the part to blurt out the required bloodthirsty details, it was a sure bet that only a loudmouth, a moron or a mug would volunteer to put his face forward and thus become so easily identifiable to rival firms. Such transitory glory inevitably translates as a limited lifespan. (The *Sun*, incidentally, once ran a hilarious series called 'Aggro Britain', which featured a snap of the Tilbury Skins from Essex, led at the time by then skin Tony Barker, a.k.a. the lead singer with the Oi! band Angela Rippon's Bum. The photographer had obviously begged them to pull ferocious faces but had managed to capture them only in mid-gurn. Rival Millwall firms reprinted the picture as a sticker bearing the slogan IS THIS MAN A HARDNUT OR IS HE COCO THE CLOWN? Tony Barker was undoubtedly a hard man, with an awesome reputation, but he'd been foolish to pose for the papers.)

Other rib-tickling press exposés came loaded with such cornball headlines as THE YOBBO, MANIACS, GAME OF HATE and WE NAME THE SOCCER THUGS, although my all-time favourite was THE BITCHES IN BOVVER BOOTS, which was about female terrace fighters. There were some, too. Yeti of West Ham went in as enthusiastically as any man. Donna never wore 'bovver boots', though.

The 1979–80 season was when leading personalities at Upton Park dropped the skinhead look for good. Andy Russell recalls, 'The police were on the lookout for DM boots, so we wore training shoes.' They also grew their hair and replaced those omnipresent Lonsdale T-shirts and sweatshirts with Slazenger jumpers and golfing tops. Soon after, they dropped straight jeans in favour of slightly flared Farah slacks, originally popular with black soul boys.

Gold chains, bracelets and sovereign rings were important accessories. Green combat jackets, popular among the terrace elite in early 1979, were ditched when they became identified with skinheads, and replaced by smart leather jackets and suede blousons.

Diamond Pringles were *de rigueur* early on too, but, like Slazengers, had been dropped by the end of 1981 as the search for different, more elitist and often more expensive gear went on.

In London, these smart young terrace tykes referred to themselves as Chaps. And, like some bizarre throwback to the days of Scuttlers and Peaky Blinders of Victorian street-gang infamy, other inner-city areas threw up similar young and working-class terrace-related cults.

In Manchester, stylised street youths became known as Perry Boys – because, although they'd adopted trainers and 'wedge' cuts, they at first refused to part with their beloved Fred Perry shirts. The Perries were around throughout the punk years and punk bashing was an occasional pastime. The first Perry Boy look was a tennis shirt under a chunky-knit burgundy jumper, with Fruit of the Loom overalls and black Adidas trainers. By spring 1980, this look had evolved into Peter Werth polo shirts, Lois jeans and Adidas Stan Smith trainers, often dyed. Eventually the Perry Boys became known as Town Boys and then simply the Boys.

In Liverpool, similar kids called themselves scallies (a contradiction of scallywags) and were to prove far more influential than their Manchester cousins. Scallies were in evidence at Scotland Road as early as 1977. Occasional *Sounds* contributor Kevin Sampson, who was one himself, says they drew their original dress influences from punk and Bowie's 'Low' look.

## STYLE WARS ON THE TERRACES: CASUAL

Like the London soul boys who were drawn to the punk scene, the scallies opted for mohair pullovers, straight jeans and plastic sandals. Their most distinguishing feature, however, was their 'wedge' haircuts, a lop-sided throwback to the Depression that hung (absurdly) over one eye. By 1978, the scallies had shed their punk touches and become essentially football-orientated. Probably ahead of the young Londoners, the Liverpool match boys became increasingly clothes-obsessed. Lois drainpipes replaced straight jeans and the lucrative cascade of changing label names began in earnest. Fiorucci, Lacoste, Inege – they all had their moments.

Liverpool FC's frequent triumphant trips to Europe throughout this era introduced many a young light-fingered scally to the joys of lifting the type of high-quality skiing and sportswear that was at that time unknown in British high street shops. (The reds were also responsible for the bizarre popularity of the deerstalker hat, adopted as early as 1979.)

These were upmarket boutiques with well-to-do customers and low or no security in place. They paid dearly for that oversight. In May 1981 the European Cup final between Liverpool and Real Madrid was played at the Parc de Paris. Quality Paris stores were divested of their wares in a manner that resembled rats stripping flesh from a corpse. Italy, Belgium, Switzerland – wherever Liverpool played the Anfield army had a field day. The practice of pouring into shops by the score and overwhelming the staff was known as steaming. And it caught on. Every international thereafter was surrounded by similar tales of English fans on a mass shoplifting spree. No wonder the Parc de Paris terraces echoed to the strains of 'drinking wine on the dole in Gay Paree' – ironically enough to the tune of 'Hurrah for the Red, White & Blue!'

In London the trendsetters – from Highbury and Upton Park – had also started looking further afield for their finery. Burberry macs were in, as were Nike trainers and Lois jeans (frayed, of course). By 1980 the French brand Lacoste ruled the roost. Andy 'Skully' Russell remembers, 'Lacoste wasn't that special – we're talking three-button pastel polo shirts – but everyone had to have one.'

Young kids would be out raiding shops and slicing off the crocodile logos with their Stanley blades so Mum could sew them onto their supermarket T-shirts. West End stores reported spates of incidents involving youths perusing their stock, swiftly cutting out the symbol and then vanishing into the hurly-burly of the tourist-jammed streets outside.

Snide (i.e. fake) Lacoste tops manufactured in the Far East were sold in pubs, clubs and markets. Meanwhile, the tastiest terrace dressers were 'checking' pricey ski anoraks.

Away games soon meant that the hot new Liverpool and London fashions rapidly found followers at every other major club. Everton and Millwall were close behind the pacesetters and, by 1981, every team had its firm of sharp-dressed ruckers. Millwall had the Bushwackers, Leeds had the Service Crew, Portsmouth the 6.57 Crew, Chelsea had their Tube Crew, Newcastle had the Mainline Express, Cardiff the Soul Crew, Spurs the GLC (Greater London Casuals), Wolves the Subway Army and so on. Middlesbrough, Aston Villa, Man City – they all had their share of casual followers. And so it went on. Even Luton had the MIGs – Men in Gear. But of course it was West Ham United who had the ICF, the Inter-City Firm, and the ICF had style.

They were the first to marry ultraviolence with sick humour. When they left behind their unfortunate, and often unconscious, victims they also left a business-style calling card bearing the motif, 'Congratulations, you have just met the ICF'.

They were called the ICF, naturally enough, because they travelled to matches on InterCity trains rather than old-fashioned coaches. Persil soap powder vouchers enabled the Chaps to travel so cheaply.

A lot of the old Secret Affair Glory Boys and hardcore Cockney Rejects ruck'n'roll fans were in the vanguard of the ICF, or resurfaced in it, including names like Skully, Danny Harrison and Andy Swallow. Also high in the ranks was Cass Pennant, a black man from Kent, who had been the first soccer fan to get a three-year sentence after a Charlton fan was left in a coma the same night as a Millwall fan was found on the lines at New Cross (cue the sick West Ham chant, 'We're all mad / We're insane / We throw Millwall under trains').

Later, Cass was 'fitted up' for the stabbing of a Sheffield Wednesday fan in promotion year. Everyone in the know knew that Cass hadn't done it. The ICF marched in protest about his jailing to Downing Street and handed in a petition with 2,000 claret-and-blue names on it.

Skully, of East End Badoes infamy, was himself charged with the murder of an Arsenal fan in 1982. He was acquitted, the murder left unsolved, although later he was to serve nearly 15 years for springing John Kendall out of Gartree Prison by helicopter.

Stabbings were on the increase in the early eighties. Stanley knives sadly became a nationwide terrace chic accessory. They were easily concealed and stabbing someone was quicker and required much less effort than fighting them. You could 'open up' someone as quickly and easily as you could zip up your Fila Terinda tracksuit.

Away from the matches, hammers and machetes were frequently wielded in street clashes. A petrol bomb was hurled at 'Millwallies' by West Ham fans at London Bridge in 1984. Inevitably, Millwall hit back. Their firms spent most of 1984 gunning for any south London West Ham, and there were ugly clashes at New Cross and Whitechapel. An ICF stalwart called Billy Gale took the biscuit for ultraviolence, however. Billy, who served with the 2nd Battalion of the Royal Green Jackets, slung a live grenade at his blue and white opponents. It was a miracle that no one was killed.

Inside the stadiums, the battle was all about reputation and territory. Away mobs wanted to 'take' the home end. The home mobs' honour depended on their keeping it free from contamination. It was often gut-churningly violent. And yet, to the participants, the violence was incidental, natural, a release/safety valve. What's more, the kids and young adults who were really into the whole bellicose business weren't the stereotype thick thugs – 'ANIMALS!' – that the outraged tabloid commentators imagined them to be. On the contrary, they tended to be sharp, hard-working and funny.

All you had to do was check out the letter pages of *Sounds*, *The Face* or *The End* at the time to realise that this was no illiterate rabble. Many ICF characters appeared regularly in the 'Jaws' columns of *Sounds* (not to mention the Channel 4 *Our Lives* series).

The first in-depth appraisal of casual appeared in the July 1983 edition of *The Face*. It was well written (with an inevitable Liverpool bias) by Kevin Sampson, but it's worth pointing out that *The Face* had turned down the same article a year before.

Robert Elms, who has tried to pass himself off as some great casual expert, had his first piece on the phenomenon published in December 1983 – and then only after the *End* collective had done a ton of his homework for him.

Now, *The End* – that was something else. The brainchild of a bunch of lovable Scouse mop-tops, including Sampson, the Farm's Peter Hooton, retired rucker and raconteur John Potter and former mod fanziner Phil Jones, *The End* first materialised in September 1981 with a print run of just 500 copies. Three years on and it was selling more than 4,000 a time.

It was easy to see why. *The End* was a rib-tickling football fanzine, more concerned with the preoccupations of terrace punters than the daring deeds of dazzling goal scorers like Graham Souness and Derek 'Gypo' Hales. In less sussed hands it could easily have degenerated into a ruckers' bible, but *The End*'s attitude to firms and fashions was mercifully tongue-in-cheek. And its letters page positively pulsated with heated debate about match-dude chic.

Nineteen eighty-three and early 1984 were when the style wars really rocketed. Tacchini, Pierre Cardin, Lacoste, Ellesse, Fila, Pringle, Dior, St Laurent, Aquascutum, Kappa, Lyle & Scott, Gabicci, Robert Klein and Armani were names to claim once the fight for the coolest, classiest casual line was on, and few designs lasted longer than a month.

Go away on holiday for a fortnight and you could come back to find your entire wardrobe had been made redundant. And woe betide the followers who failed to keep up! Elms recalls the time QPR went to Coventry away in the 1983–84 season. On the way to the ground, the 400-strong mob of Londoners were confronted by an equal number of Coventry casuals. Glaring at the opposition through the thin line of duty cops, the Rangers boys spotted a weakness. Some of the Coventry mob were wearing Fila – an Italian brand that had gone out of fashion in the capital more than a month before. In a matter of moments the dismissive chant broke out, 'My dog sleeps on Fila, my dog sleeps on Fila, la-la-la, la-la-la.'

It wasn't easy being in the vanguard of style. And it wasn't cheap, either. Like tracksuits did, like cardigans did, casual cost money. A punter would think nothing of splashing out £80 on a sweater that he might wear in public just once.

Reacting to the market, the major manufacturers updated fast and kept their designs to limited editions – but even that wasn't good enough for the real elitists: they moved on to even dearer and more exclusive lines from Head and Burberry. Wexmann slacks replaced Farahs and if you had to wear jeans, you'd better have made sure you'd snipped a three inch split up the seams at the bottom.

Simultaneously, Nike's Act trainer line replaced the normal Nike Legend and both were forgotten when DiaDdora Elite arrived at £38 a pair. New Balance and Nike Wimbledon made it in 1984, although the more sophisticated preferred crocodile-skin shoes, which went so much better with your Ralph Lauren shirt, doncha think?

Girls meantime went in for Benetton rugby shirts or Club Sport track tops. Pencil-pleat skirts were popular for a while and it was 'in' to wear gold everywhere. Flaunt it, baby! But casual was very much a male prerogative. The male scene evolved much faster and it was the social kiss of death to be seen in something passé (anyone sporting Lonsdale, diamond Pringles or Gallini T-shirts in the summer of 1984 was good for more laughs than a Jimmy Jones stag show).

Where to buy it all? Most 'outsider' journalists in London name-checked Stuart's at Shepherds Bush and left it at that. If they'd bothered to catch a Tube to Liverpool Street, got off and headed east, they'd have uncovered an Aladdin's cave of sartorial delights. There was Dice at Roman Road, Reiss at Liverpool Street, Moda 3 in Tower Bridge Road, Davis's at Mile End and Roman Road, Grants in Commercial Road, Ozzy's in Roman Road, Odyssey at East Ham, Piajer at the Angel, Cohens in Roman Road, Temples in Walthamstow and the Athletic Foot Company at the Angel.

Cecil Gee sold a lot of Armani lines too, and discerning punters were quite happy to buy their ski jackets at Lillywhite's or travel up to Nicholas Nickleby's in Oxford Street.

None of it was cheap. A good Armani sweater would set you back £90 and a Fila tracksuit went for around a ton. So where did they get the money? Some kids were professional thieves with plenty of cash to dispose of. Kids on top-whack skilled jobs who were still living at home weren't exactly short of a bob or two either. But a lot of casuals were on the dole, Maggie's Millions – how did they cope? Thieving continued to be widespread. And, in case you didn't have the bottle to nick the stuff yourself (well, it did have its drawbacks: three ICF faces including Danny Harrison ended up jailed when they got overconfident in Geneva in 1984), a thriving black market in knocked-off gear had grown up at home. Illicit factories had sprung up in Essex specifically to manufacture counterfeit casual clobber. But the Chaps running them weren't always that on the ball. Fashion atrocities sold in the Dagenham area included snide Fred Perry tops complete with Lacoste logos.

The worst crime of all, however, was 'taxing', when casuals would mug other casuals in the streets, literally stealing the shirts from their backs or the trainers from their feet. This was disapproved of when the victim was working-class, but no one minded so much when he was obviously from another tax bracket.

It was the spread of urban casual fashion to suburbia in 1984 that sparked the sudden fall from grace of the label-name game. When the posh boys picked up on it, it was time to let it go. In August 1984 the *Sunday Times* ran a feature on the young suburban middle classes decked out in Tacchini tracksuit tops and Lacoste jumpers. They'd paid for it all legit, of course, but it didn't lessen the blow. Terrace chic had passed into the hands of the middle classes and that meant it was no good at all.

The trend away from pricey gear actually began in depression-blitzed Liverpool as early as the 1981–82 season. First to go was label competitiveness – anything casual was accepted. A new 'scruff' look emerged, ironically not all that far removed from what the 'norm' at Upton Park had been in 1980.

From 1982 the scally look split in two. The youngsters still held onto their wedges and flicks, their green hooded anoraks, trainers and winter sheepskin mittens, while the older scallies began to dress 'sensibly'. They wore their hair short, sported tweed and cord jackets, suede shoes and woollen sweaters. And they smoked dope.

It was unfortunate for new group Accent that the anti-casual reaction was just biting in London when they'd just begun to get noticed by the music press as the first self-styled casual band.

Accent began gigging at the fag end of 1983 and got spotted (by *Sounds*, naturally) in spring 1984. They operated out of Stuart's, the former soul-boy emporium in Shepherds Bush, were based in Fulham and appeared smothered in fashionable label names. Live, they reminded me of a rougher Undertones, or one of the better mod bands of 1979. They ran the Casual Beat Club at the Kings Head in Fulham and, because of the way they dressed, got unfairly lambasted as a hype. In fact their self-financed debut single, 'We Are Lost', established them as a classy pop band.

Accent were a little naïve, but they believed in what they were doing totally and were genuinely dismayed when a Jam-type punk trio called the Sines from Stockton changed their image and jumped on what they obviously imagined would prove a lucrative casual bandwagon.

When the bands didn't take off, the Sines changed their name to Glory Boys (too risky!) and dressed in Fred Perry tops and stone-bleached denims.

When Accent disowned label names towards the end of 1984, at least it was because everyone around them was doing so as well.

A third casual band, an 11-piece soul outfit called the Hiss, kept a low profile rather than sully their hands by associating with the likes of the Sines. They re-emerged in 1985 as La Pel (as in the clothes shop).

EMI sniffed around Accent for a while, but none of these groups took off.

There have been other casual bands. In terms of the clothes they wore, Skully's East End Badoes, starring good-natured Terry Hayes on vocals, were probably the first, although the music they played was pure uncompromising Oi! (even though, bizarrely, Skully himself didn't go for that sort of sound). By 1983 some of the white ICF members were so into Lover's Rock reggae that they'd formed a small but dedicated movement called Cock Against Racism, which was devoted entirely to the amorous pursuit of black women.

Pete Hooton's Farm were the best of the bands spawned by casual. Genuine scallies, they specialised in tasty pop with neat trumpet touches. Suggsy produced their debut *Hearts and Minds* 12-inch EP (released December 1984 on Skysaw) to favourable reviews and a dollop of airplay. They went on to eventually notch up two Top Ten hits ('Groovy Train' and 'All Together Now' in 1990) and five more Top Forty ones. The only thing is, in line with scally wisdom, by the time of their first release the Farm had moved a long way from casual fashion, although they did maintain a 100 per cent hardcore scally following.

At the end of the day there wasn't a major casual band, just as there wasn't an authentic home-grown skinhead band in the sixties, either. In the South at least casual wasn't about anything as messy as rock bands. The casual soundtrack was contemporary black American music. They were modern-day soul boys.

Ex-casual and DJ Terry Farley says, 'In the South, casuals listened to soul. Up North they listened more to white music. But it wasn't really about that. We were football casuals — the two words were inseparable.

This was about firms of hooligans and terrace violence. It was about turning up at football and looking good.'

Eddie Piller of Acid Jazz sees it differently. 'It was a weird time. For a while in the early 1980s it was in to dress like you were on your way to play a tennis match; it was all tracksuits and designer headbands – the difference being Bjorn Borg wouldn't be carrying a tool in his trackie pocket on the way to Wimbledon. Casual was chiefly about looking good, and smashing other football fans to fuck. But a lot of those guys were seriously into the latest black sounds.'

The elite of Southern casuals favoured electro and hip-hop – the naked heart of the Bronx exposed and throbbing. Hip-hop grew out of DJ 'jams', open-air parties in the streets and parks of the South Bronx, born of deprivation and pioneered by the likes of DJ Kool Herc. Nowhere is hip-hop culture better explained than in David Toop's superbly detailed *The Rap Attack*, which tells the whole story from the sound's roots in Africa right through Afro-American rapping to the dawn of electro-funk, scratching, break-dancing and so on.

Hip-hop started out completely underground, but Deborah Harry took it out of New York and into the charts with Blondie's 1980–81 hit 'Rapture' (Number 1 in the US, Number 5 in the UK). Within a couple of years, there was enough UK interest among black and white soul boys (for black kids this was the only real alternative to the Rastafarian ghetto) for Morgan Khan to build his successful (for a few good years at least) Streetsounds empire by licensing the hottest US cuts.

Malcolm McLaren picked up on the new ghetto beat early, throwing in Trevor Horn and the rapping, scratching World Famous Supreme Team to come up with his 1983 hit 'Buffalo Girls'.

Such exposure, following on from the way Blondie and Tina Weymouth's Tom Tom Club had helped to popularise rapping, meant that few people who went to the clubs in 1984 could have avoided the real thing.

Soon, casual would ebb away, replaced by acid house, Britpop and finally the Burberry and Stone Island brands associated with the chavs.

But, for a few short years in the eighties, these deadly peacocks ruled the UK's terraces and cities. Like mod, the casual mood was to flaunt it, front it, flash it. Give it the big 'un. It was as true of the young casuals on the street corners with their ghetto blasters as it was of the older ones in the champagne bars of the cocktail pubs (which proliferated in the East End and south of the river), sitting there with their tasty tans from the Bahamas or the Greek Islands (well, Marbella was well past it, and even Puerto Banus had had its day), wearing the next wave of fashionable designer gear (Ralph Lauren, Gaultier, Gucci, Dolce & Gabbana – a mighty long way from the humble Lacoste) with their Porsches parked outside.

Wonder what the social workers made of it all ...

In a piece I wrote for *Sounds* in early 1985 I noted:

*Right now, casual style is on the way out on the terraces, even though there are still soul-boys and football head-cases willing to shell out £35 for ankle boots; and slightly less for C.17 jeans. The last letter I got from Pete Hooton spoke darkly of a flare revival, and yes he is talking trousers, even though one Liverpool lunatic has been firing tug-boat flares into rival fans at nearly every match this season. Flared trousers are one trend I would hate to see back, but you know they're coming. Levi is launching denim and cord flares later this year. Lee and Wrangler are already doing it. Gulp. Could this mean the end of cool as we know it?*

*Almost certainly. But the smart money says not for long ...*

## CHAPTER FOURTEEN

# 'DISTURBED SHOOTERS WEREN'T TRUE GOTHS'
### (HEADLINE FROM THE CHICAGO TRIBUNE, 27 APRIL 1999)

July 2004. Sidcup, Kent. A pair of tall teenagers clad head to toe in black are spotted by a gang of chavs. The kids can't be more than 14 years old; the couple are about 17. Baying like animals, the gang mass behind them, about 15 strong. Boys and girls alike, they start to hurl insults. Two of the girls pick up stones and throw them. Not to be outdone, one of the boys lobs half a house brick, which hits the lad on the head, knocking him to the floor. If it hadn't been for the intervention of bystanders, my wife included, the results could have been fatal.

For others this decade, it was fatal. This hatred and hostility is still an everyday story for anyone who adheres to a youth cult. The older teenagers' 'crime' was to be different, and in this particular case to look vulnerable. They were goths.

Goth bashing became horribly fashionable in the noughties. In August 2007, another peaceful goth couple were attacked in a skate park because of the way they looked. Robert Maltby, 21, and his girlfriend Sophie Lancaster, 20, were found with serious head injuries in the park at Stubby Lee, in Bacup, Lancashire. Their faces were so badly swollen that police could not tell which person was male and which was female. Sophie Lancaster subsequently died of her injuries. Five teenage boys, aged 15 to 17, were arrested. Ryan Herbert and Brendan Harris were later convicted of her murder and given life sentences; the three others were given lesser sentences for the assault on her boyfriend. Delivering the sentence, Judge Anthony Russell stated, 'This was a hate crime against these completely harmless people targeted because their appearance was different to yours.'

He went on to defend goths, describing them as 'perfectly peaceful, law-abiding people who pose no threat to anybody'.

In August 2008, Paul Gibbs, a student from Leeds, was offered a motorbike ride by three men as he was on a camping with a group of fellow goths in Rothwell Country Park. Quinn Colley, 18, Ryan Woodhead, 18, and Andrew Hall, 22, deliberately befriended the campers in order to attack and rob them. Away from the group, they knocked Gibbs, 26, down from the bike and battered him unconscious with a motorbike helmet.

His attackers then sliced off his left ear before returning to the camp, stabbing four of the men and robbing two of the women. Colley and Woodhead were sentenced to a minimum of two and a half years in prison and Hall to a minimum of four and a half years for what the judge called an 'evil, calculated attack'.

Paul Gibbs was left with severe brain damage. Because the ear was not found for 17 hours, surgeons could not immediately reattach it. Instead, they stitched it inside his stomach so that tissue would regrow. It would later be reconstructed by using some of the cartilage from his ribcage. The student had to learn to walk again after the surgery. It is still unclear whether the brain injuries will affect him for the rest of his life.

Such terrifying violence and prejudice appear to be regular bedfellows for one of the UK's most passive yet determinedly different subcultures.

Gothic rock incubated in London's West End in the aftermath of punk. Music weekly *Sounds* announced its arrival in February 1981 in an article by Steve Keaton headlined 'THE RISE OF PUNK GOTHIQUE'. Early bands included Alien Sex Fiend, UK Decay, Southern Death Cult and Specimen.

Quite independently, the early eighties also saw the development of the similar-looking death rock as an offshoot of US punk. In the UK, goth got rockier with the arrival of bands like the Sisters of Mercy, the Mission and the March Violets. The nineties saw boundaries blurred between goth and the 'corpse-painted' followers of black metal. The trend continued into the nineties as the subculture took root in Los Angeles, Orange County and New York. Goth music changed, broadened and welcomed new sounds. Cybergoth had more in common with technopop than death rock. But everything from seventies glam to ethereal wave was played at goth clubs. Electro-dance bands such as the Covenant and VNV Nation flourished on the goth scene.

Shock rocker Marilyn Manson (Brian Warner), one of the decade's major new stars, is often linked to the cult, but not by hardcore goths themselves. Ohio-born Manson notched up a string of big-selling singles and albums as well as film scores for hit movies such as *The Matrix*. His weird look and status as an honorary reverend in the Church of Satan gave the Christian Right in the States something else to bash the goths with and British tabs something new to moan about. According to porn star Jenna Jameson, Manson is 'enormously endowed'. And certainly when you look at him the words 'big plonker' spring to mind. His 2005 marriage to fetish model Dita Von Teese lasted just one year. It was all a might livelier than the massed ranks of insufferably dull rock acts (boring student band Coldplay, former public-school boys Keane) or the plastic pop that has dominated the British charts for what feels like for ever.

In Germany, a new subculture emerged called grufties – or, in English, tomb creatures.

The first goths were less contentious than crass and arguably less interesting. Their obvious spiritual ancestors were Bauhaus, whose seminal 1979 song 'Bela Lugosi's Dead' was the clarion call for the new cult, although Siouxsie of the Banshees was the first to use the word to describe the Banshees' new direction and she certainly created the goth look for women. Alice Cooper was a big influence and arguably Screamin' Lord Sutch got there first (not to mention Bobby 'Boris' Pickett & the Crypt-Kicker Five).

Once more, Soho was to be the launching pad of a new movement, which developed at the Batcave (at Gossips nightclub – again!). It opened in July 1982 specialising in glam rock and new wave, but before long goth sounds predominated. The club was run by Ollie Wisdom, lead singer with the house band Specimen. Robert Smith of the Cure was a regular (although he insisted they were a raincoat band). Other faces included Steve Severin of the Banshees, Nick Cave, Danielle Dax and Marc Almond. Alien Sex Fiend and Sex Gang Children played frequently. It became the haunt for the new goth movement, whose style and imagery took root here: black veils, black eyeliner, black fishnets, black boots, black corsets, black-painted fingernails, spiky black-dyed hair – you get the picture. Trousers were worn tight, boots were pointed, buckles were big. Silver flourished, and crucifixes were popular. Morbid themes of death and vampires abounded. It was fancy dress for would-be fiends.

In later years, white makeup was used to give already pale skin a deathlier pallor, and piercings became fashionable.

Simon Reynolds describes the look as consisting of 'backcombed or ratted black hair, ruffled Regency shirts, stovepipe hats, leather garments and spiked dog collars; the ensemble accessorised with religious, magical or macabre jewellery ... typically made from silver'. These including bone earrings, rosaries, pentacles, ankhs and skulls. Not fighting clothes. Goths were essentially an introspective cult. Morbid, yes, with their obsession with vampires and Victoriana; violent, no.

Not that this stopped the mass media trying to link them wrongly with atrocities like the Columbine killings and the Red Lake High

School massacre. The real killers were loners obsessed with heavy metal and the Third Reich, not goths.

True goths tend to be apolitical pacifists. They were just the latest youth-cult whipping boys demonised by lazy media.

The scene is still huge, especially in the US and Germany, where huge festivals such as Wave-Gotik-Treffen can attract tens of thousands of enthusiasts.

## CHAPTER FIFTEEN

# THE BATTLE OF WATERLOO: FOR BLOOD AND HONOUR

On Saturday, 12 September 1992, police wielding riot shields and batons closed Waterloo Station in London after anti-fascist demonstrators clashed with neo-Nazi supporters gathering to attend a Blood & Honour concert. At one stage the cops charged the rival groups with batons drawn as they spilled onto Waterloo Bridge, bringing traffic to a standstill. There were 33 arrests, 44 people were hospitalised, and some bystanders were injured; both the Underground and mainline stations were shut down and British Rail services were suspended.

Outside Waterloo, bottles, bricks and other missiles were hurled as the National Socialist skinheads fought pitched battles with Anti-Fascist Action — mostly comprising Trotskyite and Class War activists. Terrified passengers fled and two British Transport police officers were taken to St Thomas's Hospital, one with a glass wound to the face. As the rival groups spilled out along the South Bank, more refined concertgoers and musicians from the Royal Festival Hall were caught up in the chaos as the police struggled to contain and control the disturbance. Anarchists smashed up two cars.

The far Left, used to having their own way in public confrontations, had expected little resistance from their opponents this day and had spent much of the morning picking off small groups of neo-Nazis and foreign skinheads as they arrived. The police stood by while they attacked them with bricks and bottles, boots and fists.

The battered skins later regrouped in a mob outside on Waterloo bridge, but the mood among the anti-fascists was triumphant. What they hadn't realised was that, rather than fear the face-off, Blood & Honour – who call themselves *28*, from the initials 'B' and the 'H' – had not only actively planned it, they had also lined up the cavalry in the shape of the Chelsea Headhunters and assorted football casuals.

Blood & Honour had deliberately made that night's planned concert by neo-Nazi band Skrewdriver public knowledge, flyposting the message 'SKREWDRIVER BACK IN LONDON' the length and breadth of the country. The redirection point, Waterloo Station, had been displayed on them prominently. A series of phone calls from activists posing as concerned members of the public had then been made to local councils and every known Left-wing and anti-fascist organisation. Skrewdriver singer Ian Stuart Donaldson, known as Ian Stuart, was interviewed by Richard Littlejohn on London's LBC radio. This gig was always meant to be the opposite of low-key.

The plan was to lure the street-fighting Left to Waterloo mainline station. The plan worked.

The 3.15 Reading-to-Waterloo train rolled onto Platform 15 on time carrying two ferocious firms of neo-Nazis: west London *28* skinheads and the notorious Chelsea Headhunters. At the same time sympathetic firms of casuals from Millwall, West Ham and Portsmouth joined up with the bloodied battalion outside on the bridge, along with the leader guard of the British Movement.

The prematurely triumphant far Left now found themselves caught in a pincer movement, between the claws of a particularly vicious crab. Suddenly the opposition were hundreds strong and they all, in the parlance of street fighting, 'wanted to know'.

The Headhunters went into action immediately, challenging the surprised and in many cases terrified anti-fascist demonstrators, who, although larger in number, did not fancy their chances. As they retreated out of the station, the reinforced mob on the bridge charged towards them. Caught between two ferocious mobs chanting 'skinhead!' and '*sieg heil*!' most of the demonstrators turned tail and fled. The brave hardcore who stood and fought were battered with the same lack of mercy as they had shown to the enemy earlier. A police officer described the scene to the press as being 'like Custer's Last Stand'. Only police intervention saved more from serious injury.

Batons flying, the cops separated the two sides and began clearing the station of hooligans. The *28*-led mob were now between 400 and 500 strong. The tide had been turned.

*28* didn't have it all their own way, however. Earlier that day, their security chief Kirk Barker and his unit had been arrested and charged with violent disorder as soon as they'd arrived at Waterloo; and, the night before, Ian Stuart had been attacked in a Burton-on-Trent pub by a group of black activists, one of whom smashed a pint glass into his face telling him 'The gig's off, you Nazi bastard.' Later, Stuart joked on stage, 'I wouldn't mind but there weren't even any beer in it.'

The gig was not off. That morning, *28* activists had booked the function room of the Yorkshire Grey pub in Eltham, southeast London – just a short stroll from where Boy George had grown up.

Eight hundred attended the concert – with hundreds more unable to get in. Five hundred police in riot gear outside enforced the fire regulations. The anti-fascists did not show. The cops attempted to close the function room bar, but backed down after the organisers angrily protested. Skrewdriver played followed by No Remorse and the Swedish band Dirlewanger.

Against the odds, *28* had pulled off the biggest neo-Nazi rock concert ever seen in London. For the Nazi skinheads, it was their greatest triumph to date.

So who were they? Where did they come from? And what have they become?

# THE BATTLE OF WATERLOO: FOR BLOOD AND HONOUR

Ian Stuart founded Blood & Honour in 1987, taking the name from the slogan of the Hitler Youth: '*Blut und Ehr*'. (The phrase originated in the German racial-purity law of 1935, passed to 'protect the Blood and Honour of our people', which was thought to sum up what the movement *28* was all about.)

The seeds of the National Socialist rock movement had been planted in the late 1970s with the formation of the National Front-backed Rock Against Communism (RAC) (see Chapter 16, 'Blowing in the Wind'). Radicalised in the early eighties, Stuart set up the White Noise Club (WNC) with the NF, re-formed Skrewdriver as a white-power band and began organising gigs and open-air concerts under the RAC banner. Throughout 1983 and 1984 the scene flourished. But by 1986 it became clear that elements of the NF leadership had been systematically defrauding the bands.

The leading groups Skrewdriver, Brutal Attack, Sudden Impact and No Remorse split with the WNC in disgust.

The following summer Stuart launched Blood & Honour, and on 5 September the four bands played a word-of-mouth gig in Morden, Surrey, to an audience of around 500, including supporters from France, Italy and Germany. Other bands such as Skullhead, Violent Storm and English Rose joined the movement and *28* rapidly spawned major scenes in the USA with divisions in Australia, Belgium, Scandinavia and Eastern Europe.

There was no mistaking their intent: *28* gigs are blitzed in symbols associated with fascism, including the Mosley lightning flash from the 1930s, the Celtic cross, the Odal rune, the tree-of-life rune, and the three 7s associated with the Afrikaner Weerstandsbeweging (AWB) of South Africa.

It's hard to give precise figures for sales and support, as the organisation is shrouded in secrecy, but it is known that Skrewdriver sales alone made a millionaire of Herbert Egoldt, the boss of their German record label Rock-O-Rama. Even Hollywood responded with schlock movies about the neo-Nazi skins, such as the 1990 film *So Proudly We Heil*.

I spoke to London *28* members to try and understand their much-despised scene and to establish how their bands differ from other kinds of punk. The most obvious difference is in the lyrical content of their songs. As self-confessed Nazis, the *28* bands see all non-white immigration as a problem; race is a constant theme and they consider themselves to be 'the only real protest movement' because they oppose the political constraints of modern liberalism.

Many also reject punk as a term, preferring to be described as 'skinhead rock' to distance themselves, they say, 'from the middle class, drug-taking, sexual deviancy that 'punk' now seems to stand for in many quarters.' But, of course, many skinheads would adamantly distance themselves from being associated with *28*.

The type of songs played by the *28* bands range from brutal hardcore and streetpunk to ballads via black metal and standard rock songs. They are defined by their extreme viewpoint, and wear their alienation from accepted social mores as a dubious badge of pride.

A London *28* spokesman told me: 'Bands like Blackout, Legion of St George, Pureblood, Brutal Attack or Crusade could have made a "good living" if they had chosen the "non-political musical path" and ignored subjects which affected their lives the most. With the equipment and facilities now available to any RAC band being on a par with any other band of any genre, bad recordings and poor quality are things of the past.'

Did they, I wondered, ever encounter hostility to punk from National Socialist political activists, some of whom I would imagine would prefer to emphasise folk music and the classics?

'There is no hostility at our concerts between different genres or followers of music,' they said. 'In the past there was the skinhead, punk, heavy-metal rivalry, but that is nonexistent now. But there is some scorn from some "NS purists" towards skinheads and *28* and its closeness to punk; but it must be stressed we are a musical movement first and foremost. The NS purist would not attend one of our functions, nor we his. *28* now encompasses bands from every level of the Right-wing spectrum, from Nationalist to Loyalist to National Socialist.'

Of all the acts aligned with *28*, Saga — described as 'the Swedish Madonna of the far right' — is the most worrying as she manages to combine their dogmatic message with haunting melodic folk music. Is she a one-off or the start of a trend, I asked?

'The musical resistance scene is worldwide and every country has its own infra structure of bands of every type,' they replied. 'Some bands do cross national divides with their message. Saga is a ballads artist and rock singer with her band Symphony of Sorrow, Stigger, the former Skrewdriver guitarist, and John from Nemesis (a Scottish *28* band) are probably the most notable balladeers on the GB resistance scene. Woden and Blood Red Eagle are Viking Metal bands, Blitzkrieg are hatecore. Blitzkrieg and Hate For Breakfast are examples of hatecore bands.'

'In the early eighties, Red Action were probably the opposition grouping you took most seriously. Is there an equivalent of them today?' I asked.

'The UAF — Unite Against Fascism — are very vocal, but not organised in a street-fighting sense like Red Action were. *Searchlight* is more of a business venture and Class War a fashion statement of rebellion by middle-class white kids while at higher education or on a gap year. Obviously, the BNP's massive growth and entry to the main political stage has taken the spotlight from us to some extent, but times and sympathies have changed in our nation and venues that wouldn't entertain us in the past actively court us now.

'We have learnt from the past and have a good organisation in place for finding, securing and holding concerts with the minimum risk to the event and supporters.'

Presumably, I put it to them, there were many attempts by the far-Left/Class War/AFA to crush the scene. What, I wondered, were the most memorable encounters?

'The Left has tried to prevent *28* at every step for over two decades but to no avail, as the amount of concerts, attendances and bands active today are testament to. The reds' favoured tactic was and is to ambush small groups of concertgoers before or after events while en route. We have circumvented this with redirection points and by travelling en mass. The two-for-one policy of hitting back twice as hard every time one of our people has been touched has worked as the best deterrent.

'The failed attempt by mass mobilisation of anti-patriotic groups at Waterloo was the most memorable encounter. There is always a continual tit for tat of spats going on but nothing to really mention. We win some, we lose some; it is the skinhead way of life we volunteered for and, as Ian Stuart so wisely said, "Life is just a struggle when you're proud of your country, but we'll just keep on fighting as that's the way it's got to be."'

So what had the most significant setbacks been? I asked.

'28 was hosting concerts on a weekly basis, nationwide in the mid-eighties. Skrewdriver would pull seven hundred on a Thursday night in Carshalton regularly; crowds and support were massive. The police then, through a concerted effort, managed to stop nearly every concert for a three- to four-year period, which basically took away all the new blood and broke the chain, so to say. Concerts were stopped at the last minute, mass raids were held and leading figures imprisoned, but the scene has continued.'

The police have been more effective than the far-Left in tackling 28. Cops in the East Midlands arrested Ian Stuart before a major 28 outdoor festival planned for 31 July 1993 and served him with an injunction order not to perform. They blockaded the venue, seized amplifiers and confiscated sound equipment.

That September, the East Midlands Division of 28 organised what was planned as the largest white nationalist music festival ever held in Europe. Three nights before the concert, Ian Stuart Donaldson and a few friends were travelling in a car that spun out of control into a ditch. Some of the passengers endured minor wounds, one was killed instantly, and Donaldson was pronounced dead on 24 September 1993.

MI5 were suspected.

Car crashes claimed the lives of leading B&H members – including the Cardiff-based band Violent Storm. Were these, I asked, seen as accidents or sabotage?

'There is no official statement from *28* on the car crashes that have happened to more than one band, and have proved fatal to members of two. The scene seems to be split with some saying it has happened too often and always at times when something big is in the offing; others say it is mere coincidence and bad luck.'

Despite the setbacks, *28* has built up a well-established calendar of events in Britain, including an annual Ian Stuart — ISD — memorial concert.

'There have been many memorable events for many years a concert just going ahead was a victory in itself. The annual ISD is a massive affair and an unwritten battle commences every September between *28* and every foe imaginable to host the event. To date we have been successful for over a decade. In 2009 there were sixteen official *28* Ian Stuart memorials held around the world and many more independent ones. Not bad for a skinhead from Blackpool.'

The Ian Stuart memorial concert at the Bungalow Inn in Redhill, Somerset, in 2008 attracted hostile but widespread BBC, radio and national newspaper coverage.

The *Sun* reported, VILLAGE INVADED BY 800 NAZI THUGS. Reporter John Coles wrote, 'A village expecting a scooter festival found itself invaded by more than 800 Nazi yobs instead. Racist skinheads from across Britain, Germany and Eastern Europe arrived draped in swastika flags. Wearing leather jackets and army boots, they stomped through the streets chanting: "Sieg Heil, Sieg Heil."'

London *28* say, 'Bad press of the pure fantasy type as seen after the ISD 08 concert is par for the course but still we grow.'

Around the world, particularly in Italy and Germany (where 28 and Rock Against Communism are still banned) the organisation is far larger than it is in the UK. The fall of Communism led to flourishing 28 scenes in many of the emergent Eastern European nations, but London 28 expect these to recede to a hard core over the next few years.

They said: 'After an initial thrust, the dress-ups and fashionistsas always seem to disappear and leave a stronger but smaller scene. Police pressure is relentless, which means different scenes rise and fall more due to state actions than fashion changes, new music waves etc. So many concerts have been stopped over the years, losing the odd gig is more of an occupational hazard for 28 bands than a setback of any sort.'

They went on to claim that 'our magazine and CD sales suggest the British scene is growing again and could easily regain the heights of the mid-eighties.'

I can find no evidence that 28 is currently growing in the UK, however. Theirs is largely a cash business with no published accounts. Large-scale events are few and far between. But there is no doubt that Nazi rock continues to exist in this country as a resilient, self-contained and extremely well-organised underground scene.

# CHAPTER SIXTEEN

# BLOWING IN THE WIND: YOUTH CULT POLITICS

'MODS AND ROCKERS MUST UNITE TO FIGHT THE TORIES.'
Young Socialists leaflet, 1964

As we have seen throughout this book, British youth cults have long flirted with extremist politics with often disastrous results. The trend began in the late 1950s, when the Campaign for Nuclear Disarmament (CND) radicalised thousands of youth, many of middle- and lower-middle-class backgrounds. The young nuclear-disarmament protestors brightened up their annual trek to Aldermaston with trad-jazz marching bands, skiffle players and folk music. CND was launched in 1958, revitalising the postwar protest movement. The campaigners argued that Britain should disarm unilaterally – i.e. get rid of our nuclear weapons first, to inspire the others. Some Tories supported them, Enoch Powell included, but the movement was largely of the Left. In its ranks could be found Methodists, Marxists, Trots, anarchists, artists, beatniks, poets, Quakers and cynical Stalinists, who naturally had no objection to Uncle Joe keeping his bomb ...

It was very much a cross-class alliance. Academics and students marched with trade unionists; actors and churchmen with Labour and

Communist Party members. Not many Teddy Boys, though. The demonstrators had conviction, but no glamour. It was worthy, but all a bit drab. Popular, though. Their third march, over Easter 1960, was the biggest demonstration of the century up to that point, with one police inspector putting the number at 100,000.

The following year, the plainly rattled authorities banned the marchers from rallying at Trafalgar Square. The police cordon could not hold them back; violence and arrests flared and a mass sit-in was staged. The cops were left looking foolish, incompetent and ineffective. CND could have built on the chaos but instead, bizarrely, they got involved in other causes and split the 1962 march in to two.

All left-wing organisations grew from this epidemic of protest. The only ones to attract a largely working-class membership were the Young Socialists (YS), the youth league of the Trotskyite Socialist Labour League (which became the Workers' Revolutionary Party, or WRP). Throughout the sixties, the YS were consistently contemptuous of hippy values. Their orientation was strictly blue-collar. It was the Young Socialists who leafleted seaside resorts in August 1964 with the glorious message, 'Mods and rockers must unite to fight the Tories.' A sentiment as true as it was unheeded.

They were attractive to teenage yobbos, not only because they stressed trade unions and the rights of young workers, but also because they also put on good discos, gigs and football matches. However, because of the somewhat intense nature of their politics (for good reason, the WRP are known as the Seven Day Adventists of the Trot Left), their turnover was too high and their burnout rate too fast to ever retain more than a few thousand members at any one time. But at least the YS realised that socialism was about the working class, not 'red bases' in universities, homosexual self-publicity or vegetarian power. And certainly they knew how to relate to council estate kids better than the cobwebbed, decaying Communist Party whose brightest idea was to splash the Beatles on the cover of their youth rag, *Challenge*, and sell it outside their concerts as a programme.

The first big political development in the popular music of the 1960s was the rise of the protest singer. Robert Zimmerman, a.k.a. Bob Dylan, was the folk musician who broke through to rock audiences. His early songs were radical, bleak and extremely whiny. He sang 'a hard rain is gonna fall', painting an apocalyptic future of a nuclear winter that never happened. The pessimism caught on. Barry McGuire had a hit the following year with 'Eve of Destruction' while Zager and Evans echoed the downer mood, wondering in song if mankind could survive as long as the year 2525.

If only *Dads Army*'s Private Frazer had recorded a novelty single based on his 'we're all doomed' catchphrase, he'd have made a mint.

Donovan was Britain's answer to Dylan, with the big-selling protest song 'Universal Soldier', which blamed the poor old squaddies for every war in history (very much 'Tommy this an' Tommy that an' Tommy 'ow's yer soul? ...' forgetting the rest of Kipling's rhyme: 'but it's the thin red line of 'eroes when the drums begin to roll').

Away from the bleating balladeers, real pop excitement could be found out at sea in the shape of pirate radio. The recent Richard Curtis film *The Boat that Rocked* is supposed to tell the story of this radical time. In 1966, British pop music was at its height but the BBC played only 45 minutes of it a day. The gap was filled by the pirate DJs until, in the movie, they are shut down by a typically stuffy Tory-style politician, played by Ken Branagh with an OTT moustache, a posh accent and a butler in tow. Any kid watching the film today would assume that the Conservative Party banned the pirates to stop them rotting the nation's morals. In fact it was a Labour government who killed the pirate stations. And Tony Benn, now the revered face of the Socialist Labour Left, was the Postmaster General who declared the pioneers 'a menace' for the crime of opening up the airwaves to popular music ...

It was Benn, then known by his rather grander birth name of Anthony Wedgwood Benn, who drove the pirates underground. Labour's 1967 Marine Broadcasting Offences Act made it an offence to advertise or supply an offshore radio station from the UK, forcing

Radio Caroline to relocate to Holland. There were even plans for MI5 to knock out the offshore broadcasters – even though they were outside British waters. It was only the pirates' huge popularity among the young that persuaded the authorities to back off.

As Benn noted in his diaries, the Tories had refused to act against the stations because they 'had some sympathy with pirate entrepreneurs'.

The stations were forced off air eventually – Caroline was fatally nobbled by falling advertising revenue – but their enterprise changed the face of radio for ever, liberating the airwaves and forcing the BBC to launch Radio One (Britain's state-run radio station) as a Caroline clone.

*The Boat that Rocked* is built on a gross inaccuracy. It was socialist Labour, not the capitalist Conservative, who waged war on pop.

That didn't stop many of rock's leading icons dressing unashamedly to the Left. The Who's Pete Townshend was a former Young Communist; John Lennon, a multitalented millionaire Marxist revolutionary; and Joe Strummer's brand of rose-tinted Stalinism counterbalanced punk's inborn nihilism.

From Dylan to Billy Bragg, from the MC5 to Tom Robinson, the Left-wing tradition in popular culture is not only unavoidable, it is also the accepted orthodoxy, and rarely challenged. Capitalism may rule the head of pop music but socialism has its heart.

Without doubt, Lennon was Britain's most important revolutionary songwriter. The Beatles were long-time Labour supporters, but John was radicalised by the antiwar movement, the Paris uprising of May 1968 and his relationship with the very middle-class Japanese 'artist' Yoko Ono. At first he was cautious and a pacifist. John's song 'Revolution' denounced people fired by hatred. He and Yoko had their ludicrous 'bed-in' for peace; he grew his hair and returned his MBE. But Lennon was tempted by violent solutions too. His confusion is reflected in the two different versions of 'Revolution'; in the first he counts himself out of having anything to do with destruction and in the second he replaces 'out' with 'in'. Influenced by the squawking Ono, John's native Scouse socialism crystallised into something harder.

In an interview with Tariq Ali and Robin Blackburn, published in the International Marxist Group paper *Red Mole*, Lennon explained that he had thought at first that the new wave of working-class pop stars meant that society was loosening up and that the workers were breaking through, adding, 'I realise in retrospect that it's the same phoney deal they gave the blacks [whom] they allowed to be runners or boxers or entertainers. The same people have the power. The class system didn't change one bit, leaving the same bastards running everything.'

John's bleak, almost painful solo song 'Working-Class Hero' reflects that view. His explicitly socialist anthem 'Power to the People' rejected reformist solutions, demanding that 'we' had better get on with the insurrection right away. The Nixon-bashing 'Gimme Some Truth' on the *Imagine* album continued the theme. 'Imagine' itself is said by many to be the ultimate socialist pop hymn. I could never stand its utopian dopiness.

John's politics went gaga when he and the fragrant Yoko relocated to New York in 1971 and started hanging out with middle-class Yippie leaders Abbie Hoffman and Jerry Rubin. As he associated with no end of fashionable causes, John's focus rapidly moved away from class. The result was the embarrassing, empty and occasionally ludicrous agitprop sloganeering of the double album *Some Time in New York City*, in which Lennon espoused feminism (with the dubious 'Woman is the Nigger of the World'), Attica prison rioters and Irish nationalism. On 'Sunday Bloody Sunday', John sings about 'Anglo pigs and Scotties' and declares, 'Repatriate to England all of those who call it home'; while 'The Luck of the Irish' is utterly twee old cobblers, with a lyric about leprechauns. Yoko's offerings, such as 'Sisters O Sisters' and 'We're All Water', were particularly dire and the album died on its arse. It was all a far cry from the never-released joke version of 'Get Back' once recorded by the Beatles, pirate copies of which have long been circulated in rock circles.

Lennon became target number one for the FBI, and the Nixon regime attempted to deport him. Shaken, John dropped out of politics and spent five years as a 'feminist househusband' before returning to music just months before his assassination.

The history of pop politics is a catalogue of blunders and embarrassments. Consider the high watermark of the 'counterculture', the grand folly that was the Woodstock festival of August 1969. This hippy hiatus came dripping with dippy idealism. Woodstock 'Nation' was supposed to be youth culture's great stand against the Man; the zenith of flower-power achievement. Two hundred and fifty thousand largely stoned or tripping enthusiasts turned up to a field in New York State. But no one had given much thought to the catering. It was a disaster until President Johnson stepped in. The authorities didn't send in the National Guard: they dropped food parcels.

Local women's groups made sandwiches and farmers donated grub. But, irony of ironies, it was the US Air Force that kept the hippy nation from going tits up ... Woodstock was a con, with Altamont its tragic punchline. And, even as the myth was being recycled in print, on film and on record, the reality of the 'Hippy Dream' was looking increasingly bleak. Haight-Ashbury, once seen as the ultimate advert for Californian sun-soaked love-and-peacenik living, degenerated into a festering sore of smack abuse, prostitution and mugging.

Similarly, the Black Power movement, passionately espoused by white middle-class radicals, degenerated tragically into black racism.

Their most extreme white equivalents were the Youth International Party, or Yippies, the Weathermen and the White Panthers, who came into being specifically to back up the Black Panthers. John Sinclair, the self-styled 'Minister of Information' for the White Panther Party, formed a rock band in Detroit called the MC5. Sinclair painted them as urban guerrillas plundering 'the straight world' for money to fund their revolution. Their debut live album, *Kick Out the Jams*, was sensational. But when Sinclair got busted, copping a ludicrously heavy ten-year sentence for giving two free joints to undercover Feds, the band swiftly dropped the revolution and moved on – to commercial failure.

More than 40 years on from the 1967 Summer of Love, we can see how little good the hippies actually achieved. The short spell of political liberalism they contributed to rebounded with the Right-wing Reagan administration and the rampaging Moral Majority. The creed of 'Free Love' (a.k.a. no morals) backfired with the catastrophic global spread of herpes and the arrival of AIDS. Drug culture (tune in, turn on, cop out) bequeathed the upper-class sport of snorting cocaine at £60 a gram, while cheap heroin ravished the ghettoes, sapping the will to fight back. And America's retreat from Indo-China led to the rise of the butcher Pol Pot in Cambodia and a new genocide.

The hippies themselves just cut their hair and moved into business, the media, law and politics – their rightful place as mature middle-class adults. Meet the new boss …

In Britain it was much the same, except here the hippies were far more influenced by traditional Left-wing politics and the Marxist- (and post-Marxist-) inspired Paris students. The long-term result was a major influx from the careerist middle class into the Labour Party and local government, which accelerated Labour's decline among working-class voters, contributing to the rise of Essex Man and his guru, Margaret Hilda Thatcher, and later the BNP.

The image that best sums up the hypocrisy of the era for me is one of John Lennon crooning 'imagine no possessions' while renting a whole apartment in Manhattan just to store his wife's furs. It says a lot for the common sense of working-class kids at the time that the majority of us paid no attention and got stuck into Desmond Dekker instead.

The Left didn't have it all their own way, however. In the USA, the presumed unity of the antiwar movement was shattered for ever when those brutal Right-wing barbarians, the Hell's Angels of California, laid into student protestors at Berkeley in the Autumn of 1965 and then offered to fight the Vietcong. Sonny Barger wrote to President Johnson, saying, 'Dear Mr President: On behalf of myself and my associates I volunteer a group of loyal Americans for behind the line duty in Vietnam. We feel that a crack troop of trained gorrillas [sic] would demoralise the Viet Cong and advance the cause of freedom. We are available for training and duty immediately.'

Later, Elvis, the King of Rock'n'Roll himself, famously offered his services to Richard Nixon in the battle against narcotics, subversion and 'the hippy element'. Elvis wrote to the president in 1970, asking to be made a federal agent at large in rock'n'roll circles; they met shortly afterwards, but the King never got his badge and there was never to be a legion of Ted Feds. Which is, on balance, a shame.

The 'revolution' didn't wash for everyone. David Bowie caught the mood of the post-1968 generation when he wrote off his older brother's tastes, sniffily dismissing the Beatles and the Stones as 'that revolution stuff'.

It was just a shame that he went on to briefly flirt with fascism. Particularly contentious was the time the Thin White Duke *sieg-heil*ed fans and photographers at Victoria Station when he returned from Berlin after the European leg of his Station to Station tour on 2 May 1976 (some fans returned the gesture). It was no isolated moment. In an interview published in the following September's *Playboy*, Bowie referred to Hitler as 'the first rock star' and praised his stage presence. He also stated that Britain was 'ready for a fascist leader' (possibly a thin, white Duce?).

Later, a calmer chameleon blamed excessive cocaine consumption for his springtime-for-the-Führer flirtations. By the end of the year, Bowie was laughing it all off. In 1977, he denied them vociferously. But the damage had been done. Swastika chic caught on big time. Malcolm McLaren might have argued that punks adopted Nazi symbols to agitate straight society and 'negate their power', but that didn't stop Siouxsie Sue singing 'too many Jews for my liking' on 'Love in a Void', a sentiment the Banshees later tried to atone for with the 1980 single 'Israel'. And Right-wing youth were undoubtedly attracted to the new movement because of it. *Socialist Worker* ran a debate on whether punk was Nazi – I defended punk, citing the Clash as the true spirit of the movement. But the National Front were on the rise. For years their youth wing, the YNF, had put it about that various stars were 'closet' supporters of their race-based nationalism. Poor old Rod Stewart's name was dropped, completely without substance. Bowie's gesture was enough to give them concrete ammunition. Eric Clapton's drunken outburst at a gig in Birmingham that August gave them more.

Clapton, a brilliant blues guitarist whose third solo hit had been a cover of Bob Marley's 'I Shot the Sheriff', told his audience that Britain was becoming overcrowded and urged them to vote for Enoch Powell to prevent the country becoming 'a black colony'. Later, Clapton defended his position, saying, reasonably enough, that it wasn't racist to be concerned about unfettered immigration; he also admitted that he'd been drunk and pissed off because an Arab had touched up his wife's arse.

Roger Huddle, a printer at *Socialist Worker*, and Red Saunders, a Trot theatre performer and photographer, had been kicking about the idea of holding a Rock Against Racism concert ever since Bowie at Victoria. Eric's speech, coupled with concern about the rising NF vote, spurred them in to action. Huddle and Saunders wrote to the music press opposing Clapton's comments and asking for support for a Rock Against Racism campaign. Hundreds replied. They came up with the slogan, 'Reggae, Soul, Rock'n'roll, Jazz, Funk, Punk – Our Music' (cruelly snubbing the UK folk, country and blues scenes) and 'NF = No Fun'. The first issue of the RAR fanzine *Temporary Hoarding* heavily featured the Clash. Both Huddle and Saunders were SWP members and local branches helped organise shows. Carol Grimes from Vinegar Joe was a frequent performer, but the RAR network of gigs helped to build and break bands as diverse as the Ruts and Steel Pulse (RAR roller-coasted alongside punk, the rehashed hippy ideas of its leading members being balanced at first by punk's anger, realism and energy).

Nineteen seventy-seven also saw the launch of the Anti-Nazi League. Unlike Rock Against Racism, which had been a roots-up development, the ANL (or Anal to its detractors) had been formed by the SWP central committee specifically as a front organisation (leader Tony Cliff liked to refer to the SWP as 'the cog within a cog' of the broader-based ANL and Right to Work Campaign, drawing in less committed folk to activity that helped to win them over to the full-blooded Bolshevism of the party). Punks, soul boys and soccer yobs rallied to the cause, uniting with young blacks and the usual mobs of mouldy hippies and middle-class professionals to stop the NF marching through Lewisham in August 1977. (See Chapter 4, 'Anarchy in the UK: Punk and the Battle of Lewisham). Together, RAR and the ANL became a mass movement. More than 30,000 (the organisers claimed 85,000) marched the six miles from Trafalgar Square to Hackney's Victoria Park in spring 1978 to attend the first Anti-Nazi League Carnival. The line-up included the Clash, Steel Pulse, X-Ray Spex, Jimmy Pursey (solo – the rest of Sham refused to come) and the inevitable Tom Robinson Band. TRB were *the* RAR band.

Cambridge-born ex-choirboy Tom Robinson was a decent enough fellow, but unworldly. He was never a punk. He'd been in a folky acoustic trio called Café Society whose only single was 'The Whitby Two-Step'. TRB formed in January 1977 and were a pretty average pub-rock band. Their rapid growth, and signing that same year, was more to do with their politics than their music; although the apolitical 'Motorway' was a decent song. Robinson epitomised the trendy rent-a-cause mentality of student Leftism and consequently won massive support from the media. His lyrics were right on and naff.

Tom worked through every fashionable cause going. There was 'Right on Sister' (about feminism), 'Sing If You're Glad to be Gay' (cringe if you're not) and 'Martin' (a real piece of patronising piffle delivered in puke-worthy mock cockney). It sure lacked the punch and certainty of the Clash's political anthems such as 'White Riot', 'Career Opportunities', '1977' and the revolutionary 'Remote Control', which is not only dismissive of MPs – all denounced as fat and old – but of Parliament itself; democracy, it's so bourgeois, dontcha know?

RAR and ANL claimed that 35,000 attended their Northern Carnival in Manchester (with Buzzcocks, Graham Parker and Misty in Roots) and that 100,000 were at the second London carnival with

Sham and Elvis Costello at Brockwell Park, Brixton, in September. Police estimates of the crowd numbers vary significantly. The NF used the cover of the Brockwell event to stage a march of their own in east London. Not enough revellers could be mobilised to stop them. The second carnival was to be RAR's greatest achievement. Tory leader Maggie Thatcher gave a speech reflecting Claptonian fears of being 'swamped by an alien culture' and, in April 1979, was duly elected. The NF were beaten, not by the Left, but by a radical element of the free-enterprise right. Demoralised they lost momentum, split into three rival factions and have never looked dangerous since.

Meanwhile, the organised far Left switched focus. Not too surprisingly, RAR, who had been formed by self-confessed hippies, drifted into soggy politics. They launched the ludicrous Rock Against Sexism while continuing to book and patronise Rastafarians, the most misogynist grouping of people in Britain this side of the Andy Capp Fan Club. The ANL went the same way, sprouting laughable subsections along Vegetarians Against the Nazis lines. But what really scuppered the campaigners was the defection of leading rock performers who were profoundly pissed off with the way the SWP were using them and the ANL to recruit and convert their fans.

At the beginning of 1979, the YNF attempted to reverse their flagging fortunes by fighting the Left at their own game, launching their own 'umbrella' alternative to RAR: Rock Against Communism. It was not a success. Very few bands were willing to commit themselves to RAC's self-styled crusade to 'kick out the reds, Pakis, blacks and Jews' and the ones that did were uniformly dire. Leeds bands the Dentists and the Ventz were the most notorious. Other bands involved included Tragic Minds, White Boss, Column 44 and the piss-poor Afflicted (who never played outside of one doss-hole of a pub in Deptford). The re-formed Skrewdriver would have been a feather in their cap, but at the time Ian Stuart Donaldson was torn between his true beliefs and his possible career. He pulled out of RAC's showpiece gig at the Conway Hall in August 1979 and Skrewdriver split shortly after.

The far-Right element among the skinheads, both supporters of the NF and the more blatantly Nazi British Movement, had to be content with disrupting other people's gigs. The summer of 1979 saw the worst series of incidents, with Labour Party Young Socialist and Young Communist League concerts suffering the most. Attacks on popular bands like the Ruts and Stiff Little Fingers did little to enhance the BM's standing among unaligned punks and skins, however. And in east London they met their match in the Cockney Rejects and their firm, who took them on and battered them spectacularly on three occasions (see Chapter 8, 'White Riot? The True Story of Oi!'), although it should be stressed that the Rejects hated all politicians equally.

It was unfortunate for the YNF that their leaders undermined their recruitment drive. John Kingsley Read condemned football hooligans, stating that they should be 'whipped until the skin falls off their back'. Johnny Rotten was also condemned in NF publications, described as being 'no better than a white nigger'. And in 1981 David Carr wrote, 'It is our duty as white nationalists to expose the alien and anti-British forces behind the punk trend.' Yes, that'll get the kids flooding in. The only music that met with tacit racial-nationalist approval was the electronic sound that gained popularity at the start of this decade, post-Kraftwerk. 'Electronic music,' commented Spearhead, 'combines many of the strains of classical and traditional Aryan music in a modern package; popular it may be, but only amongst the thinking white youth who represent the better type of Briton in this decadent country today.'

At national party level, former YNF organiser Joe Pearce and his cohorts in the 'political soldier' faction staged a coup, taking over the NF and evicting tubby long-term National Activities Organiser Martin Webster (using his homosexuality against him). Pearce's faction were heavily influenced by a group of Italian neo-Nazi terrorists and preached a workers-orientated brand of Brownshirt philosophy.

Towards the end of the year, Ian Stuart was co-opted onto the party's national directorate. He put a new band together as Skrewdriver in 1982, before finally coming out as a National Socialist in 1983. That year the NF relaunched their Rock Against Communism campaign with Skrewdriver as the headline act. The Front also launched the White Noise Club (WNC), releasing records on their own White Noise label. Other bands followed and this time they were musically competent: Brutal Attack, No Remorse, the Ovalteenies, London Branch, and Peter & the Wolf.

The resurgent far Right turned its fire power on Ken Livingstone's GLC (Greater London Council). On 10 June 1984, the GLC organised a free Jobs for Change open-air concert at Jubilee Gardens on London's South Bank. The Smiths headlined, supported by Billy Bragg and the Redskins – the SWP-supporting soul band who aimed to make Marxism danceable. Halfway through the Redskins set, the stage was invaded by about 50 neo-Nazi skins, led by Chubby Chris Henderson, who attacked the band and beat up their security. Another mob of Nazi skins arrived later and had to make do with attacking Hank Wangford.

Emboldened, Skrewdriver released an album called *Hail the New Dawn* on the German label Rock-O-Rama. There was no longer any ambiguity in their lyrics: 'I believe in the white race,' Ian Stuart bellowed. 'A race apart – we've got a mile start.' (He'd have needed a mile start up against Tommie Smith or John Carlos.) The white race let Stuart down, however, when the WNC swindled him and the bands out of thousands. On the rebound, he formed Blood & Honour (see Chapter 15, 'The Battle of Waterloo') who later revealed, 'The WNC defrauded all the bands and especially Ian Stuart out of an awful lot of money. While this was denied at the time, with the subsequent years and Ian's death many of the WNC have now come clean about the amount of money that was "diverted".'

An unsavoury racist element in British youth cults can be traced right back to 1958 when some of the working-class Teddy Boys of west London were in the red-knuckled vanguard of postwar Britain's first major race riot (See Chapter 1, 'In the Beginning There Was the Ted'). Some racists adopted rockabilly because they erroneously believed it to be the only real 'white' component of rock'n'roll. In fact, rockabilly, or country rock, as it was originally known, was actually the most complete integration of black R&B and white country, which formerly hadn't used drums at all. Presley was the first performer to fuse the two folk styles, his 'Sun Sessions' being perhaps the finest example of the genre (claims that the King was a racist have been regularly ridiculed by the many black performers who knew him personally. Elvis was hugely popular with black American record buyers. Between 1956 and 1963 he had more than 30 hits in the *Billboard* R&B charts, including six Number 1s; and in turn Elvis was always quick to praise black artists from Lavern Baker to Arthur 'Big Boy' Crudup).

Never ones to allow the facts to blur their prejudices, the racist 'Rebels' adopted rockabilly in its entirety, and, following the success of the Sun collection *Sun Rockabilly Volume 1*, many majors raided their back catalogues to get in on the till ringing. For the hardcore racists, the real thing was far too tame, and a black market developed in the mid- to late seventies for imported records by obscure country artist Johnny Rebel, funded and produced by the Ku Klux Klan with titles like 'Coon Town', 'Nigger Hatin' Me' and 'Send Them Niggers North'. What the records lacked in quality or composition was compensated for in the rebels' eyes by their commitment to that race-hate tunnel vision.

Many Teds disliked rockabilly and were known to boo it. Later in the decade Ted DJs like Geoff Barker made a principled stand against racist elements. Charlie Gillett, probably the country's leading authority on rock'n'roll and soul, spoke out against them too. And in the Battersea area of south London, a left-wing Ted called Pete Chambers tried to get a Teds Against the Nazis group off the ground.

Shortly afterwards, in 1979, the 2-Tone bands took up the RAR message and physically embodied its spirit (see Chapter 7, 'Rude Boys Outta Jail'). While the Oi! bands, with their message of unity between 'skins, punks and Herberts' (terrace hooligans), or skunks, attempted to bring working-class youth together to fight against common enemies such as unemployment, low wages and police oppression.

SWP in a modern liberal democracy to operate the kinds of strictures needed by the Bolsheviks when they were on the verge of the revolution in 1917's feudal, autocratic Russia (the SWP claimed to be Trotskyist but had evolved an all-controlling, self-sustaining ruling elite that Stalin would have been proud of). The Party branded them 'adventurists' and 'squadists'. Some were expelled; the rest left in sympathy and set up Red Action.

One leading member was Micky O'Farrell, a dedicated anti-unemployment campaigner, full-time cockney red Man United hooligan and part-time protest singer. In his 'Letter From Brixton Prison', O'Farrell argued that the middle-class composition of groups like the SWP, and its about-turn ditching of populist campaigns such as RAR in favour of industrial work after Thatcher's 1979 election victory, had contributed to the resurgence of far-Right groups at street level.

Like the Black Panthers before them, Red Action realised that the 'lumpen proles' would provide the muscle for any Right-wing revolution and so it was important to win their hearts and minds, as well as those of the industrial working class. O'Farrell wrote, 'It may well be easier to fob off a naïve young proletarian with simplistic nationalistic arguments than the much more complex revolutionary ideas, but this is no excuse for the total failure of the Left to relate to these people in any way socially, politically or culturally.'

I remember having a conversation with him in the early eighties. I opined that the professional-class composition of the SWP had resulted in their 'Marxism' becoming a radical petit bourgeois ideology. O'Farrell put it more succinctly: 'They're all middle class wankers,' he said.

Red Action threw themselves into activity, fighting the neo-Nazis on the streets and trying to relate to the kinds of kids who worked on building sites, rucked at football matches or were lost to the dole. Later they formed Anti-Fascist Action as a front organisation. At heart they were thugs. They enjoyed violent confrontation with their ideological opposites, the 'Fash', seeking it out for its own sake, and usually came 'tooled up' with coshes, hammers and pick-axe handles.

They used 'anti-fascism' to justify their lawbreaking (and jaw breaking), just as the far-Right used exaggerated patriotism and defence of the realm to excuse theirs.

Like the Front, Red Action realised the potent appeal of rock music. Their magazine, called *Red Action*, featured interviews with rock radicals like the Redskins, Attila and Burial. It 'got' Oi!, and defended it, as well as arguing for a militant socialist alternative in language that was succinct, easy to read and nonpatronising. In 1984, Red Action organised an Oi! tour to support the miners' strike featuring Burial and Red London, a Geordie group who crossed Oi! with soul and socialism.

Red Action's pro-yob, trendy-baiting attitudes were reflected to an even greater degree by fanzines such as *Stand Up and Spit*, run by Teething Tim, a political activist and the toaster with the Anti-Social Workers. Smothered in quotes from the Cockney Rejects (who would have hated Tim's politics), the 'zine advocated Oi!, skinhead reggae and direct action, ridiculing 'social worker' politics. Slogans like 'Reds Against Trendies' and 'Trendy Left Drop Dead' competed for space with attacks on wealthy 'parasites' and pleasant song lyrics such as 'If I die on a Nazi street / There'll be ten dead Nazis at my feet.' Reading it made it seem a mighty long time since the terraces of Spurs had echoed to songs like 'Blair Peach's body lies a-mouldering in the grave and the National Front goes marching on / Glory, glory Adolf Hitler, and the National Front goes marching on.'

I sympathised with some of Red Action's arguments at the time, principally their class focus, but their bloodlust and support for Irish terrorism was less easy to accommodate. You wouldn't catch me slinging shrapnel into a collecting bucket for the IRA, who with their bombs in Birmingham and Woolwich had declared war — not on the British state but the young English working class.

In December 1983, six random people were killed by an IRA bomb at Harrods in Kensington, which blasted through central London streets. Seventy-five others were injured. Yes, they're to blame for all the hurt, misery and inequality in the world, those bloody Christmas shoppers.

Ten years later, Harrods was bombed again; and within a week a second Semtex device was detonated on a Network South East train to Ramsgate. The bombers, Jan Taylor and Patrick Hayes, were both long-term English members of Red Action.

All the leading members of Red Action, known as the 'Stewards Group' from their time protecting demos in the late seventies, had at different times been in court, on a range of charges, including grievous bodily harm 'with intent'. They cheerfully admit that they are 'tooled up' when they attack 'the Fash'. But this was a different level of violence – albeit one correctly identified as a possibility by the SWP when they expelled them for adventurism. Their journey from 'fighting fascism' and supporting Irish nationalism to waging guerrilla war on society had proved a short one.

When the police burst into Hayes's basement flat in Walford Road, Stoke Newington, and arrested the pair, one of them fired three shots at the oncoming officers, missing all of them. Among the items found in the flat were a box containing 22lb of Semtex, handguns, a sock full of bullets, several electronic detonators and timing devices, and keys to a lock-up garage in Muswell Hill from which a large quantity of homemade explosive was later recovered.

At the end of their trial the following May, both were sentenced to 30 years for the Harrods and Ramsgate train bombings. Hayes was also linked forensically to several huge lorry bombs of the type, which destroyed the Baltic Exchange and devastated Bishopsgate, including one that failed to explode under Canary Wharf.

Six years later David Copeland, an engineer and a former member of the BNP, killed two people and injured more than 60 with three nail bombs placed in Brixton, Brick Lane and a Soho gay pub. Amazing what misery you can cause with those self-justifying ideological blinkers on.

At the tail end of 1985, a group of well-meaning left-wing musicians launched Red Wedge with the aim of drumming up support for the Labour Party. It was the brainchild of those morose monkeys Billy Bragg, Paul Weller and Jimmy Somerville from the Communards. Other acts rallied to join the Red Wedge joy fest on the road, including the Smiths, Tom Robinson, Jerry Dammers and Lloyd Cole. At the general election of 1987, the Conservatives were returned with a 102-seat majority.

The Tories had a secret weapon though. Cilla Black. Oh, and Rick Wakeman.

The Red Wedge enthusiasts curled up in embarrassment.


Elsewhere the buccaneering spirit of the old pop radio pirates reasserted itself in the rave scene that emerged in 1987. Smiley culture. This underground 'acid house' electronic dance scene developed via raves – unlicensed parties within the 'Magic Roundabout' of the M25 – which mixed house music with the thrills of MDMA, better known as ecstasy (or just E), a drug that had first caught on in US gay dance clubs. Once again, the press and politicians were excited into orgies of outrage, partly because of the sometimes deadly dehydrating side effects of the drug, mostly because it was a cash-in-hand business and no one was paying tax. Many of the young entrepreneurs running the London rave scene were former ICF football hooligans who had followed the Cockney Rejects. As a significant youth-cult sidebar, one positive side effect of Es was to take the violence out of football for years. No one wants to fight when they're loved up, matey.

Grant Fleming recalls his amazement at attending his first rave at the Clink – a converted prison in south London. Carlton Leach and associates were running the door, so it looked like a West Ham operation. 'The music was banging,' he says. 'People were spangled, really off their pancake. The dance floor was a dungeon full of ravers going for it in an ocean of dry ice and flashing lights. Then something really strange happened. I saw Jacko, one of Millwall's top faces, and one of our lot, and they're shaking hands. They we're not alone. As I looked around I saw gangs of rival hooligans hugging each other – heavy firms from north, south, east and west London not just tolerating each other but actively loved up with each other. Six months before, they'd have been ripping off each other's head. They would never have been in the same room together peacefully. Now, no one was fighting. It was unheard of – until ecstasy. 'Things have changed,' my friend Kenny said. 'No one's bothered about that any more'. And for a while that was how it stayed.

The Shamen, formerly a rock band from Aberdeen, were one of the first to turn techno and bring acid house into the mainstream. They topped the charts in 1992 with an ill-disguised hymn to ecstasy, 'Ebenezer Goode' (''E's good, 'e's good, he's Ebenezer Goode …').

Meanwhile, a new and extremely brutal scene emerged – US rap and hip-hop. A 1988 concert at Nassau Coliseum on Long Island, featuring Eric B and Rakim, Kool Moe Dee, Doug E Fresh and other rappers, was the scene of robberies, stabbings and a homicide, violence that led to a ban on rap concerts at the venue. For a while you couldn't attend a rap concert without entering by way of a cordon of police, a metal detector and a frisking, with more police and security guards stationed inside the hall. As rap's popularity grew in the 1990s, the violent posturing of the artists turned real.

An East Coast–West Coast feud developed, pitting Death Row Records, based in southern California, against New York's Bad Boy Entertainment. The feud escalated from a battle of words to a bloody war. Its two most prominent casualties were the rival rappers Tupac Shakur and Notorious B.I.G. Both of the young black stars were shot multiple times while sitting in the front passenger seats of their vehicles and were rushed to the hospital by their entourages. Notorious B.I.G., a.k.a. Biggie Smalls, gunned down in LA, was dead on arrival. Tupac Shakur was shot in Las Vegas. He lived for six days and underwent multiple operations before succumbing to his wounds. In both cases, witnesses refused to come forward and help the police with their enquiries. Gang enmity between the Bloods and the Crips appears to have played a part in both murders. In May 2009, another rapper, called Dolla, was shot and killed outside an LA mall.

It made mods and rockers look like the good old days.

Run DMC had the first breakthrough hit in the UK when they teamed up with veteran rockers Aerosmith for the 1986 smash 'Walk This Way'. But it took three white kids to take the new sound and a new look to suburbia – three middle-class Jewish lads called the Beastie Boys. They'd been a New York punk band called the Aborigines but struck gold in 1987 with an unholy marriage of rap, rock and frat-boy humour. Hits like '(You) Gotta Fight for Your Right (to Party)', 'She's On It' and 'No Sleep Till Brooklyn' made them household names. The overreaction of the British press was absurd, especially when the worst thing their fans did was nick car hood ornaments and insignia to wear as jewellery – a far cry from the bling years to come. The *Daily Mirror* even ran a dubious story about the group snubbing handicapped kids at an airport.

Hip-hop was huge and remains so to this day. In the nineties it mutated into gangsta rap. The same white liberals who had hated Oi! were wetting themselves over rappers, who shot each other, wrote misogynistic and gay-bashing songs and made anti-Semitic statements. Leaving aside Biggie Smalls and Tupac, Snoop Dogg has a rap sheet that makes the aggro of the Cockney Rejects seem small beer.

Marshall Mathers III, better known as Eminem, was dubbed the Elvis of Hip-Hop – a white boy from Michigan who went triple platinum in 1999 with his *Slim Shady* album, selling 1.5 million records in the first week of release. But big-selling black performers like the Grammy-winning Puff Daddy (Sean Combs), Busta Rhymes (Trevor Smith Junior) and 50 Cent (Curtis James Jackson III) continue to set the pace. In the naughty noughties, leading hip-hop acts branched out into hardcore porn. Snoop Dogg was first. His 2001 adult movie *Snoop Dogg Doggy Style* was the year's bestselling blue DVD. Scores followed.

And who among us wouldn't want to get buck naked with the Buckwild Girls?

The middle-class British Left did not approve. The hippy tradition had reasserted itself in the eighties and nineties with new preoccupations: Greenham Common, the focus on minorities and the right of hairy-legged, man-hating women to call their gender 'wimmin' and so on. Later, the SWP lost the plot completely, teaming up with the Muslim Association of Britain (MAB) in the Stop the War Coalition. MAB are hostile to pretty much every value the far Left hold dear: democracy, feminism, gay rights, atheism ... their stated aim is to establish an Islamic state in the UK, with the right to impose the death penalty on any Muslim who renounces their faith. So much for the rights of man!

While blathering on about 'cultural equivalence', the Left have managed to give respectability to the kind of Right-wing intolerance they have been fighting since the 1960s.

'Gay rights' became the *cause célèbre* of the late eighties and nineties. One of the first bands to be denounced were US rockers Guns N' Roses whose song 'One in a Million' moaned about immigrants and gays, linking the first to terrorism and the second to AIDS. (Aussie rock band Rose Tattoo also reacted against multi-culturalism; their song 'Revenge' complained about newcomers to Australia who don't speak the lingo or respect the country's traditions.)

Many rap and reggae artists were enthusiastically anti-gay, causing much confusion on the left. Which minority to support? Gay activists won the day and albums by artists such as reggae stars Buju Banton, Beenie Man, Elephant Man, TOK, Vybz Kartel and Bounty Killer were denounced and a campaign was launched to ban their music. Brighton was the first to forbid sales of 'homophobic' albums in music stores. 'Freedom of speech ... ceases to be valid when you are talking about incitement to murder,' said Brighton and Hove councillor Simon Williams – although to date no action has been taken against Tom Jones for 'Delilah', Twisted Sister for their Falklands song 'Shoot 'Em

Down', or ditties glorifying Stalin, Che, the IRA or Osama Bin Laden. Some murderers are more equal than others.

Jamaican academic Dr Lez Henry argued that, if the gay activists' claims were true, then the genre would be inviting violence against everyone. He said, 'In reggae dancehall culture everything is the recipient of violence. From the sound systems to the person who plays the set, to the unfaithful baby mother, to the person who looks at you wrong. It's not just gays.' Jamaican professor Carolyn Cooper agreed:

'A parent will say to their child, "Me a go kill you wid licks today," and the parent doesn't intend to actually kill the child. It is a statement to suggest the seriousness of the offence that the child has committed. It's not meant to be literal – it's a metaphor. We come from a culture in which verbal power is very important so that people who do not even have guns will be singing: "Boom bye bye in a batty bwoy head." What they are doing is asserting their sense of displeasure with homosexuality.'

The extreme AIDS misinformation campaign of the eighties may have triggered the anti-gay backlash. In the UK, even the Conservative government were bamboozled by the 'we're all at risk' line, issuing leaflets that informed shocked spinster pensioners of the dangers of overenthusiastic anal sex.

Elsewhere, the crusties flourished. The high tide was the anti-poll-tax rally in Trafalgar Square on 31 March 1990. It turned into the worst riot in central London for a century. By the end of the action, plumes of black smoke engulfed Nelson's Column. There were 340 arrests and 113 were injured, including 45 police officers. Twenty horses were also hurt. Cars were overturned and set alight, and four Tube stations were shut for safety reasons as police tried to clear the streets. Demonstrators, including Class War activists and Crass-style anarchists, attacked cops with bricks and cans. Firemen attempting to extinguish the blazes were pelted with wood and stones. Shop windows were smashed and many businesses had their contents looted.

Violence erupted just after 4pm following a peaceful march against the poll tax that saw up to 70,000 protesters take to the streets. A group of protesters involved in a sit-in at Whitehall, close to the Downing Street entrance, refused to move after requests from police and stewards. As police arrested offenders, placards and cans were thrown from the crowd and the trouble spread to Charing Cross Road, Pall Mall, Regent Street and Covent Garden. Photographer Steve Eason described the scene as being 'like the tapestry of the Battle of Hastings with sticks and missiles flying through the air and police officers in gladiatorial poses'.

David Meynell, deputy assistant commissioner of the Metropolitan Police, in charge of the operation, said a peaceful march had been 'completely overshadowed by the actions of about 3,000 to 3,500 people in minority groups'. He said they 'without any doubt at all' had launched 'a ferocious and sustained attack on the police'.

The influence of the Crass collective lives on in relatively harmless anti-globalisation campaigns and protests against motorway development.

Dreadlocked 'eco-warrior' Swampy (Daniel Hooper) became the public face of the movement in 1996. Not too surprisingly, he came from a nice middle-class home in Berkshire.


In 1997, John Major's Tory government was kicked out and replaced by Tony Blair's New Labour project. Quite a few people who should have known better were taken in. Like the Beatles before them, the Oasis boys were briefly bamboozled into sharing their spotlight with Phoney Tony. But Cool Britannia was a con, Tone's been wearing Rupert Murdoch's ideological bloomers ever since, and he stumbled towards the end of his time in power amidst a mounting tide of sleaze, spin and recrimination for the fiascos of Iraq and Afghanistan. After posing with the gullible Gallagher brothers, Blair went on to cosy up to any fading pop stars who would give him a free holiday: Cliff, the Bee Gees, anyone who'd have him really.

In 2001, 9/11 understandably stoked a patriotic backlash in the

USA. Country singer Toby Keith penned 'Courtesy of the Red, White & Blue (The Angry American)' that branded 9/11 'a sucker punch' and warned Al-Qaeda and its sympathisers that Uncle Sam's righteous wrath would soon rain down on them in a terrible vengeance.

On the strength of that single, Keith's album *Unleashed* debuted at the top of the *Billboard* 200 chart, elbowing aside the latest *Now That's What I Call Music*.

Quite what any of it had to do with the invasion of Iraq remains uncertain; but the attacks on the US inspired many other songs. Neil Young wrote 'Let's Roll' – a tribute to courageous passengers on Flight 93, who fought back against the hijackers – while Bruce Springsteen found his form and wrote a whole album about it.

There was a brief backlash against country artists the Dixie Chicks after they told a London audience, 'We're ashamed the President is from Texas' on the eve of the invasion of Iraq. There was a backlash against the Iraq war, too, of course. The 'American Idiot' of Green Day's superlative Top Three hit was George W Bush. But there are pro-Bush artists too. The Right Brothers, from Nashville, Tennessee, have recorded songs including 'Bush Was Right', 'Stop Global Whining' and 'I'm In Love With Ann Coulter', a love song about a statuesque, Left-bashing, Cruella de Vil-style US columnist.

Worldwide, large charitable causes replaced politics at the heart of pop, attracting the usual mob of earnest, ethical and tedious egotists. 'Live Earth' was the latest fiasco as the music biz embraced the great global-warning con. Live Earth … from the people who cured African famine and made poverty history … just don't mention all the planes, trains, private jets, limos, trucks and tour buses that it required. Live Earth's carbon footprint equalled that of a small country.

I guess it gives Saint Bob something to do when he isn't advising the Conservative Party. He's not quite as irritating as that chump Bono, self-styled rock ambassador to the world. Pop and politics; no good has ever come of it and I doubt if it ever will.

# CHAPTER SEVENTEEN

# THE NOUGHTIES: HOODIES AND CHAVS

The new century saw the growth of a new teenage folk demon to torment the sleep of Middle England: the hoody. He is the Ted of our times, with the drape jackets and quiff replaced by a simple anonymous cloth hood. The garment was seen as proof of criminal intent by hysterical commentators and in May 2005, the Bluewater shopping centre in Greenhithe, Kent, banned shoppers from sporting either hoodies or baseball caps (although it didn't stop the shops there from selling them). Labour's John Prescott, then deputy prime minister, boosted the moral panic by saying that he'd felt intimidated by a hoody gang at a motorway service station. But not so intimidated that it had put him off his pies.

The hooded top dates back to New York's hip-hop culture in the late 1970s. Later, it was adopted by kids on the skate-punk scene. In the UK, it is associated with the young working, unworking and dangerous classes who became known dismissively as 'chavs'. The chav look consisted of brand-name tracksuits, white trainers, hoodies and designer accessories – usually Burberry caps and scarves – augmented with gold rings, chunky bracelets and neck chains. Bling. Burberry discontinued their baseball caps in 2004 in a bid to distance themselves from the latest manifestation of yob culture. Girl chavs wore large earrings, fake tan and heavy makeup, and had their hair pulled back in a tight ponytail, known colloquially as a 'Croydon facelift'. The look was captured perfectly by Matt Lucas in his *Little Britain* character Vicky Pollard, a tubby, morally lax, unmarried mum in a Kappa tracksuit.

The chavs' music of choice was hip-hop, although they had some time for jokey punk-pop bands like Blink 182. Their natural enemies were the cops, emos, goths and students. The Kaiser Chiefs laid into this new street-urchin generation in 'I Predict a Riot' which mocked, among other things, a man in a tracksuit, under-dressed women and chip-eaters. There's nice, sophisticated, university-educated Ricky Wilson trying to get a taxi home while all these horrible oiks attempt to shag each other between mouthfuls of saveloys – don't you feel his pain? Tsk. The Clash wanted a riot, the Kaiser Chiefs are terrified one might break out and ruin their social life. Still, it went down well with student audiences.

A website called ChavScum was set up offering a 'user's guide to the ASBO generation'. Mostly, it involved the middle-class writers sneering at council-estate kids. Julie Burchill argued that the word 'chav' was an anti-working-class putdown; a form of 'social racism'. Or, as we used to call it, snobbery.

Communications Professor Angela McRobbie, from London's Goldsmith College, put the appeal of the hoody down to its promise of anonymity, mystery and anxiety. 'Rap culture celebrates defiance,' she said, 'as it narrates the experience of social exclusion. Musically and stylistically, it projects menace and danger as well as anger and rage. The hooded top is one in a long line of garments chosen by young people, usually boys, to which are ascribed meanings suggesting that they are "up to no good". In the past, such appropriation was usually restricted to membership of specific youth cultures – leather jackets, bondage trousers – but nowadays it is the norm among young people to flag up their music and cultural preferences in this way, hence the adoption of the hoody by boys across the boundaries of age, ethnicity and class.'

Football hooliganism returned in the nineties and over the last few years has become quite an industry. Cass Pennant wrote his autobiography and then a book on the ICF, another on Portsmouth's 6.57 crew and a fourth on England's away firm. Scores of former hooligans followed suit, with the likes of Martin King's Head Hunter Books, which published books on the Cardiff Soul Crew and the Swansea Jacks as well as Chelsea. (And also did a sideline in Head Hunter clothing, although the ICF-related Longshanks got there first.) Next came DVDs, big-budget movies (*Football Factory*, *Green Street* and Cass Pennant's biopic *Cass*, among others).

In 2006, a TV series called *Real Football Factories* featured the re-formed Cockney Rejects. In 2007 a film called *The Rise of the Footsoldier* was made about Carlton Leach – the original cover model for *Strength Thru Oi!*. Shane Meadows's skinhead movie *This Is England* was also released that year. A film about the Cockney Rejects called *Join the Rejects – Get Yourself Killed* is set to follow.

Hooliganism wasn't only a spectator sport, either. In August 2009, a Carling Cup match between West Ham and Millwall at Upton Park resulted in a 44-year-old Lions supporter being stabbed in the chest in Priory Road. Inside the stadium there were shocking scenes of 'large-scale trouble' involving hundreds of fans. Fights broke out at 6pm and were still raging five hours later. Missiles were thrown at officers but none were injured, and West Ham fans invaded the pitch three times.

At 11pm there were still several hundred hardcore Hammers supporters outside the stadium chanting and bombarding police with crates and bottles. One man from Harrow, north London, was stretchered away after being hit with a dart to the head.

ICF members later blamed a Sky News TV report for the trouble. One told me, 'The reason we kicked off was Sky had reported that a West Ham fan had been killed. By the time we found out that this wasn't the case, the damage had been done.' The press reacted with disgust. The *Sun* labelled the fans 'yobs' who were 'dragging soccer back into the gutter'. The *Mail*'s Martin Samuel likened the fighting to a horror film.

About 200 riot police and 20 mounted officers were at the ground and a police helicopter circled the area. The Press Association quoted an unnamed 19-year-old saying he saw a police officer being kicked on the ground. Eyewitnesses told of hooligans trying to rip out bollards and lighting 'small fires'. Aaron Smith, from Hemel Hempstead, who was at the game, said, 'I saw one man cornered by at least a dozen Millwall fans before kick-off. Terrifying scenes.'

And a Millwall fan told the BBC, 'It was like a war zone outside the stadium. There was fighting all around. I brought my kids with me tonight and they've seen some violence that is indescribable.'

One noticeable aspect of the fighting and the pitch invasions was that it wasn't just teenagers involved. Most of those involved appeared to be in their thirties, forties and early fifties.

It was the same story at the Glastonbury festival, where the year's star line-up could have been the cast of *The Last of the Summer Wine*. Punk icons like Iggy Pop and John Lydon are now on TV flogging insurance and Country Life butter. It's a crying shame. Meanwhile, British rock's excuse for a rebel is Pete Doherty of Babyshambles, and formerly of the Libertines, who is more known for his heroin consumption, his vacuity and his love life than his music.

Doherty is living proof that you can shovel down narcotics by the bucket and still be as dull as ditchwater.

In the US, the reaction against grunge took the form of a spirited punk renewal, with bands like Green Day and the Offspring coupling spiky rhythms with hooks and melodies. Californian three-piece Green Day showed an obvious debt to bands like the Clash, the Ramones and the Buzzcocks. They sold 10 million copies of their 1994 third album *Dookie*, going on to far greater success with their sensational seventh album *American Idiot*, a Bush-bashing rock opera released 10 years later, which took them to another level of global fame. Left-wing bands such as the excellent Rancid and the Dropkick Murphys now flog the legacy of the Clash, the Specials and the Pogues back to a grateful British public.

I wonder how many who buy them are over 40. The Rebellion festivals in Blackpool are populated with ex-skins and ex-punks rubbing beer bellies with middle-aged punters, unable to leave behind the fashions of their youth.

Teenage violence persists, of course. In the inner cities, it is more savage and deadlier than it has ever been, but the gangs are no longer linked to music or football. They are more to do with ethnicity and territory. In east London, Somali street gangs clash with Russian street gangs and clash over turf rights with their Bengali equivalents.

South London streets are particularly notorious thanks to black British gangs like the Peckham Boys and the Younger Peckham Boys from the North Peckham and Bell's Garden council estates. Their main rivals are the Ghetto Boys from Deptford and New Cross. Shootings and stabbings have become commonplace. Funded by the drug trade, their arsenal is known to include Mac 10 sub-machine guns. The killers of Damilola Taylor were Younger Peckham Boys. At the time of the murder in 2000, they were aged 12 and 13.

Hooligan violence has reverted to how it was before the Teds and pre-rock'n'roll. It's territorial again, but with deadlier weapons.

Meet the new hate, same as the old hate.

The cults remain but they are no longer the exclusive property of teenagers. Maybe something young and exciting is waiting around the corner to shock and delight us. But I doubt it. Music is no longer the prerogative of youth. In that sense, the age of the teen is over; and the age of the youth cult is, too.